T0367872

GOD DID IT

HEALING TESTIMONIES ACROSS TIME AND RELIGIONS

ROSE ANN PALMER, Ph.D.

iUniverse LLC
Bloomington

GOD DID IT
HEALING TESTIMONIES ACROSS TIME AND RELIGIONS

iUniverse books may be ordered through booksellers or by contacting:

iUniverse LLC
1663 Liberty Drive
Bloomington, IN 47403
www.iuniverse.com
1-800-Authors (1-800-288-4677)

ISBN: 978-1-4917-3371-4 (sc)
ISBN: 978-1-4917-3372-1 (hc)
ISBN: 978-1-4917-3373-8 (e)

Library of Congress Control Number: 2014908300

Printed in the United States of America.

iUniverse rev. date: 06/10/2014

For John Hubbard

I am sure this is what Rose Ann wants.

John Palmer, Ph.D.
Rose Ann's husband

Proclaim God's marvelous deeds to all the nations.

Psalm 96:3

Contents

Author's Note

Think of this book as a bottle of one-a-day vitamins for your soul. Each page tells the story of at least one person healed through prayer. As you read, you will become more and more convinced that God is alive and eager to interact with you, and if you need it (and who doesn't?) to heal you, too. He wants you to go to the doctor and take medicine, of course. Doctors and medicine are His usual instruments of healing.

Don't nag God. Ask once, take the focus off yourself, and focus on Your Father. If it makes you feel better, write down the request. God wants to heal you. God is always knocking at our doors trying to get in to heal us. He loves you more than you love yourself. Spending prayer time praising and thanking the Father opens you up to receive His healing love. Maybe when Jesus told us, "Love the Lord thy God with thy whole mind, thy whole heart, and thy whole soul," He gave more than spiritual advice. He may have been showing us a way to physical self-healing as well. Jesus was telling us to glow with healing joy.

Introduction to Rose Ann Palmer: Charismatics Babble, Fall Down, and Stage Cures

Roman Catholic Charismatics make up the Pentecostal arm of the Catholic Church and include in their worship prayer forms that date back to the time of the Apostles: Charismatics pray in tongues, are slain in the Spirit, and expect healing, or as scoffers say, "Charismatics babble, fall down, and stage sham cures." Despite being sneered at by those who've never felt the power of the Holy Spirit coursing through their own bodies, Charismatics continue to imitate the first Christians and have fun doing so.

I'd dismissed the movement as weird at best or at worst dishonest, staged by actors brought in for faked healings. What did we need it for anyway?

Then one autumn night over ten years ago, job-related research brought my husband and me to St. Michael's Church in Brooklyn, New York where the most powerful experience of my life took place under a basketball hoop at a prayer meeting held in a parochial school gym. Since that night, my life has been divided into two parts: before the experience and after the experience. For a long time, I couldn't speak about it without bursting into tears, overwhelmed that I had felt the presence of God in my own body. Even now I cry as I type, recalling the sensations that changed my faith from "I believe" to "I know."

While hootenanny music blasted, the congregation sang loudly, clapped, and moved in time to music from guitars, banjos, a keyboard, tambourines, drums, and a trumpet. I realize now they were working themselves up loving God with their whole hearts, their whole minds, and their whole souls as Jesus directed.

Then after about half an hour of songs of praise and thanksgiving, a side door opened and the healing priest, Father Robert DeGrandis, a dark-haired man of medium height, strode in and walked across the gym. "Do you have a heart condition?" he asked a young man in the middle of one of the central rows.

People from the youth's prayer group cheered. The man had come hoping for a healing, and Father had heard a word of knowledge [the Charismatic gift of "knowing," of receiving direct wisdom and knowledge from Heaven] that the boy, a total stranger, was healed. The woman next to the youth put her arms around him and people got up from bridge chairs to congratulate him. Father moved on to another. I don't remember now what the complaint was; I was too flabbergasted by what was going on.

Then Father DeGrandis took out a small jar of Holy Oil and said matter-of-factly, as if asking for a newspaper, "Holy Spirit, send down Your tongues of fire." The priest directed everyone on the right side of the gym to stand facing the wall on the north side, eyes closed, hands raised. We weren't on that side, but my friend, Mary, kicked off her shoes and rushed up anyway. I watched people get up from their chairs and assemble: hands up, eyes closed, facing the wall, behind each person a man designated as catcher.

Father DeGrandis walked slowly down the line between the gym wall and the people, anointed each on the forehead in the name of Jesus, and then placed his arm behind each one's back to help the catcher break their fall. And most of them did fall: one after the other like dominoes, boom, boom, boom, boom—slain in the Spirit [when the Presence and power of God comes directly at you causing you to fall]. Mary collapsed backwards into the arms of a burly stranger, who caught her under the arms and lowered her gently to the ground. The northern perimeter of the gym floor was covered with the bodies of those slain in the Spirit.

Would this happen to me? I'd seen holy cards of saints lying in a fetal position, figurative arrows piercing their hearts, but those slain in the Spirit in the gym were all regular people like me. Like them, could I let go and let God fill me and fell me?

Once fawning over Father DeGrandis, I'd said, "You are a gift to us, Father, a genius, like Mozart."

He laughed and said it had to do with the music ministry.

"I've been doing this for over thirty years, and I've observed that if people have been praising and thanking God with hymns of praise and thanksgiving for about half an hour, they are wide open and the Holy Spirit can just rush right in," he'd said.

Those few who hadn't fallen staggered, looked groggy, remained swaying in place, or walked slowly back to their seats, but the majority of people were lowered to the ground gently by the line of catchers who then moved on to the next section.

Whatever was happening, I wanted in. When Father signaled for our side to come up to be blessed, I prayed like a little kid, "Now me, Lord. Now, me," jumped up from my bridge chair, and stood with the others facing the wall on the west side of the gym, eyes closed, hands raised. My husband, an experienced catcher, stood behind me.

When Father approached, I opened my eyes as the ones to my right fell one after the other. I was afraid of falling down and I'm ashamed to admit it, but I said to Father DeGrandis, "The bigger they are, the harder they fall." I wanted the blessing, but I didn't want to fall down.

The priest laughed, anointed me with Holy Oil in the name of Jesus, and moved on. I felt a stirring in my heart as if someone were stirring a cup of tea with a teaspoon. The stirring was accompanied by a feeling of peace and happiness so deep that I thought, "This is what Heaven must be like."

I wanted the feeling to go on forever. With bodies on the gym floor to the right and left of me, I stood, eyes closed, hands raised, enjoying the beautiful feeling. Then my husband, the catcher, decided that I was not going to fall, that it was safe to leave me standing there, and moved down the line to be anointed himself.

When I sensed that he'd moved, I was afraid I'd fall and decided that I'd try to move across the gym floor back to the east side of the gym and sit down to enjoy the beautiful feeling. Hands still up in the air, I staggered slowly across the gym like a drunken robot.

Meanwhile, the people who had fallen the first time were beginning to get up and were double dipping, lining up again in front of Father DeGrandis, who blessed them a second time as they fell into the catcher's arms once more.

Head turned watching me, Father blessed a double dipper without looking at him. The man fell into the catcher's arms, unseen by the priest as his eyes followed my progress across the gym. Like a parent tying one child's shoelaces while observing the other child eating dinner, Father called out, alarmed, "Are you all right?"

"I'm . . . fine . . . Father," I said, holding on to the beautiful feeling and pronouncing each word like a tightrope walker trying to communicate from the high wire. I reached my chair and closed my eyes, delighted that the beautiful feeling had survived the trip across the gym.

Everyone thought the disciples were drunk after the Holy Spirit came among them on Pentecost. I felt drunk. I sat, eyes closed, for another fifteen minutes or so, enjoying the feeling when a noise disturbed me. I made a funny observation based on an uncharitable thought, laughed, and the feeling evaporated.

Years later I asked a medical doctor, who had been in the CIA, if any drug could be applied to the skin that would cause that reaction. He said, "Not that quickly." As you can see, it takes a lot to convince me of the authenticity of such phenomena.

What had happened to me? Was this baptism of the Holy Spirit? I don't think so. When I asked Father DeGrandis, he didn't say anything.

Whatever it was, it was the most important experience of my life. For many months, I was like the Ancient Mariner, telling my story to anyone I met. For many months, I would burst into tears speaking about the experience. Why?

The nuns told us that God dwells within us and is always there nurturing, loving, and listening to us. I believed them, found joy in prayer, prayed continuously, and followed the rules set up by the Creator for our happiness, but never had a physical sensation that God loved me back.

I loved God with my whole heart, but it felt like unrequited love. I imagined to the Lord that we look like ants in an ant farm. I wondered how He could tell the Rose Ann ant apart from all the other millions of ants. I was grateful for what God had done for me, for giving me life, health, food, religion, family, education, for all the bounty that life in America provides, but it seemed group bounty. We're all blessed. We're all nourished. There didn't seem to be anything personal about it. I imagine a lot of Americans feel that way.

Now my life is divided in two parts: before the experience and after the experience. B.E., I knew He was there, that He made the universe, that He was out there in the big beyond, that He dwelt within me as well and loved me, but maybe the way a man with many, many wives must love his many, many children. I never felt unwavering belief that He knew my name, let alone would communicate with me, would stir within me and make His Presence felt, would say through that beautiful feeling, "See, it's true. I'm here all the time and I love you, too."

The message is not just for me, it is for you also. Now, A.E. (after the experience), I am constantly on the alert for communication from the Lord.

Sounds nutty, right? Think of the relationship you have with your pets. You try to communicate with them as best you can based on the limitations of the animal. I keep in mind the relationship between my dog, Fifi, and me. I would say to Fifi, "Don't run out when I open the door."

I knew she couldn't understand why I was not letting her out of the house without her leash. I did the best I could to let her know I loved her and cared about her and wanted the best for her, but all my Fifi understood was her water dish and her food bowl and going for walks and my cuddling her. To Fifi, I was smell and sound and sight and love. Communicating was not easy. God is constantly trying to communicate with each of us.

Since the experience, I am less fearful, more trusting, empowered, because I know He is *really there all the time*. And that is the big message.

He wants to communicate with us, but we have to be alert. We have to watch where he pulls the leash. Does He want us here? There?

"Speak, Lord, Your servant listens."

The experience was so profound that I felt compelled to return the next day for Father's Saturday workshop. I had a lot of work to do and didn't have time for anything that would sidetrack me, but like a drug addict, nothing existed of greater importance than getting another fix. Nobody would go with me so I drove by myself into Brooklyn the next day into a dangerous neighborhood, back to St. Michael's gym. Nothing could have stopped me from returning to the scene of the experience.

I arrived just in time for the first workshop which was on, of all things, "Speaking in Tongues," a phenomenon I considered wacky, with one exception. Years ago I had gone to a Charismatic prayer meeting run by Trinitarian nuns. Their prayer in tongues was beautiful, like "lake water lapping with low sounds by the shore" (Yeats). For years, I'd searched unsuccessfully for a prayer group as beautiful as that one.

With that one exception, speaking in tongues [the praise of God in language given by the Holy Spirit] seemed strange, but Father DeGrandis made it seem natural, had an organized way of teaching it, and got results. He stood in the gymnasium in an aisle formed between rows of folding chairs among an audience of about two hundred people. I sat in the back near the last row, attentive, because the experience of the night before had shown me that Father DeGrandis was a powerful instrument of the Lord. I wondered how such a sensible man could be involved in something I considered off the wall.

Saying that speaking in tongues was like driving an old Ford, you have to crank it up, crank it up, crank it up, he rotated his arm as if cranking the engine on an imaginary antique car.

"You're not embarrassed to put on party hats and make fools of yourselves on New Year's Eve; you shouldn't be afraid to make fools of yourself by trying to pray in tongues."

("But why?" I asked myself.)

"Begin with the word 'Alleluia' (which means 'Praise God'), focus on the Lord, and repeat the word over and over."

He asked those new to tongues to stand up, close their eyes, and raise their hands in prayer. Feeling cold and clammy with embarrassment, I stood up as did about forty other people. When I closed my eyes, I was less embarrassed.

He explained that repeating that word over and over again while focusing on God may result in emission of sounds that come from somewhere inside of one, but have not been formulated consciously by the individual emitting them.

"The Spirit prays within you, according to Romans 8:26: 'Likewise the Spirit helps us in our weakness; for we do not know how to pray as we ought, but the Spirit himself intercedes for us with sighs too deep for words.'"

("How scary," I thought.)

Then he asked those experienced in tongues to check whether or not the new ones were really experiencing tongues. When they were, he said to tell the new ones to sit down.

We began repeating the word "Alleluia." I said it over and over again, and after about five minutes the syllables turned into "la, la, la, la."

My eyes were closed and I was focused on the night sky, on the immensity of the starry, starry world that the Lord had made.

Psalm 8

O Lord, Our Lord, how majestic is Thy Name in all the earth! . . .
When I consider Thy Heavens, the work of Thy Fingers,
The moon and the stars that Thou hast made
What is man that Thou art mindful of him or the son of man that Thou visitest him?
For Thou hast made him a little less than the angels . . .
Thou hast put all things under his feet . . .
The beasts of the field, the birds of the air, and the fish of the sea . . .
O Lord, Our Lord, how majestic is Thy Name in all the earth!

A man walked up behind me between the folding chair and me and put his hands on mine. I was shocked. A complete stranger stood, his front to my back, his palms pressed against the backs of my hands. He whispered, "Not yet" and walked away!

I felt ashamed, as though I had failed a crucial test. It took me a few minutes to recover my focus on the Lord and begin again. Meanwhile, the sound of tongues filled the gymnasium. The sound rose and fell, beautiful beyond any musical program. Waterfalls of sound washed over us as people praised in concert harmony. Each seemed to have an individual "tongue," but the whole was an orchestra in perfect harmony, like angels on a riff.

I thought of the lines from "The Rime of the Ancient Mariner" describing the spirits of the dead sailors grouped around the mast and singing hymns of praise: "Round and round went that sweet sound . . ."

I "la, la, laed" away valiantly. A woman slid in behind me and placed her hands on the backs of mine, waited a few seconds, and then said, "Not yet."

When I opened my eyes at her approach, I saw other standees being tapped on the shoulder and told to sit down, but there I was, looming above the crowd, still not doing it right.

More time passed and the concert increased in volume until I thought they would raise the roof with the power of their glorious music. A third woman slid in behind me, placed her hands on the back of mine, and finally tapped me and said, "Sit down, you have it."

I may have had it, but I felt nothing, none of the powerful ecstasy of the night before. I sat down and looked around me. The others were belting out their praise in nonsense syllables blended harmoniously in magnificent music.

In the row next to where Father DeGrandis stood was a young woman in a business suit who had been standing with us newcomers and now sat sobbing hysterically. When Father signaled to the group to stop, he asked the woman to testify about what had happened to her. She sobbed into the microphone that she had had the most powerful experience of her life.

At a point in repeating the word "Alleluia," she felt that some Force within her had taken over her vocal bands, and that the sounds coming from her had been completely under the control of the Holy Spirit.

I still hadn't had an experience like that, but was open to it and realized that it must be because I didn't have tongues readiness yet.

What is "speaking in tongues?"

In *The Gift of Tongues*, Father DeGrandis quotes Agnes Sanford's book, *The Healing Gifts of the Spirit*:

> But if one forgets oneself completely and fixes the mind upon God, letting the words that come unbidden to one's lips flow as they will, then this gift can be most wonderfully therapeutic in the healing of the soul. For out of the depths we cry unto the Lord and the Lord who dwelleth within the depths hears our cry and His love flows over us in a way we have not known before. Moreover when we do not know how to pray, then the Spirit within us prays with "groaning that cannot be uttered," or as we might say, with sounds that cannot be expressed in our own language—and we have a serene knowledge that out of the deep unconscious we are praying according to the will of God. And from the feelings that accompany our prayer we sense that we are being lifted up more closely into His being than we have been when tied to the chains of our own understood tongue.

My original question still had not been answered, "Why?"

Intrigued by this question, I attempted to pray in tongues again. As Father DeGrandis recommends, I focused on the Lord and repeated "Alleluia" until the sounds became something else. Concentrating on beautiful scenes from nature, I watched the sky in my mind's eye and praised the Creator in my heart. The sounds changed to something heavy with vowels and suddenly I was weeping as I brought to God the hurts of my life. I felt a deep inner healing as a result of this profound experience.

I know virtually nothing about it, but think of speaking in tongues as white noise blocking out our own thoughts and allowing God's thoughts to come through.

Every day I thank God for the experiences of His Presence received through Father DeGrandis.

One especially powerful experience came when my son and I were giving Father DeGrandis a lift to Long Island from a magnificent cathedral in a poor section of Manhattan. Climbing steep stone steps, we turned to look at the tenements and warehouses around us before entering the packed cathedral. Still on their feet several hours after Mass, people from the Philippine ministry waved their arms in time to the music as they shouted out hymns of praise and thanksgiving. The cathedral was ablaze with the fire and glory of Pentecost.

My son and I looked around in wonder as we walked down the center aisle under magnificent stained glass windows with waves of powerful music pulsating: praise, praise, praise. The sanctuary was covered with the bodies of those slain in the Spirit and double dippers were lining up in front of Father DeGrandis who stood quietly at the marble altar rail. I lined up with them, hoping for a repeat of the experience in St. Michael's gymnasium. The others all fell, keeping the catchers scurrying. My son and I were not slain in the Spirit, but the memory of those people ablaze with joy in the Living God is indelibly etched in my mind. How glorious it is to see the Power of God manifested through His people.

Father Robert DeGrandis

Massachusetts's native Father Bob DeGrandis did not start out in the healing ministry. From 1959 to 1969, fresh out of the seminary, he worked in the civil rights movement in Miami (Florida), New Orleans (Louisiana), and Birmingham (Alabama) as a member of the Society of St. Joseph, an order of priests who work with African-Americans. Although the work was satisfying, Father felt uneasy with his role, identifying himself more as a social worker than as a proclaimer of the gospel. He felt powerless and ineffective.

Then late in 1969, the *National Catholic Reporter* published an article about Catholic Pentecostals: priests and nuns praying in tongues and laying hands on people for healing. His interest piqued, Father Bob read *Catholic Pentecostals*, a book describing how the Holy Spirit comes upon us and moves us as was described two thousand years ago in the book of Acts. He knew he had found what his spiritual life needed.

After becoming involved with Catholic Pentecostals, Father DeGrandis saw his prayer life blossom. The Lord Jesus baptized him in the Holy Spirit. The sacraments and the Mass held new dynamism. The New Testament took on deeper meaning. The Holy Spirit renewed him in a powerful way, giving greater vitality to his daily Holy Hour. He began bringing people together to study Scripture and pray.

Then miracles started happening. During prayer meetings, people noticed that long-term health problems were vanishing. Everyone who participated in Bible study and being prayed over was healed. Symptoms of arthritis or sinus or headache or whatever disappeared.

Father got so caught up in the healing power of the Holy Spirit that he began inviting people to come up for laying on of hands after Sunday Mass. Usually the whole congregation would respond, and he'd move along the altar rail laying hands on each individual.

All kinds of things began to happen. Father DeGrandis prayed with one woman whose son had come back from Vietnam and locked himself in his room. Dirty and disheveled, he refused to come out for months. The day after the group prayed, the vet came out of his room, cleaned himself up, and went job hunting.

Emboldened by such obvious signs of the Presence of God, Father began a prayer meeting in his own parish. Hearing of extraordinary healings, many affluent white people from over the mountain started coming down to Father's parish in the ghetto. Robert DeGrandis knew this was it! The Spirit of God was doing what no human had been able to accomplish: Blacks and Whites were acting like brothers and sisters, singing and praying together. Many said this was the first time they had related as equals. Father called it an authentic spirituality of the New Testament, built upon the Holy Spirit.

At this pivotal point in his life, Father Robert DeGrandis made a deep commitment to the Catholic Charismatic Renewal, but influential people in his parish didn't like what he was doing. Angry parishioners criticized him for introducing spontaneous prayer, singing, and clapping. Father was transferred back to New Orleans.

Despite the setback, that year he was invited to minister in Puerto Rico where for the first time he really experienced the power of God.

"As I went around the island talking and praying with people, there were tremendous healings. They blew my mind. Every time people complained of pain, we would simply pray and the pain would leave. People with difficulty walking would move normally after prayer."

During that trip in 1971, he was invited to speak to a group of priests on the island of St. Croix. At a little prayer meeting up in the mountains led by an American priest, Father Mike Kostak, Father Bob testified to being baptized in the Spirit [a renewal or actualization of the Graces of our baptism], gave the priests a "tongues workshop," laid hands on each of them, and prayed for a release of the Spirit. It wasn't until 1982 that he saw the results of that seed-planting experience when he heard that Father Mike Kostak now preaches worldwide on the Charismatic renewal.

Another seed sprouted in a well-known television personality, Mother Angelica. When Father DeGrandis was in Birmingham in 1969 praying at a Poor Clare monastery, he said to the Mother Superior, "This Charismatic renewal is beautiful. People are really melted by the love of God."

She responded, "We don't need all of that. We have the Holy Spirit. We have everything."

One day Barbara Shlemon and he prayed over Mother Angelica. A few nights later, the nun received the gift of tongues while sitting in bed reading the Gospel of John. Within two weeks, every nun in the monastery had been baptized in the Spirit. Mother Angelica founded the nationwide Eternal Word Television Network (EWTN). In her biography she calls Father DeGrandis a young, aggressive Josephite priest who bugged her to let him pray over her.

Father planted another seed in Eddie Ensley, a young Presbyterian seminarian, who went to Father's prayer meeting because there was nothing Charismatic in his own Church. Later in 1975, Father heard Eddie give his testimony. He became a Catholic, traveled around the country giving talks, and is the author of *Prayer That Heals Our Emotions* and also *Sounds of Wonder*, a book on tongues.

On a year's leave to examine his ideas, Father Bob made a thirty-day retreat, then went to Mexico for two months to study Spanish. In January 1973 while in Mexico, he was invited to the island of Grenada.

"The prime minister was a man very much involved in the occult and very erratic. He said, 'I'm going to throw out all of the priests on the island.'

14

"There were only 26 priests for 65,000 people. We started the house of prayer and began training prayer group leaders, feeling that in a few months the Church would be thrown off the island.

"We went into different towns as we were invited and said, 'Give us eight or ten people to start with.'

"We would usually get 150 people the first night . . . The people were so simple and so close to God and nature that by the middle of the first prayer meeting they would be baptized in the Spirit, and by the end of the first prayer meeting they would be praying in tongues. (I remember one Catholic theologian who admitted it took him more than two years to come into the gift of tongues!)

"That time in Grenada bore fruit. A woman stood up in a Miami conference in November 1985 and said, 'When the communists took over Grenada, the prayer groups met and prayed and prayed for deliverance. Finally the Americans invaded. We feel that the American invasion of Grenada was a direct response to the intercession of the prayer groups.'

"President Reagan said once that the invasion of Grenada was a response to the prayers of the people of that island!"

Father Bob confided that he hears the Lord speak to him in a variety of ways, but only once has he heard Him speak audibly.

Before he left Grenada, a woman from Jamaica, Ivy Alovees, said, "We'd like you to come to Jamaica."

"At one o'clock in the afternoon, I heard an audible voice, 'Go to Jamaica.' So I went to Jamaica and did the basic teaching of the Charismatic renewal that flourishes today.

"From Jamaica I went to the Dominican Republic . . . When . . . I knocked on the door, the Lord said to me interiorly, 'I want you to pray over the first person who comes to the door for the gift of healing.'"

For many years, that woman, Maria Sandigiovani, traveled all around the world with the late Father Emiliano Tardif in a powerful team-healing ministry.

When Father DeGrandis returned to parish work in Mobile, Alabama, he taught a continuing education course on "Healing Prayer." From an initial enrollment of 80 persons in 1975, it grew to an enrollment of 400, Catholics and non-Catholics, and continued from 1975 to 1983, even though Father left Mobile in 1976. Doctors would send terminal cases to the prayer class; many are alive today.

In 1979, Father went from Mobile to New Orleans. He was told he could not become a pastor because he would alienate some of the people. When he notified his superior that he had decided to join another community, he was given a small conservative parish in Texas, outside of Houston.

Father promised himself he'd be very low key. "But it was hard to be low key. I formed a prayer group. We had 60 people that really had a deep experience with the Lord. They were a powerful group. Within eight months there was a petition to get rid of me, and I was transferred. I asked a leader of the parish why they did not like my ministry. One of her comments was that I 'forced Charismatic renewal down their throats.'

"I said, 'Give me one example.'

"She responded, 'You always tell us to read the Scriptures.'"

In 1979, Father DeGrandis went to see the new superior general who answered Father's prayers of ten years by suggesting that he work full time in the Charismatic renewal. He says, "I have seen powerful conversions, miraculous healings and deliverances in 19 countries around the world. I have seen terminal cancer healed, blind eyes opened, teeth repaired, arthritis, anorexia and all kinds of crippling diseases disappear through the power of God. He confirms His Word with signs and wonders."

A young girl testifies to the healing of her eyes in the following witness, reported in the *National Enquirer*, February 15, 1986:

Dear Father DeGrandis,

I am writing to you in regard to the healing I received while at your service at St. Paul of the Cross Church in North Palm Beach, Florida.

Before I went to the service I was praying that my eyes would be healed, but my mother told me that tonight is going to be more spiritual healing than physical healing. So I attended just out of curiosity.

While I sat in the pew watching you perform miracles in front of everyone's eyes, doubt was coming into my mind. All I can recall is that from out of the blue you nonchalantly pointed to the section of the church where I sat, but as I looked at you it seemed as if your finger pointed straight at me. That is when my heart started to pump. You see, I have had bad vision/astigmatism all my life. When your hand reached out to the section of the church where I sat, I heard the words come out of your mouth, "A person in this section has distorted vision and is now feeling pressure against the eyes. If this is you, please rise." As I heard these words . . . I felt a tingling sensation in my eyes. I was also in my own little world with Jesus. I stood up. You asked me my name, age, and how long I had had the problem. Tears started to roll down my face as I answered, "I'm Karyn Sharkey. I'm fourteen years old and I have had distorted vision all my life." I sat down utterly amazed at the experience I'd just been through. Days later I told my friends and everyone I knew. Some started putting negative feelings in my mind and making me feel unsure, but my parents kept reassuring me and telling me, "God chose you because of all your faith and He wants you to spread this wonderful happening to everyone."

Mommy told me we had received an appointment card telling me it was time for a checkup the day before the service took

17

place. So the following Tuesday we (my mother and I) went to the eye doctor. He did not know what wonderful things had occurred in my life. As he looked at my eyes and looked at my file he said, "Is this the right file? You do have astigmatism, don't you, Karyn?" No reply, just laughter. As he kept examining my eyes he looked puzzled and asked, "Have you had an operation?" I said, "No." Then my mother and I started to laugh and he asked, "What is it?" My mother and I told him what I experienced. He examined my eyes some more and sat down while saying, "I'm an atheist, but I believe in what I see. You have 20/20 vision. You can go home and throw away your lenses." After hearing that terrific news, we burst out of the office, not waiting to call close relatives up north. We spread the wonderful news all around town. I thank and praise God for this wonderful blessing and all the blessings in my life.

Note: My mother went to the optician's office where my contacts and glasses were made. She asked, "Can Karyn ever have 20/20 vision?" The optician replied, "If she is fitted properly with contacts." My mother said, "I mean without the aid of anything?" He said, "It can never be." My mother proceeded to explain to him what had happened. He said, "She would have to have had two healings—one because of the shape of her eyes and second because of her vision."

I am witnessing this wonderful happening all over the country. May God bless you and your beautiful ministry.

Karyn Sharkey

As Father DeGrandis says, Jesus heals today.

"If we believe in a personal God, we believe in miracles. We believe in a personal God who is love, and love always seeks what is best for the beloved."

Father relates the story of five-year-old Mary Peissner of Pleasant Hill, California, who was knocked twenty-five feet when hit by a car. Her mother, Betty Peissner, rushed outside to find her in a coma.

"I leaned over her unconscious body and whispered in her ear, 'Mary, did you give your hurt to Jesus?'"

"She opened her eyes, looked at me and said, 'Yes, Mom, I did.' Then she lapsed back into the coma.

"The doctors . . . said she had broken ribs and a ruptured spleen. There would be three hours of surgery and she might die.

"That's when the miracle happened. A short while after reaching the hospital, Mary came out of her coma. Subsequent X-rays showed that the spleen had been miraculously welded together as had her ribs. I was surprised and the doctors were flabbergasted."

Linda Schweiger of Richland, Washington told Father DeGrandis of being healed of multiple sclerosis, severe depression, and food allergies when a woman prayed over her at a "Life in the Spirit" seminar [to lead people to new life in the power of the Holy Spirit].

"She felt power and light go through her body and heard the Lord say, 'It is time.' Later the Lord showed her that the power and light were His compassion flowing through the compassionate hearts of the woman and the backup prayers who joined in praying in the Spirit."

Of course everyone is interested in miracles. Father DeGrandis demystifies the secret of tapping into the healing power of God: Open yourself up to His healing power by forgiving all who have hurt you, and then praise and thank the Creator with your whole heart. When you are wide open, the Holy Spirit can rush in to heal you.

While giving a retreat in Arizona, Father John Hampsch, C.M.F., dashed into the dining room for a quick cup of coffee. After putting instant coffee in a cup and filling it from a hot water urn, Father Hampsch felt severe burning pain in his throat. When the priest staggered into the kitchen, the cook showed him a container labeled Deadly Poison-Fatal if Swallowed. She had been soaking the inside of the urn with a caustic chemical.

Poison Control urged them to rush him to the nearest hospital. They said if he got there in time, he might live, but would have permanent throat and voice damage. The retreat house was in a rural area too far out for ambulance service.

"While Father Hampsch waited for the car to take him to emergency, he sensed God saying to him, 'Turn to My Word, there is healing power in My Word.'

"I responded silently, 'Lord, I've never done this before, but when one faces the possibility of dying, it is easy to elicit greater faith. I claim, in faith, your words of Mark 16:17-18 . . . signs will accompany those who believe . . . when they drink deadly poison, it will not hurt them at all.' Within less than a minute, the pain stopped and I felt perfectly normal.'"

✌∽

Robert DeGrandis, S.S.J., *Testimony of Father Robert DeGrandis*, 19-21, 25-27.

Robert DeGrandis, S.S.J. with Linda Schubert, *The Gift of Miracles: Experiencing God's Extraordinary Power in Your Life* (Ann Arbor, MI: Servant Publications, 1991), 25, 67, 78, 114.

Father Emiliano Tardif and My Husband, John Palmer: Surprise! You're Healed

Father Emiliano Tardif wore street clothes. Like all priests, he was forbidden by law from wearing clerical clothes in public in Mexico and had not had time to change into religious garb when he arrived at Providence, Rhode Island's, T.F. Green Airport in May 1993 for the 25ᵗʰ Anniversary Conference of the Catholic Charismatic Renewal in the United States. The conference drew a huge crowd to Providence's Civic Center, a large indoor stadium.

Tapes show bishops, crosiers in hand, leading the procession into the arena, then stopping in amazement to look around at the size and power of the crowd singing "We are one body, one body in Christ." The lyrics in English, Spanish, Haitian Creole, French, and Italian harmonized powerfully.

In the bleachers, Dr. John Palmer, an amateur videographer, filmed the event and gave no thought to asking for healing. John considered himself healthy, despite a painful tear in the rotator cuff in his right shoulder that kept him awake night after night for six months. He prayed and focused on his camera. Then, John says, "Father Tardif said the crowd was too large for him to lay hands on each one of us, so he'd do a group service. As Father spoke in Spanish, his words were translated into several languages sentence by sentence.

"Father raised his arms and said, 'We are very fortunate, God is healing people today,' and began to call out healings. When the priest raised his arms, I felt uncomfortably hot. I thought, 'They're crazy. With all these people here, they turned the air conditioning off and turned the heat on.'

"Then I felt intense heat in my neck and right shoulder and down my arm into my hand. The nun in front of me took out her hearing aids and said she could hear. A deaf man to my right, part of a group being signed to, said he could hear, but what really blew my mind was a man in a wheelchair whose prayer group had carried him into the men's room earlier in the day. You knew he wasn't from central casting because the men carrying him were his neighbors. They said he'd been paralyzed in a car accident years ago. The paralyzed man got up from the wheelchair and walked for the first time since the accident.

"These were just a few of the healings near me. There were others all over the stadium. I couldn't believe what I was seeing. There wasn't any difference in my shoulder. I wasn't even thinking about it because I didn't feel I had anything wrong with me compared to other people there.

"When I woke up in the hotel the next morning, my shoulder was pain-free and has been ever since. There were probably other delayed healings like mine multiplying those seen by everyone during the service."

I had opposed John's trip to Rhode Island. How could he drive all that distance from New York with one good arm? When my husband returned and walked down the driveway waving his right arm over his head, I knew something spectacular had happened at Father Emiliano Tardif's healing service. We thank You and praise You, Lord, for showing Your loving Presence among us!

Father Emiliano Tardif: Healed in Spite of Himself

Emiliano Tardif was dying of tuberculosis in the Dominican Republic. He collapsed at a Christian Family Movement meeting on June 14, 1973 as a result of sixteen years of overwork as the country's Provincial for the Missionaries of the Sacred Heart. Rushed to the

National Medical Center, he was diagnosed with acute pulmonary tuberculosis.

Unable to work, Father Tardif decided to go back to Quebec where he was born and raised. In Canada, through July, the priest had biopsies and X-rays at a specialized medical center. All tests confirmed the prior diagnosis: acute pulmonary TB had seriously damaged both of Father's lungs. He was to be hospitalized for a year of treatment and rest before doctors would even discuss the possibility of releasing him from the hospital.

A priest from *Notre Dame Magazine* took Father's picture for an article intended to illustrate how to offer up suffering and be a prayerful patient. The title of the article was "How to Live as a Sick Person." Ironically, by the time the article was published, God had totally and completely healed Father Tardif who left the hospital fifteen days before the issue was released.

On the same day the priest-writer visited, five laymen from a local Charismatic prayer group came to pray over Father Tardif.

"My two sets of visitors had two entirely different points of view: the first, that I accept my illness; the second, that I recover my health."

Emiliano laughed at the Charismatic renewal, so he accepted the Canadian Charismatic prayer group's ministrations out of courtesy, never believing a simple prayer would be enough to heal him. He felt it ridiculous. The laymen quoted the Scripture, "Lay hands on the sick and they will recover."

They told the priest with certainty that they would lay hands on him and the Lord would heal him. Then they moved towards Father Tardif, who sat in a rocking chair, and put their hands on his head in Jesus' name. Embarrassed, Emiliano asked them to close the door.

"They closed the door. (It was too late; Jesus had already entered the room.)"

As the men prayed, Emiliano Tardif felt great warmth in his lungs. He thought it was another attack. "No, it was the burning love of Jesus that was touching me and healing my damaged lungs. There was a prophecy during this time of prayer. The Lord told me, 'I will make you a witness of my love.' The living Jesus was giving life not only to my lungs, but also to my priesthood and to my whole being."

Three days later, the priest felt fine. His appetite was good, he had no pain, and he wanted to go home. The doctors gave Father a test that showed he was healed, but made him stay another month searching "for the tuberculosis that had got away." Confounding the doctors, Father Tardif left the hospital weighing 110 pounds. He left with no medication, no prescriptions, no precautions, no special care, in perfect health.

*   *   *

Father says God heals even though we have little faith. God is large enough to make up for tiny faith and heals us with the faith we have. We don't need more. God's Love is all we need. Focus on how much God loves you. He loves you more than you love yourself. You are His child. Know that God wants to heal you. Feel His Love.

Father Tardif: Labeled a Nut

After a year spent studying the Charismatic renewal, Father Tardif was assigned to a parish in Nagua, Dominican Republic. There Father testified about his own healing at a prayer service for forty people. Then he invited the sick to come forward to be prayed over. Two were healed.

Of course, word spread! Afflicted people came from neighboring towns, the blind, the deaf, and deaf-mutes. Each week there were healings.

In August 1974, Donna Sara was sent home from the hospital to die. As Father prayed over her, the dying woman felt intense heat in her womb, wept, and knew her illness had disappeared. Two weeks later, doctors declared her completely healed. Donna Sara returned to the prayer group bringing burial clothes her children had prepared for her wake.

Opposition to the healings began. Annoying some parishioners, large numbers of people came to church singing joyfully on the way. All this activity in Nagua turned off some priests. Because Father Tardif believed in the healing power of Christ and prayed in tongues, they said, "Father Emiliano may have been cured of his tuberculosis, but he's certainly crazy now!"

However, God said in prophecy, "I am pouring out My Spirit through you. It is a devouring fire that will fill the entire city. Open your eyes and you will see signs and wonders that many have longed for."

"There were so many miracles that we were unable to keep count of them."

Father Tardif's first word of knowledge was, "There's a woman here who is being cured of cancer. She is feeling a great heat in her womb." No one came forward. Ashamed to enter, the woman he spoke of, a prostitute, hid outside behind the fence. The next day, she went to the microphone, wept, and testified. Two operations had not worked.

The healed prostitute told others. So many prostitutes were evangelized that 80% of Nagua's five hundred houses of prostitution closed their doors. Brothels became houses of prayer. "Nagua used to be a city of prostitutes, but now it's a city of prayer."

On June 10, 1974, Father was sent to replace a pastor on vacation in Pimentel, a rural town with few paved streets. The pastor reluctantly gave Father Tardif permission to form a renewal group. Then the pastor left. Father invited people to hear the testimony of his own healing from TB. Two hundred came, bringing their sick on stretchers.

One man had been unable to walk since breaking his spine five and a half years before. "The man on the stretcher began to sweat and tremble. Father remembered when God healed him, he felt heat. The priest said to the man, 'The Lord is healing you. Get up in the name of Jesus. You are healed.' I gave him my hand and he looked at me with surprise and with much effort got up and started to walk slowly. Father shouted, 'Continue walking in the Name of Jesus, God is healing you.' The man took one step at a time and reached the tabernacle, weeping and thanking the Lord. He went home carrying his stretcher under his arm. Ten others were healed that night. Father Tardif says, 'Speak less of God and more with God and He will slowly transform the world.'"

Father Tardif: "The Resurrected Christ Walks Among Us"—Police Protest

Each healing brought more people. Three thousand came to Pimentel for the second gathering. The huge congregation spilled over from the church, filling the street.

During prayers for the sick, Mercedes Domingues, blind for ten years, felt intense cold in her eyes. On the way home, she could see a little. The next day, Mercedes was completely healed.

"She started telling everyone. If the Lord had opened her eyes, who was she to keep her mouth shut? Her healing made a great impact on the people of Pimentel."

Seven thousand came the next week. Sick people professing the love of Jesus filled the park beyond San Juan Baptista Church. An enormous number were healed.

"When we ask for something, He gives us everything. There is no limit to His power or to His love. He does not heal just two or three, He is infinitely more generous."

Traffic was overwhelming. The police protested, demanding the meetings stop. However, the police chief's wife, sick for twelve years, had been healed. Insisting the meetings continue, the police chief assigned eighteen extra policemen to keep order.

Twenty thousand people attended the fourth meeting on July 9, 1974.

At nine o'clock in the morning, people had begun arriving by bus and truck from all over the country. "The crowd was so big that we had to set up loudspeakers and put the altar on the roof."

A policeman, partly paralyzed after a stroke, was healed that night. After that, the police were solidly behind the meetings.

Deaf for sixteen years, a woman from Pimentel heard ringing and then heard perfectly. Another local, unable to walk, had been reduced to crawling. He was cured. More than one hundred people that Father knew about were healed that night.

"We were experiencing just what we had read in the Bible. It was the risen Jesus walking among us and saving His people."

Forty-two thousand arrived for the fifth gathering. People traveled from all over the Dominican Republic, from Puerto Rico, and from Haiti. Crowds covered the highway. Loudspeakers were inadequate.

The size of the crowd frightened Father Tardif. People tried to touch him, pulled off all his buttons, and almost crushed him. Prophetic words were given for Father: "Evangelize My people. I want a people of praise."

This gathering got extensive newspaper, radio, and television coverage. Talking it over, the Bishop and Father Tardif agreed there would be no more big gatherings. Father began forty-five small prayer groups in different parishes in Pimentel. The entire town became a house of prayer. Father began taking Wednesdays off so people would learn to follow Jesus, not Father Tardif.

"The Lord continued to heal the sick."

As an example, from 1974 to 1984, a single prayer group at the home of Guara Rosario on Colon Street recorded 224 cases of physical healing. In one day, November 13, 1975, twenty-two healings were noted. Soon the prayer group stopped writing them down because "there were too many." Father Tardif noted that there were no longer many healings in that prayer group because there were no sick people. All had been healed. Father Tardif says, "It is simply the gospel repeating itself."

Father Tardif Calls Himself "The Donkey that Brought Jesus to Pimentel"

"The Lord infiltrated the mass media . . ."

God healed the mother of a television announcer in Pimentel on Palm Sunday, 1975. The reporter told the story of the miracle to the television audience.

"The Lord then reached into the Chamber of Deputies where he cured a deputy to the National Assembly of a problem in her neck."

More favorable publicity came on October 15, 1975, when the bishop of Pimentel responded to questions of the authenticity of this and other testimony concerning Father Emiliano Tardif when asked by the French magazine, *Il Est Vivent* [*He is Alive*]. The bishop wrote that the testimony was authentic. *Il Est Vivent* published an article on the healings at Pimentel in Issues 6 and 7.

However, severe criticism loomed ahead. On July 16, 1975, God warned Father Tardif that he would be ridiculed and persecuted, but not to worry.

When three months had passed, the pastor returned to find big changes at San Juan Baptista. Everyone from policemen to children was abuzz with the good news of the healing power of the living God.

The day Father left Pimentel to return to Nagua, he saw a little donkey in the street stop, snort, and show his teeth. It smiled at him as if saying, "You're just the donkey that brought Jesus to this town . . .

The glory . . . (was) never intended for you . . . (it) was intended for the One whom you carried."

Father Tardif went back to Nagua filled with joy. Then the attacks God had warned him about began. Through it all, Father was confident in Jesus and felt peaceful. The secretary of health accused Father Tardif of being a charlatan. Others called his healing ministry "sorcery." Radio and television commentators called him a liar and a fanatic and made jokes about him, and in twenty-four hours the press was waging war against the healing priest. So-called psychologists said there was nothing miraculous about the cures; they were caused by group hysteria. Father Tardif challenged them to organize meetings to cure all the sick people in the country.

Neighboring priests asked Father's provincial to banish him from the Dominican Republic. They felt he was hurting the pastoral organizations and emptying their parishes. One told him there were too many miracles. So many miracles seemed crazy. His enemies contended that there were few miracles at Lourdes, but through the ministry of Father Tardif there were many, too many.

Father responded that the measure of our faith is the Gospels. Saint Mark's, the oldest of the four Gospels, tells of eighteen miracles and healings in the first sixteen chapters. "If we removed the signs of power from Mark's Gospel, only one or two pages would be left."

In August 1975, Father wrote an article entitled, "It's Christ's Fault" for *Amigo del Hogar*, a family magazine. In it Father explained that Jesus heals, not Father Tardif.

* * *

Like Father Tardif, let us pray to empty ourselves of all that keeps God's Love from filling and healing us. As we forgive those who have hurt us, let us remember how Jesus forgave those who betrayed and murdered Him. May the light of Christ's forgiveness grow within us and light the world with His Love.

Father Tardif: On the Road with Jesus

The Dominican Republic's National Bishops Committee endorsed Father Tardif, despite vicious attacks on him from all sides. Invitations to preach poured in from all five continents. Father hit the road with Jesus, proclaiming: Jesus lives today!

Invited to give a retreat in Jánico, Dominican Republic, in a parish with low church attendance, Father preached to a half-empty church.

". . . lying on the floor was a man who looked like a rag doll. Both hands and both feet were paralyzed, and he was unable to eat or walk by himself." Distracted by the man's pitiful state, Father started the service by praying for him.

"As soon as we started to pray, he began to tremble and sweat. I remembered that I had also felt a penetrating heat when the Lord healed me. So I said, 'Stand up! The Lord is healing you!' Then I took him by the hand and told him 'Walk!'"

After the healed man walked to the sanctuary, he wept as he told the congregation he had not walked in nineteen years. Father Tardif said if he had known that, he wouldn't have dared tell the man to stand up. The next day the church was so full that some had to listen from outside through the windows.

Father changed his method of preaching. He began to restrict his talks to testimony to the power of the Lord as he had witnessed it most recently.

"The marvels of the Lord are so numerous that one lifetime is not enough to tell all what He has done in the past ten years."

In Montreal in June 1977, 60,000 people filled the Olympic Stadium. Cardinal Roy, six bishops, 920 priests, and the mayor were present. Over one hundred persons in wheelchairs sat together near the altar.

While the whole stadium prayed for the sick and praised the Lord, Rose Aimee, a victim of multiple sclerosis for eleven years, got up and walked.

"On the other side, a man got up from his wheelchair, and then another and then another! In all, twelve cripples left their wheelchairs and began to walk!"

Everyone wept. The headlines in the biggest newspaper in the city announced the news: "Sensation at Olympic Stadium. Cripples Walk." Another Montreal newspaper, *Le Journal*, said, "The Bedridden Get Up and Walk."

The next day, when Father was asked on television if he felt the healings were due to mass hysteria, Father said, "Well, explain to me why no cripple ever got to his feet in a baseball or a football game, and why no cancer victim has ever been healed while his favorite team was winning."

In 1981, Father preached a retreat for 320 priests in Lisieux, France. He was very intimidated by the presence of learned men like Cardinal Suenens and Cardinal Renard.

"Father Tardif said, 'Don't leave me alone, please, Lord.' Fortunately, that first night the Lord healed a priest who had suffered from phlebitis and that ended the discussion. I remember how he pulled up his trousers legs in the dining room and showed both his legs completely healed."

Of this Cardinal Renard said, "The Church is a permanent Pentecost, not a permanent rationalization."

Our God lives!

Father Tardif: The Secret? Abandon Yourself to God and Praise Him

Contrasting the Living Jesus of Power, Love, and Light with the textbook Jesus, Father Tardif tells a joke, "One day, Jesus asked his disciples, 'Who do they say I am?'

"Simon Peter stood up and said, 'You are the eschatological theophany which ontologically sustains the intentionality of our subconscious and interpersonal relationships.'

"Jesus opened his eyes wide with surprise and asked, 'Whaaaaat?'"

In 1975, Father was invited to be the Dominican Republic's delegate at a big Charismatic conference in Rome. His superiors felt someone native born should go in his place. Disappointed but obedient, Father rode on horseback to a village in the Dominican Republic in the hills. While praying in tongues for the sick, the word "epilepsy" kept popping into his mind. Finally, he took a risk and asked, "Is there someone here with epilepsy? The Lord is healing you now!"

The local headmistress of the school finally raised her hand after a long period of silence. Her fifteen-year-old daughter stood next to her trembling and sweating. The girl, epileptic from birth, was healed completely. Her sickness never returned.

God had granted the word of knowledge to Father Tardif, a gift far more useful to Father's ministry than the conference in Rome. Father describes the word of knowledge as an inner certainty that monopolizes your being and remains for a long period of time. ". . . you are certain of something, which you know doesn't come from you, but through you." To prove it is genuine, it must be accompanied by testimony confirming its validity. He cites examples of its occurrence in Scripture: Nathan looking into King David's heart (2 Samuel 12:1-15) and Peter with Ananias and Sapphira (Acts 5:1-11).

In November 1982, 5,000 people gathered in Tahiti for a Mass under the stars. After Communion, Father prayed for the sick. The whole throng prayed in tongues. Words of knowledge came as they sang in the Spirit. Father was surprised by the precision of one: "There is a person here who has come to Mass for the first time . . . She has a pain in her spinal column on the fourth vertebra. A coconut hit her in the back. Right now you are feeling . . . tremendous warmth there. The Lord is healing you. You will soon be able to give witness of a complete healing." Sentences had come to Father like tissues coming from a tissue box.

At an even larger gathering the next day, people testified to healings of the day before. A Protestant woman, who had attended her first Mass, had been injured and healed just as Father had said. While knocking down coconuts for tourists, she had been hit on the back by a coconut that damaged her fourth vertebra. The bones had fused. Her doctor did not know how to operate for that condition. At Mass the night before, she felt warmth, trembled and cried, feeling the Presence of God. She had been healed. Her pain was gone.

Father tells of seeing workers producing enough electricity for all of Paraguay at an enormous hydroelectric complex. Yet at night, the workers' houses were lighted by candles. No power lines connected their houses to the plant just a few feet away. Father says let's not be like that. Let's tap into the Light of Christ. Abandon yourself to God and praise Him. He heals His people in a climate of praise.

Father Tardif: How Big is God? Thiiiis Big!

Try this on for size. Father Tardif taped nine television programs for CHOT-TV, Ottawa, Canada, during the summer in 1982. The half-hour programs were to be aired at the end of the year. Words of knowledge came to Father during the last program. He said, "There's a man alone in a hospital. He has a very severe back problem. The Lord is healing him. He is feeling a great heat in his back. He can get up and walk."

On the way home, Father realized the program wouldn't be transmitted until several months later. Father laughed at God's sense of humor. The man to be healed while watching the show had not even gone to the hospital yet.

The words given Father were validated by a letter he received January 16, 1983. In June, God had given Father the knowledge of a healing that was to take place on December 18 and Father had said, "Right now."

"The Lord is not limited by time . . . He is the Eternal Present!"

Father says miracles ". . . show us the power of God, so that we can abandon ourselves to Him in every facet of our lives."

He visited a police captain on his deathbed. Captain Munoz had not eaten solid food for fifty days, but drank rum every three hours.

"We prayed for him and . . . he stopped drinking immediately! He didn't even have to go to the hospital for detoxification. I found myself remembering Wisdom 16:12: 'No herb, no poultice cured them, but it was your word, Lord, which heals all things.'"

Shouts and curses sounded outside the church the day after Captain Munoz was healed of alcoholism. Father found women lining up their drunkard husbands to be prayed over. Oddly, that day there were more drunkards in church than in the bars.

Father says from 1858 to 1978, only sixty-four miracles were officially recognized by the Church at Lourdes. Miracles are healing that are medically impossible. Healings speed up the healing process that might alternately have occurred over the long run if medicine, surgery, or convalescence had intervened. Not all healings are miracles. At Lourdes in the year 1972 alone, 5,432 healings were recorded.

Anita Siu de Sheffer of Santiago, Chile, experienced a miracle. She lost her senses of taste and smell through a cerebral lesion caused by an automobile accident ten years prior. Doctors in the best hospitals in the United States told her the fibers transmitting these senses could not be reunited surgically. Only a miracle could help her.

At a healing Mass in Panama, Father received these words of knowledge, "There is a woman here who is suffering from a very difficult condition. She is going to be healed in her sleep tonight, and tomorrow she will be able to give us testimony of a complete cure."

The following morning, Anita was awakened by the smell of roses outside and the aroma of coffee from the kitchen. She could taste her breakfast. After ten years, the woman had been totally and permanently healed.

"The Lord Jesus had done what no doctor in the world was capable of doing. He is Lord of the impossible!"

Man's Solution: Toenails Fall Out. God's Solution: Arthritis Goes Bye-Bye

Maria Teresa Galeano de Baez of Paraguay wrote Father Tardif on August 25, 1981 telling of her miracle. Severe pains in her ankles, knees, and wrists were diagnosed as rheumatoid arthritis. Mrs. Galeano went to the United States for treatment at an arthritis center. Her specialist, Dr. Alonso Portuondo, confirmed the diagnosis and told Maria that her illness was incurable. A treatment of gold salts was recommended to check its advance. Side effects soon appeared: ". . . sores broke out all over my body, and my hair and my toenails fell out. Slowly the number of platelets and white cells in my blood started to decline." At this point, Father Emiliano Tardif arrived in Paraguay.

When Father prayed for healing at the Church of St. Alfonso, Maria could hear her heart beating and thought it would explode. At his prayer service at the church in Coronel Oviedo, a tremor ran through her body. Father Tardif announced that two women were being healed of arthritis at that moment and asked them to kneel down to prove it to themselves.

"By the time Maria saw Father for the third time at a Mass, her pains were gone and she had stopped all medication. At the airport when he left Paraguay, Father prayed for her once more."

"Father's final words to her were, 'Don't say, "I've got arthritis," say, "I had arthritis,"' because you are healed."

New lab tests proved Maria really was cured. Dr. Nicolas Breuer, her doctor in Asuncion, said, "I have to say that there is a Superior Being, way beyond the bounds of science for whom nothing is impossible." Even bone damage to the joints had disappeared. It was a miracle.

Many healings took place in Tahiti where Father Tardif ministered from October 21 to November 14, 1982. One miracle blessed a blind man who began to cry during a Mass for the sick. While drying his eyes, the blind man realized he could see.

This miracle so deeply impressed Gabilou, a famous singer in the Pacific, that the celebrity repented, confessed his sins, and received the Eucharist. Jean Gabilou gives his testimony publicly. Healed spiritually, the singer now evangelizes, reaching out to youth, living and singing for Jesus. "Jesus is also the Lord of singers and artists."

Father Tardif: Do You Believe that God Can Heal You?

Sick of hearing about miracles, a priest in the Cameroon reluctantly attended a retreat for priests given by Father Tardif at Sangmelima. The turned-off priest was healed of chronic arthritis so severe that he had been unable to tie his shoelaces. Father Tardif laughed because suddenly the priest who had not wanted to hear about miracles couldn't stop talking about them.

"Our attitude must be that of unconditionally placing ourselves in the hands of a loving Father. He has a wonderful plan for each one of us."

At a conference in Quebec in 1974, Father Tardif gave a workshop for two thousand people. Father left his desk to shut the door and saw Helen Lacroix, a stranger, in a wheelchair. She had been unable to walk for five and a half years. The woman said they wouldn't let her in because the hall was too full. Father pushed her wheelchair into the conference hall and closed the door behind them.

He talked about the importance of witnessing to wonders God has worked in our lives. A doctor rose and said that before claiming a miracle, medical certification was necessary, as in Lourdes. Father protested that if someone feels he has been healed (as Father had himself been healed of TB) ". . . you can't expect him to wait for a doctor's opinion before giving thanks to God."

The doctor argued on eloquently using vocabulary so highfalutin that Father did not understand some of it. As the doctor was speaking, Father Tardif said, "God touched the woman in the wheelchair that I had brought into the hall. She felt power flow through her. She got up and began to walk down the aisle alone.

"After an automobile accident five and a half years earlier, she had had a delicate operation in which her kneecaps had been removed. As a result, she was incapable of ever walking again."

When the crowd quieted down, Father said to the protesting doctor, who was the most moved in the group, "Jesus must have thought that since Father Tardif was unable to answer you, he would do it Himself."

Father urges that we keep our eyes on the Healer and not on our own healing. He says we must have faith in Jesus, not faith in our faith. "The greatest act of faith is to begin to believe that God is bigger than the little faith that we have, and that he doesn't depend on us."

* * *

"Praying in the name of Jesus is not just saying the name of Jesus, but having the confidence of knowing that He is in us and we are in Him and the Father always hears us. Some people when they are praying for healing . . . sing or repeat the holy name of Jesus over and over again. There really is health and power in the name that means 'God saves.' We know that the word of God does exactly what it says."

Father Tardif: Mommy Says "Yes"

Father Tardif says pray simply, the way a child asks his mother for something. The child doesn't say, "Mom, if it's best for me, and if the cholesterol won't hurt me, can I have an egg, please?" You should ask knowing you are going to receive. Remember, Jesus said, ". . . believe that you have received it, and it will be yours." (Mark 11:24)

On June 13, 1975, Father was in a rush. He had worked a full day, had just ended a prayer service, and was hurrying out of a tiny chapel deep in the tropical countryside of the Dominican Republic. A little girl stopped him. She led her mother by the hand. The child asked Father Tardif to pray for her mother. Father was a little annoyed. He had just finished praying for the sick, and the mother and child had been in the congregation.

The child explained that her mother was deaf and didn't realize that Father was praying. Father felt sorry for them. They were poor simple country people, probably both in their bare feet. Even though Father didn't have time, he signaled for them to sit down on a pew, put his hands on the woman's ears, and said a simple prayer, 'Lord, heal her, but hurry up, please, because I've got a lot of work to do!'

"Then I bent over and asked the mother, 'How long have you been deaf?' She answered: 'For eight years.'"

"Father was surprised she answered. He assumed she'd be unable to hear him. He spoke again, even more quietly. "'You seem to be a very good mother.'

"She smiled. The deaf woman had heard me! Even better, the Lord had heard our unusual prayer! The woman had felt a quick breeze enter her ears and they cleared."

"Even before there is a word on my tongue, behold, O Lord, You know it all." (Psalm 139:4)

The next healing story focuses on forgiveness as a way of opening a path for God to rush in to heal us. For ten years, Olga G. de Cabrera of Guatemala suffered intense pain in her arms and legs. Her extremities were gradually becoming deformed. She visited fifteen doctors looking for a cure for an unnamed condition, probably some form of arthritis. Olga's condition was so desperate that one doctor had suggested amputating her left leg.

She became a total invalid on May 1, 1976, and expected to spend the rest of her life in bed or in a wheelchair. At a Mass for the sick, when prayer for inner healing of past hurts began, Olga started to cry. She experienced deep forgiveness of all who had injured her. When Father Tardif prayed for physical healing, Olga sensed something saying, "Get up and walk." She felt intense heat throughout her body as people do when being healed. Then she started to shiver. With tears in her eyes, the crippled woman began to walk toward the altar. "Glory to You, O Lord, King of the Universe."

*   *   *

Memorize God's promise: "Long before they call I shall answer; before they stop speaking I shall have heard." (Isaiah 65:24)

Father Tardif: Two's Company, Three's a Healing—Mega Praise Power

There were physical healings at every retreat between 1978 and 1988, but Father Tardif saw greater fruits from group prayer than when praying for people alone. Community prayer has special power.

Fifteen people journeyed together from their little tropical village to one of the big meetings at Father Tardif's church in Pimentel, Dominican Republic. The number of healings attracted so many people that the congregation had grown from 40 at the first meeting to 40,000 people by the fifth meeting. Imagine the healing power of 40,000 praying people.

As the group of fifteen men and women traveled on foot, by pickup truck, or bus, they prayed and sang hymns praising and thanking God. By the time they got to the meeting, praise had fully opened them to the Holy Spirit. At that meeting, they were all healed. It wasn't until they returned to their village that the group realized that each one of them had been healed of something. Father Tardif yearns for the day God will cure all who are sick as Jesus did in the Gospel. (Matthew 8:16)

"Deep healing . . . (comes) . . . only when we enter into a permanent communion with God, so that he can purify and sanctify us."

At sunset, after many wonderful healings at a service led by Father Tardif, people left the stadium in Brazzaville, Congo. Singing joyfully, they headed home. The guard started to turn off the lights. He saw a woman deep in prayer among the empty seats in the silent stadium as singing faded in the distance. Next to her sat her six-year-old son, his crutches propped on either side of him.

The guard told the woman to leave, but she said she couldn't. Her son hadn't been healed yet. Touched, the guard let her stay. The mother prayed for more than two hours.

"At 8:15 p.m., the little boy got up on his own two feet and began to walk without his crutches, a tender and beautiful sight in the pale moonlight. This is the perseverance in prayer that Luke's Gospel speaks about (11:5-8)."

But what kind of prayer? Was this two hours of petition? No! Father recommends abandonment accompanied by prayers of praise. He quotes the end of the prayer of Charles de Foucauld, abandoning himself into the Father's hands, ". . . For I love you, Lord, and . . . surrender myself into your hands . . . with boundless confidence, for you are my Father."

Father Tardif says, "You cannot imagine the physical and inner healings that have been achieved by . . . abandonment accompanied by prayers of praise . . . Praise the Lord always and for all things."

* * *

"I tell you solemnly once again, if two of you on earth agree to ask anything at all, it will be granted to you by my Father in heaven. For where two or three meet in my name, I shall be there with them." (Matthew 18:19-20)

Father Tardif: Giving God a Blank Check

Don't keep petitioning God. Praise Him.

"When we praise, we always receive what we don't necessarily receive when we ask."

Don't beg God for your recovery. Abandon yourself unconditionally into our Father's loving hands. Father Tardif illustrates this with the story of a priest who was finally healed after having prayed for relief from a peptic ulcer for four years.

In June 1981, the missionary was raced to the hospital because of severe hemorrhaging. He left the hospital three days later with medicines, a strict diet, and a fixed meal schedule. It was impossible for the man to stay on the diet because he was a traveling preacher. As a result, the priest was hospitalized again, this time with four peptic and one duodenal ulcers, duodenal nodules, severe gastritis, and a hiatal hernia. He needed an operation, though it was not an emergency.

"When the priest left the hospital, he began hemorrhaging again. Fearful that this meant an immediate operation, he began to complain, saying, 'Lord . . . You know . . . I can't keep to my diet because I have to travel to different . . . countries preaching . . . You know that we can't always have the same meal timetable . . . You who could heal me so that I might continue to preach your word, look how you are treating me.'

"At that precise moment, I clearly heard the voice of the Lord saying, 'Why do you fear the night that brings you to a new day?'

"That voice was, for me, spirit and life . . . I abandoned myself, without conditions, to His plans for my life and, if necessary, for my death . . . I had signed a blank check so that he could do whatever he liked with me . . . I knew with the certainty of faith that a new creation would be announced with the coming dawn. So I went back to bed and slept peacefully. I knew that at that moment the Lord had done something to my whole life. A few weeks later I was feeling so well that I stopped taking my medicine and bothering about my diet.'"

Six months later, a gastroenterologist in Houston told the priest that no operation was needed, the ulcers had healed. Two years later, he felt fine, didn't need any medicine, and ate whatever he wanted. The priest attributes his recovery to abandoning himself into the hands of his loving Father.

Father Tardif has seen more healings when he prays in tongues than when he prays normally. He believes praying in tongues puts us in God's hands unconditionally, giving God a blank check.

Invited to appear on *The Minute of God*, a one-minute television program in Bogota, Colombia, Father complained that three minutes were given to advertising beer, but only one minute to God. He prayed rapidly. When finished, Father opened his eyes, looked at the clock, and realized he still had 30 seconds, so he prayed in tongues. According to Father Diego Jaramillo, a great Charismatic preacher, several people in the television audience were healed.

*　*　*

When we don't know how to pray as we should, "the Spirit Himself prays for us with groanings that cannot be expressed in words." (Romans 8:26)

Father Tardif: Looking Foolish Before 65,000 People

Father Tardif prayed in tongues before 65,000 people in a Montreal, Canada stadium at the second Charismatic Congress. As he prayed in tongues, Father repeated words of knowledge popping into his head. Among the healings he announced was, "There is a seventy-four-year-old mother seated in front of her television at home. At this moment, the Lord is giving her back her sight."

Upset, a priest friend chided Father for saying a blind woman was watching television. It was illogical. The next day, Father Tardif visited his family outside of Montreal. A relative told him the eyes of a local blind woman had been healed while she sat in front of her television the day before trying to follow the audio of the healing Mass.

Father Tardif met the woman, Mrs. Poulin, exactly seventy-four years old. Despite treating her for retina problems, doctors had declared the woman's illness progressive and incurable. When Father gave her word of knowledge on television, Mrs. Poulin felt intense heat in her eyes.

Though her vision had been restored, she still couldn't see well enough to read. Father said, "The Lord doesn't do things by half measures. Let's pray so that you can also read the word of God."

Three days later, Mrs. Poulin called to say she was reading the Bible.

Father said, "The gift of tongues (in the stadium) had put me at the disposition of the Lord, so that he could communicate what he was doing."

In Cameroon in Africa, Father felt as if he were back in the Dominican Republic. "It was the same climate, the same landscape, and the same God performing his wonders."

The mother of a five-year-old girl who was unable to walk testified at Mass in the cathedral: her daughter had started walking. The woman's neighbors all knew the little girl could not walk.

"When the child walked up to the altar, there was a storm of applause in the cathedral . . . people began to cry and to praise the Lord. Jesus also lives today in Africa!"

A word of knowledge revealed, "There is a sixteen-year-old boy here who is deaf in the left ear. The Lord is healing him."

Of course, the teenager couldn't hear the message because he was deaf, but this didn't stop the Lord. The boy came up to the altar at the end of Mass and told the congregation that he was sixteen years old and had just been healed of deafness.

At the cathedral in Yaounde, Cameroon, a bank worker, who had worn pebble-thick glasses for nearsightedness for thirteen years, was restored to normal eyesight. When she went to work without her glasses and told her co-workers, they all came to Mass. Four thousand people attended the service. Father had to have the altar moved outside.

During Mass, a little girl whose left arm had been paralyzed was healed. A policeman was slain in the Spirit and rose up with a healed spine. The Mother Superior of an African religious order also rested in the Spirit and was healed of an ulcer.

"There were so many healings that it would be impossible to count them all."

Our God reigns!

Father Tardif: Jesus is Alive and You are His Witnesses

In 1981, Father Tardif witnessed the Presence of the Risen Christ on all five continents. In November, back in Santo Domingo, 42,000 people from 1,500 prayer groups in the Dominican Republic demonstrated at Olympic Stadium in honor of Christ the King.

"At 11 o'clock, I spoke on 'Jesus is Alive' and immediately afterward . . . the team . . . prayed for the numerous sick . . . at 2:30 we heard many, many testimonies. Among others, I saw a man who, due to a heart attack, had been paralyzed down the left side, and couldn't walk without crutches . . . healed completely during the prayers for the sick. At 2:30 he climbed the steps of the platform, alone and without his crutches. Sobbing, he thanked the Lord who had just healed him."

On the road again, at a retreat in Monterey, Mexico, Father celebrated a Mass for the sick at an open air shrine where 6,000 people surrounding the altar were drenched by continuous rain. After Communion, God healed a stroke victim who had lost the power of speech a few years before.

"The Lord freed his tongue and the man started to shout, 'Glory to God! Glory to God!'

"Everyone who knew him was amazed and he was brought up to the microphone to give his testimony. At that moment, two cripples got up and started to walk. One of them came to the microphone to give his testimony while his parish priest wept with joy. Many of the priests who were concelebrating with us were overcome by emotion and were crying as well. I was so happy. I shouted, 'Jesus is alive, and you are His witnesses.'"

In 1982, in French Polynesia, some people from the farthest islands sailed for three days to get to Father Tardif's five-day retreat. The last week of the missionary's month in Tahiti, he gave a talk every evening, then celebrated Mass, and prayed for the sick with 3,000 to 5,000 in attendance. Instead of giving a sermon, Father would give testimonies of people healed the night before.

"The testimony that struck me most was that of a man who was completely blind in one eye and almost blind in the other. He was due to have an operation soon. During the Mass for the sick, he saw a great light fill the church, just as the host was raised up, and his eyes were opened. He had been healed."

*   *   *

"The deaf that day will hear the words of a book and, after shadow and darkness, the eyes of the blind will see. But the lowly will rejoice in Yahweh even more and the poorest exult in the Holy One of Israel." (Isaiah 29:18-19)

"Let the wilderness and the dry-lands exult, let the wasteland rejoice and bloom . . . They shall see the glory of Yahweh, the splendor of our God. Strengthen all weary hands, steady all trembling knees and say to all faint hearts, 'Courage! Do not be afraid. Look your God is coming . . . He is coming to save you.'" (Isaiah 35:1-4)

Father Tardif: Jailbirds Sing with Joy

Father Tardif was jailed once with others in Yugoslavia and three times alone in Congo. In October of 1983, Father went to Medjugorje, Yugoslavia where the number of healings attracted the attention of the National Security Police. At Mass for 3,000 people on Tuesday, Father said a prayer for the sick, "From the first moment, the Lord began to heal the sick, and they came up to give their testimonies at the end of Mass."

Healings attract a crowd. On Wednesday, 8,000 attended Mass. News of amazing healings reached the authorities. They were not pleased.

"On Thursday, there were 14,000 people, but we were . . . in jail!"

At lunchtime on Thursday, three men had swaggered over to the food stand to arrest Father Tardif and his two companions as they finished their meal. The three frightened men were rushed to Citluk, a few miles away, tried before a judge, and then locked up for preaching without government authorization. Hour after hour passed. They had no idea what was going to happen to them. At 5 p.m., when one of them asked for a glass of water because it was so hot, the guards said there were no glasses. When they sang hymns, guards rushed in and ordered them to stop. After Father's and his friends' suitcases were inspected, they were given twenty-four hours to leave the country. The clergymen borrowed money for a taxi, hurried 150 kilometers to Zadar, and escaped by boat to Italy.

Cardinal Emile Biayenda of Brazzaville, Congo was not so lucky. In 1977, the Marxist police took Cardinal Biayenda for questioning. He was never seen again.

Locals in Congo were alarmed when Father Tardif was arrested, alone, three times. Despite dangerous conditions, Father Tardif preached for fifteen days in Brazzaville.

"I have never seen so many people healed as in these retreats. The only place that can be compared to the Congo . . . is French Polynesia . . . The signs in the Congo were even more arresting and surprising.

"The first night in Brazzaville, one of the words of knowledge Father received was, ' . . . a man here . . . suffers terribly in his right leg. He is lame . . . it is difficult for him to walk at all. At this moment he is trembling and feeling . . . great heat in his leg. The Lord is healing you. Don't be frightened . . . You're being cured. In the name of Jesus, stand up and walk.'

"There was a long moment of silence. No one among thousands . . . moved. Not everyone understood French so Father Kombo translated what I had said into the local dialect. Suddenly a twenty-eight-year-old man got up and began to leap like a deer. His foot was bandaged. He had suffered for years from a pain in his right leg and had been so lame that he couldn't work. His right foot was still bandaged as he stood up before the people, but now his limp had gone, once and for all. Everyone started to clap and praise the Lord. They had all seen 'the glory of Yahweh' burst forth before their very eyes."

There were many, many other healings. Among them, a blind man recovered his sight. A ten-year-old girl, deaf and dumb from birth, heard and screamed in panic. As in Yugoslavia, news of healings reached the authorities. By the end of the retreat, 5,000 were attending. The National Security Police were fascinated. Trouble loomed ahead.

Healings Put Father Tardif in the Slammer: Congo

Phenomenal healings at Linzolo outside Brazzaville began God's triumph in Congo. The following Sunday, at the cathedral in Brazzaville, 2,000 celebrants, too many to fit inside the church, forced Father Tardif to say Mass outside in front of the cathedral. At the prayers for the sick, intense heat swept over a paralyzed man who had been unable to move for eight years as a result of a hemiplegia.

"A word of knowledge invited him to get up. To the amazement of everyone, he got to his feet and walked up to the altar by himself. At the microphone he sobbed as he thanked the Lord. He had been healed!"

Then each day for two days, Father Tardif moved to a different church. In front of St. Peter's Church, with thousands in attendance, God healed two cripples. One, paralyzed for two and a half years, a thirty-five-year-old woman brought in on a stretcher was healed after Communion. The woman held Father's hand as she climbed the three steps of the podium. She danced before the altar.

"The crowd went wild with joy. At that moment, a crippled man whose family had carried him there, also got up by himself, and very calmly walked up to the altar. There were all sorts of healings."

By Tuesday, the crowds were so large that Father had to go to a 15,000-person capacity stadium in the parish of St. Ann. By 3 p.m., the huge stadium was filled to overflowing with more people outside than inside, a crowd of over 30,000 people. There were many healings. Among them, Father remembered a child born deaf who was healed in the stadium.

"His father, a professor at Brazzaville College, threw a party that night, and invited all his friends to give thanks to God for the miracle. The next morning he went to the central office where he was registered as a member of the Communist Party, handed in his party card, and told them, 'I don't need this any more. God exists. He healed my son.'"

A member of the government came under cover of darkness to warn Father Tardif that the National Security police were growing uneasy. Government spies began tailing him.

Emiliano flew to Punta Negra, 700 kilometers from Brazzaville.

"During all the ten years that I have been in the healing ministry, I have never seen so many blessings poured out on an assembly as I saw during the celebration of the first Mass for the sick in Punta Negra. The lame walked, the deaf began to hear, the dumb shouted, and the blind recovered their sight. We tried to make a note of all the testimonies so that we could choose some of them to bring to the microphone. There were more than 100 healings in the first Mass!"

A Protestant pastor, paralyzed after suffering a hemiplegia several years earlier, arrived in a taxi and was carried in on a chair. The next day, testifying to his healing, the pastor rose to his feet without any help, approached the microphone, and gave thanks to the Lord with all his heart.

Father was to finish his tour with Mass in a stadium with a capacity of 40,000. The night before the concluding Mass, Father Tardif was arrested. The Marxist National Security police did not like the way Father was disproving Marx's claim that God is dead.

Father Tardif: In Jail for Jesus

Friends in the Communist party told Father Tardif, "Marx is dying."

Father laughed, but it was not funny. Three National Security policemen came to the door at night, just as Father was about to go to bed exhausted, to be taken for questioning.

The Jesuits with whom he stayed wouldn't let Father Tardif go alone. Six years before, Cardinal Emile Biayenda had gone with the police at night alone and had never returned. Three Jesuits accompanied Father Tardif.

His crime: A stamp was missing from his visa. He was accused of entering Congo illegally, by canoe or by swimming. Father had never mentioned politics in any of his talks, but he didn't have to. Each of the hundreds of healings spoke of the existence of a Loving God.

Father Tardif was questioned for two and a half hours. The other priests were also interrogated. Father Tardif told Father Kombo jokes while they waited. Annoyed by the priests' laughter, guards made them sit in different corners, like naughty schoolchildren. At five o'clock in the morning, the four priests were returned home, but Father Tardif was placed under house arrest. The government hoped to prevent Monday and Tuesday's assembly of 40,000 at the stadium.

"The Communists were getting fed up with the signs that proved over and over again to the people of the Congo that the gospel is true, that Jesus is the Messiah, and that there is no one else, only Jesus who saves."

Father was interrogated again for three hours Monday night. On Tuesday, thousands assembled for a Mass of thanksgiving and healing in Revolution Stadium. People came from as far away as Cameroon and Zaire. There were murmurings when people heard Father Tardif was under house arrest and would not appear.

Tuesday evening, police interrogated Father Tardif from 7:30 until 11 p.m. Finally released from house arrest at 10 a.m. on October 12, 1983, Father took the boat across to Zaire and freedom. He had been interrogated three times.

When Father told Cardinal Malula of Kinshasa, Zaire, of the healings in Congo, the cardinal was amazed. He said, "Father, how do you explain this?"

"I replied, 'It's because the gospel is true.'"

In Zaire on Sunday afternoon, Father Tardif concelebrated the Eucharist with Cardinal Malula and his priests for a congregation of 10,000 at the People's Palace built for Mao Tse-tung as an advertisement for Marxism. There were so many healings that another Mass was offered the next day. Over 30,000 people attended.

"I was reminded of the prophecy that the Lord had given us back in Pimentel in the Dominican Republic when we asked him why He had sent us so many people and He said, 'Evangelize my people. I want a people who lift up their voices in praise.'"

There were beautiful testimonies of healings on Sunday. At the end of Mass, the cardinal gave his blessing and it began to rain. It had not rained in Zaire for many months and the people saw the rain as another blessing. They left singing happily.

"Let the wilderness and the dry-lands exult, let the wasteland rejoice and bloom." (Isaiah 35:1)

Marx is dead. Jesus is alive!

Father Tardif: Jesus is the Messiah

"In a blink of the eye, a trumpet will sound, I will meet Him face to face . . . there beside the walls of Zion, the holy city."

But Father had years to go before the trumpet sounded. In 1985, Father Tardif began a new book, carefully selecting and organizing his best testimonies from the preceding few years and storing them in a briefcase. He brought it with him while giving retreats in Venezuela. At a stadium in Caracas, Venezuela, Father Tardif preached before 10,000 people.

"Such was the faith of the people that healings started to take place even before we had begun the prayer for healing."

While Father preached, thieves broke into his car and stole everything, including his briefcase with the precious folder containing irreplaceable testimonies. He said to the Lord, "Lord, if you want us to write this new book, you will accomplish more healing. The testimonials we had can get lost, but we can never lose you."

Calling Jesus the light of the world, Father begins his new book with the first healing he witnessed of someone born blind. It took place in Mbandaka, Zaire, at a service for 15,000 people.

". . . an eight-year-old girl who had been born blind suddenly began to shout, 'I can see. I can see!' She was immediately surrounded by the people who were close to her. Then she asked, 'Who is my mother?' A pair of open arms, a pair of eyes filled with tears, and a maternal smile gave her the answer. Then in her mother's arms, the little girl said in a loud voice, 'Oh Mom, how beautiful you are.'" Jesus, light of the world, had taken the child out of terrible darkness. He can transform even a congenital ailment.

A journalist, Maria M. Perez, reported about healings she witnessed on March 24, 1987 in Espíritu Santo, Mexico. "Father Tardif announced many cures of people suffering from skin diseases, spinal problems, and others of the shoulder, the eyes, hearing, cancer, the heart, arthritis, asthma, the kidneys, and many other complaints."

Undoubtedly, the cure that most impressed those present was that of an eleven-year-old child, Alejandro Anguiano Contreras, who had been almost totally blind when he came to the meeting.

The boy had undergone four operations. Doctors had told Alejandro's mother, Mrs. Maria Contreras, that her son could not be treated and should be placed in a school for the blind. During prayer for the sick, the child opened his eyes and realized he had regained his sight.

"Then will the eyes of the blind be opened . . ." (Isaiah 35:5)

Father Tardif says, "If today Jesus opens the eyes of the blind. It means . . . We are indeed in the messianic times!"

Father Tardif: Empty Wheelchair

God healed nineteen-year-old Giovanna Manzo of Laureana, Italy, on July 6, 1986. A rare disease caused Giovanna's bones to crumble from birth. At forty days old, the infant's femur fractured. Seven operations and four years in the hospital did not help. Doctors warned that by adolescence, the girl would die or be left paralyzed. Though poor, her parents took Giovanna to the Rizzoli Orthopedic Institute in Bologna where she had eighteen operations, the last when she was fourteen years old.

Giovanna became bitter, contemplated life in a wheelchair, and decided on suicide. She thought that God, if He existed, must be cruel. The teenager planned to end her life by throwing herself off the balcony. Just as her wheelchair reached the railing and she was about to kill herself, two girls from a prayer group, Rossellina and Sabina, arrived uninvited. Giovanna raged at them about her suffering. They spoke gently about Jesus' love for her. Giovanna felt warmth throughout her body. She accepted the visitors' friendship, but insisted they not talk about Jesus. The girls left and returned later that day with twenty other smiling, gentle young people who brought food for her and visited.

"I smiled that day, the first time in eighteen years."

Rosa Maria suggested they pray together. Giovanna did not want to but agreed out of gratitude for their kindness.

"During the prayer that followed, Rosa Maria asked Jesus to tell us if he wanted to heal me. She opened the Bible and read that passage about the paralytic who could not get down into the pool by himself when the angel stirred the water, but Jesus came and healed him. (John 5:1-18) When she had finished reading, all of them were crying and hugging me, assuring me that Jesus was going to heal me. I could not understand. I thought that it was all a joke." [They must have opened the Bible in a random way for a word from God concerning her healing.]

In September, Giovanna had another life-threatening surgery, grafting ten centimeters of bone to the thighbone. The drug used to graft the bone was so strong that the treatment had to be stopped for fear of causing lung collapse. When Giovanna saw the doctor again, the bone had grown and the wound had healed. The young woman began to ask herself if Jesus really was looking after her.

The following summer, Giovanna became part of a prayer group where she began to talk to God as to a close friend. At a retreat given by Father Tardif, she witnessed many cures. One of Giovanna's friends complained to God that He was healing people from other countries and other cities, but had not healed anyone local. Then Giovanna heard Father Emiliano announce, "At this moment, the Lord is carrying out a major healing. Jesus is healing a cripple." She felt intense heat rising through her legs.

Alessandra, who sat next to her, cried out, "It's you, Giovanna, it's you!" The afflicted girl couldn't take a step in faith.

"You are feeling intense heat in your body," Father said. "In the name of Jesus, stand up."

Thinking not of herself, but of Jesus for whom nothing is impossible, Giovanna got up and for the first time in her life went to the altar all by herself. She climbed the altar and glorified Jesus for what He had done for her. The wheelchair is now empty.

Father Tardif: Doctor Healed

Medical student Myriam Lejeune of Lyon, France, ruptured a disk lifting a patient. The head of neurosurgery diagnosed her condition immediately, but for reasons Myriam can't fathom, delayed the operation for 48 hours, causing irreversible damage.

"An ankylotic spondylitis had formed on the scar of the herniated disk. This was confirmed by medical diagnosis, biological tests, and X-ray examination."

In excruciating pain, Myriam faced creeping paralysis that would gradually extend throughout her body. She suffered terribly and lost all hope.

Then in Strasbourg, France, Myriam joined a Charismatic community where she learned to accept God's love and to forgive.

Myriam completed her medical studies. Although pain persisted, the young doctor adjusted. Dr. Lejeune saw all the neurosurgeons in France without result. She spent nights walking to alleviate attacks.

Then along came Father Tardif!

In 1981, Myriam went with her parents to a service conducted by Father Tardif in Geneva. Dr. Lejeune's agony was so severe on the trip that she sometimes cried with pain as she lay in the vehicle transporting her.

"While praying for the sick, Father Emiliano said, 'There is an invalid here who is suffering a lot from the spine. That person is now feeling heat rising from the spine to the head.'

"I . . . began to pray for the person who was beginning to receive that blessing. Then, filled with wonder, I began to think, but Myriam, that's what you are feeling.

"A wave of heat was running along my spine and spreading across my head. It was marvelous!" Her healing had begun.

On the drive home, Myriam was able to sit up in the car, but her complete cure was gradual. Over six to eight months at first, Dr. Lejeune had two nights without pain, then one week, then only sporadic pain. Finally the pain was gone. Dr. Myriam Lejeune of Lyon, France, testifies that Jesus healed her completely.

On the other side of the world in a neighborhood of Moca, Dominican Republic, Jose Ramon Rosario Sanchez, sick from birth, suffered severe pain from aplastic anemia. Doctors determined his condition incurable.

At the age of twenty-two, Jose had been bedridden for four years. He entered the Salvador B. Gautier Hospital in Santo Domingo, hoping to regain his ability to walk. Dr. Gonzales Cano, a specialist in aplastic anemia, said the marrow of Jose's spine had been so severely affected that walking would inevitably cause a stroke. Dr. Cano told Jose's parents to take him home and help him adjust to life as an invalid.

Three years later on June 17, 1975, Father Tardif paid a surprise visit. After praying over Jose, Father ordered the man to rise from the chair in which he had been sitting for four years. Jose took a few steps. Covered with sweat, the invalid walked. His brother said, "We were amazed . . . Jose was walking."

The house was filling with people. Many cried. Others clapped. Jose's brother was dazed. Jose, the healthiest of men, has been traveling to other cities giving testimony. "Nobody (in Moca) doubts anymore that God has complete power in this world."

Through Father Tardif, From Stretcher to Bicycle

In Cordes-sur-Ciel, Dominican Republic, Fernande Gobert went from stretcher to bicycle.

A teacher with a vocation to enter the Benedictine convent, Fernande's plans changed in July 1975 when extremely painful sciatica from a herniated disk forced her to be hospitalized for surgery. Continuing pain and further operations caused her to leave the convent to teach as a lay person.

Experiencing constant pain and problems moving about, Fernande felt lucky to be able to get around at all. Then things got worse. More operations put her in bed in permanent pain. The woman could no longer sit and could take only a few steps using a cane. At a medical dead end, Fernande said, "I was due to spend the rest of my life on a bed of pain."

Six more operations failed to bring relief. Doctors began to give her morphine twice a day to help her cope with excruciating pain.

In the middle of that agony, the members of a prayer group began to visit and pray with Fernande. On September 16, 1982, a sister from the prayer group made the "mad" suggestion that Fernande go to Cordes-sur-Ciel where Father Tardif was celebrating the Eucharist.

With no thought of how painful the trip would be, the desperate woman traveled with the nun to Cordes-sur-Ciel by ambulance. Fernande must have been opening the Bible at random for a word from God because she says, "While praying, the Lord gave me the reading about the healing of Hezekiah (2 Kings 20:1-11) but I did not pay much attention to it."

This selection reads in part: ". . . tell Hezekiah, the leader of my people . . . I have heard your prayer and seen your tears. I will heal you. In three days you shall go up to the Lord's temple."

At Cordes-sur-Ciel, Father Tardif spoke on the Real Presence of Jesus in the Eucharist. Then the priest gave testimonies of healings which had taken place after a sick person had received the Eucharist.

At Communion, two brothers carried Fernande on her stretcher from the back of the church to the altar. Father Tardif knelt down to give her Communion.

"Then he asked Jesus present in the host to heal me. Finally, he placed the ciborium on my head and said, 'Lord, one day a woman touched your garment and she was healed. We know that you are present in the Holy Eucharist. Touch your child and heal her as you healed the woman with the loss of blood.'"

He told Fernande she had to make an act of faith by getting up and beginning to walk.

"I took his hands and rose from my stretcher. With his help, I started to walk. Then he let go of me and I took five steps by myself. I could not do more. Then Father added, 'The Lord has healed you. Take ten steps tomorrow, even if it hurts. Little by little you will feel that you are healed.'"

Two years later on September 5, 1984, Father Tardif received a postcard from Lourdes saying Fernande had ridden with friends by bicycle over 280 kilometers to Lourdes in thanksgiving for her healing. The grateful woman married and resumed her career as a math teacher.

Father Tardif: The Lame Leap like Stags, Lepers are Cured

"Jesus is the same yesterday, today, and forever. What he did 2,000 years ago, he does again in our own time because he has the same power today as yesterday."

On the island of Mauritius in 1985 at a huge prayer service featuring Father Tardif, a sixty-year-old man, barely able to walk even with the aid of a cane, got up and walked. When he had given his testimony before 10,000 people, he began to run.

". . . then another also abandoned his cane and there was yet one more who was walking. It was almost too much to see so many people who had previously been lame walking in all the aisles, some with their crutches raised up in the air, others without their canes. Our God is generous."

In Sangmélima, Cameroon, Father Tardif prayed with three hundred patients in a government leprosarium. Father was quite upset to witness all that suffering. ". . . the scourge of leprosy eating away at human flesh. Some had had their limbs amputated . . . others were blinded . . . and the smell of rotting flesh was overpowering."

When Father returned to the Dominican Republic, a nun who was a nurse at the leprosarium wrote Father Tardif to tell him that the

Lord had healed ten lepers that day. The healed lepers returned to their villages giving testimony to the goodness and power of God.

In 1975, Helene Gaspoz, forty-three years old, of Evolene, Switzerland, suffered from terminal bone cancer confirmed by thorough medical examinations. Mrs. Gaspoz suffered severe pain in her back, then her legs became paralyzed. The woman spent three months in bed without being able to move her head.

On June 1, 1975, she met Father Tardif at Sion, Switzerland. Helene had gone to the meeting to pray not for herself, but for her husband and three daughters. Mrs. Gaspoz felt the excruciating pain she suffered meant she would die soon.

When Father spoke the word of knowledge, Helene did not realize right away that he was talking about her. She had not asked to be healed.

"I suddenly experienced a sensation of intense heat flooding my body. My daughters told me I had become red all over. After the meeting, I noticed that my back was not hurting and that I did not need to find my balance for walking. Some friends who had come with their son who was a doctor said to me, 'But Helene, you're boiling.'"

By the time Mrs. Gaspoz arrived home, she realized she could turn her head. That night, Helene could turn in bed without difficulty for the first time in years. On waking the next day she was a new woman. All pain had vanished and her mouth was not full of blood as it usually was when she woke up. Helene got up without any help, feeling as light as a feather. The joy-filled woman ran to wake up her whole family shouting, "The Lord has healed me!"

Healed after ten years of sickness, Helene Gaspoz prayed, "Thank you, Lord! You are marvelous! We cannot doubt your resurrection anymore. You prove to us every day that you are living among us. Alleluia!"

Father Tardif: Ho Hum, Another Cancer Healed

On December 7, 1984, Don Pedro Martinez from northern Mexico got unexpected results from the latest tests for his bone and prostrate cancer. His urologist said, "Don Pedro, you are not well; you are extremely well!"

In 1987, Pedro began to have problems with his right arm and leg. Then he developed intense pain along his spine, which strong painkillers did not help. Regular injections prevented him from fainting with pain. Some specialists in medical centers in Mexico and in the United States blamed his kidneys, others his weight. They all agreed he should be operated on in Houston, Texas.

Pedro underwent two operations. He was losing all feeling in the lower extremities and had sharp pain. So ill that he was not allowed on regular flights, Pedro had to fly by air-ambulance.

The operations were fruitless. He was worse than ever: unable to move and numb from chest to feet. After the operations, family members increased their visits. Unknown to Pedro, he had been given only three months to live. During the last operation, doctors found cancer had spread to his bones and prostate. His case was hopeless.

Pedro began losing weight at an alarming rate. Pain medications kept him unconscious for the most part. Pedro lived past the three-month deadline and was taken to Monterrey. Doctors there said not to have illusions. He was terminal. For several months, he received radiotherapy at Monterrey, Mexico.

In Monterrey, Pedro was visited by a prayer group. They spoke of the love of God and laid hands on him for a new outpouring of the Holy Spirit. The experience of Baptism in the Spirit [which makes real and revitalizes our Baptismal graces] was powerful: Pedro Martinez was deeply touched.

On November 22, 1984, Pedro and his wife flew to a rally in Guadalajara where Father Tardif was to appear. As usual, Pedro was in his wheelchair.

On stretchers, in wheelchairs, some carried in the arms of others, thousands of expectant pilgrims milled around the stadium singing hymns. Limping hordes on crutches and canes waited joyfully for the gates to open.

Sixty thousand people witnessed cures as Father Tardif prayed for the sick. A man walked with his crutches raised high. A blind woman regained her sight. The healings went on and on until finally Father announced there were only five minutes left. Pedro's wife prayed, ". . . If today is not the day for him, do not allow him to get discouraged or to weaken in faith."

Then Father announced five healings. One of the men was being healed of bone cancer and should wait two weeks before testifying. ". . . he was going to feel intense heat throughout his body."

Pedro was covered with sweat. He felt as if fire were consuming his body. He knew Father was talking about him.

Eleven days later, the radiologist in Monterray suggested re-examination by new radioactive material. Samples of his bones were re-examined by the radiologist and the oncologist. They looked everywhere for cancerous spots on his bones. Pedro's radiologist said, "Medicine is good, but not as good as this. You are cured. There is no need for more radiotherapy."

Father Tardif: What's the Matter? You Deaf?

In May 1986, after prayer for healing, Father Tardif heard a teenage girl with a frantic look on her face screaming in the midst of 26,000 people in the stadium of Mbandaka, Zaire. Deaf and mute from birth, the teen was astounded when she suddenly heard songs and praise. The girl screamed while trying to block her ears.

The next day, the healed girl testified using words learned that day: "Thank you God . . . Alleluia."

Her sister stood next to her, answering Father's questions as the healed girl testified by her smiling presence. When Father asked how old the former deaf-mute was, the girl was unable to answer, not yet comprehending language. Her sister answered for her, "Fourteen years old."

Then the formerly speechless girl repeated what her sister had said, "Fourteen years old." Now that the teen heard spoken language, she would learn how to speak.

The next story, the healing of Celia Covarrubias of Irapuato, Mexico, sounded so incredible that the first time Father Tardif told it, he was warned the story would make him a laughingstock. However, a year after being healed, Celia armed herself with her medical reports and testified before 15,000 people in a Mexico City stadium.

"Some twenty years ago, I began to suffer from a cholesteatoma (tumor) in the left ear . . . infection set in.

"In 1978, I underwent a trepanation and my inner ear was removed. I thus lost all hearing on that side."

As the infection progressed, a second trepanation became necessary. Her inner ear bones were scraped. The main concern of doctors was eliminating the infection that was still spreading.

In January 1986, Celia began a Life in the Spirit seminar through the Charismatic renewal. In February 1987, at a rally in Querétaro, Mexico, as Father Tardif prayed for healing, Celia prayed for her family and friends. Resigned to her hearing loss and accustomed to hearing with one ear, she said, "Lord, here I am. You know what I am lacking and you know what I've got too much of. I place myself in your hands." She did not ask any particular favor.

As Father mentioned that a thirty-eight-year-old woman had been healed in her left ear, Celia felt intense heat and heard a loud noise. She blocked her right ear, the good one. To her surprise, she heard normally with her left. Celia asked the woman next to her if the volume on the public address system had increased. The woman said, "No."

Had God healed her? "What is certain is that though there was no medical possibility of hearing, I could hear perfectly with my left ear.

"It's been two years since I was healed. The doctors have conducted new hearing tests and cannot explain how I am able to hear.

"Now my problem is . . . how to proclaim to the whole world that we have a God who . . . has given us his only Son, how can he not give us everything else?"

People Healed by Reading: Father Tardif's Book, Jesus Lives Today!

A friend praying in tongues over Father Tardif began to laugh. She envisioned lots of people rejoicing as they read a book written by Father Tardif. Time passed. When Jose Prado asked Father's permission to publish his teachings on cassette, Father suggested Jose help him write a book, *Jesus Lives Today!*

"I would like to thank God for these last ten years of evangelization ministry," said Father Tardif.

Jose and Father Tardif visited those healed in La Romana, Nagua, and Pimentel, Dominican Republic, to document their testimonies. By the time of his death in 1999, Father had witnessed hundreds of thousands of healing in fifty countries. There were even long-distance healings God worked as people read *Jesus Lives Today!*

Although Father Tardif never visited Hungary, in February 1988, Eszther Molnar was healed in Budapest while reading *Jesus Lives Today!*

"My right hand was not well, with tendonitis . . . Then one day I had to stop working altogether because I could not hold anything in my hands. That is when I started to read your book. I reached the chapter where you mentioned that you had offered the Eucharist for readers who are sick. I did not read but rather prayed that simple prayer. I felt myself being bathed in the power of the Lord and felt compelled to raise up my hand during the prayer. Very quickly a flow of heat ran through my arm and at that very moment my pain vanished. Not only was my right hand healed, but it is now stronger than the left one."

Augusto Cesar Victoriano Baldera, a twenty-two-year-old cadet in the Dominican Republic Air Force, was also healed while reading *Jesus Lives Today!* On October 8, 1984, admitted to the Ramón de Lara Hospital of the Dominican Air Force with severe back pain, Augusto had lost all feeling in his right leg. Eventually he had to use a wheelchair. Doctors found a herniated disc between the fourth and fifth vertebrae. After fifteen days in the hospital, the cadet was discharged. Doctors ordered six months rest. He was devastated. A fighter pilot with many parachute jumps to his credit, Augusto could no longer walk by himself.

He began reading *Jesus Lives Today!* at midnight and had only read nineteen pages when he felt he needed to pray. "I began to pray quietly. Then, unwittingly, I found myself . . . praying aloud. [He woke up his brother] . . . my brother . . . was also praying for me. At that very moment, I experienced a feeling of peace and quiet within myself as well as a gentle tingling throughout my body. I called (to) my brother and told him . . . 'my body has become less stiff.' Then I sat up and began to bend forward on my bed. When I realized that the Lord was beginning to heal me . . . I called out to my brother . . . 'Let's . . . give thanks to God.' At about one o'clock, my cousin woke up . . . [the brother said].

"'The Lord is healing Rudy' . . . My cousin . . . burst out 'Glory be to God.' At three . . . my mother joined us in our thanksgiving. The Lord healed me that night. The doctors say it is unbelievable." At the time of his testimony, Augusto had made six more parachute jumps, logged fifteen more hours piloting a jet fighter, played sports and enjoyed good health. He was a witness among the cadets.

"I now belong to a new army which proclaims this truth, 'Jesus is alive and He gives life to His own.'"

Father Tardif: Why is One Healed and Not Another?

"We receive healing as a free gift, so who are we to ask God, 'Why do you heal this one and not that one?' We are not healed because we deserve it. Healing is gratuitous, a gift from God.

"The testimony of Josefina Guzman from Zapotiltic, Mexico, shows that we are healed because we are ill and not because we deserve it on account of our good works."

For a number of years, Josefina felt weak all day, was short of breath, and could not do her housework. Her husband called her lazy.

A doctor prescribed a small brandy each morning for low blood pressure. Brandy was too expensive, so Josefina drank a small beer, felt better, and began to drink throughout the day. She became an alcoholic.

When Alcoholics Anonymous told Mrs. Guzman the first glass was her problem, she knew her situation was impossible. ". . . if I didn't drink, I could not work, but if I didn't work, my husband would beat me."

Josefina knew only a miracle could heal her, but the woman thought miracles were for another age, not for today and for good people, "not for drunks like me."

At a renewal prayer group, she learned that God still works miracles today, but her health continued to deteriorate. Dr. Ismael Espejo gave her a pap test on May 24, 1984. Josefina had advanced uterine cancer. The disease was in its fifth stage and had spread throughout her pelvis. Her case was hopeless.

Josefina went to a healing Mass celebrated by Father Emiliano Tardif at Guadalajara, Mexico.

During prayer for the sick, Josefina felt a hand touch her lightly on her left shoulder. In November 1984, the dying woman attended another rally at Jalisco, Mexico. Sixty thousand people praised the God of marvels. When Father Tardif began the healing prayers, he cautioned the crowd that Jesus would heal many, but not all. Josefina thought to herself that she would not be healed. ". . . you are a drunk and do not deserve it."

Father Tardif announced that five persons were being cured of cancer and one was a woman with cancer in her belly. Josefina shouted out, "It's me." She was sure the Lord had cured her.

On January 4, 1985, the doctor declared her completely healed. Josefina shared Father Tardif's words, "Jesus is master of the impossible!" A final examination was to be given on July 10, 1986 to confirm her healing. Mrs. Guzman no longer drank. The Lord was now her strength and her fortress! She is willing to share her medical records with all who ask.

Father Tardif: One to a Customer?

A policeman rose up, very touched at a retreat in Quebec, Canada when Father Tardif received a word of knowledge that God had healed a person deaf in the left ear. "It's me. I could hear nothing from my left ear but now I can do so perfectly."

The second night, a word of knowledge revealed healing of pain in the spine caused by an accident. Father Tardif asked who was feeling great heat in the back. He said, "Get up and you will see that your pain has disappeared." The same policeman from La Sarre rose. With tears in his eyes, the officer said he no longer felt pain.

The third night, Father said, "There is someone here who suffers pain under his toenails. Your feet are feeling hot, very hot, and the Lord is healing them for you." The policeman rose a third time. The man had not even known the name of his illness, gout, but the pain was gone.

The others on retreat didn't want the police officer back on the fourth day. They felt he was hogging healings. Father Tardif explained that the power of Jesus touches each one. "He has given us a sign that we can place our trust in his love. Our God dispenses many blessings to all his children."

Fifteen days later at a retreat in Montreal, Canada, the police officer testified to his triple healing: hearing, spinal column, and gout. Father Tardif urges us to ask God for a complete healing. Don't feel He's limited to healing only one ailment.

"God gives generously always beyond our expectations."

The policeman had moved away from God, but the experience of healing touched him and all his family. He subsequently became a leader in the Charismatic renewal.

God's sense of humor popped up before thirty thousand people in a stadium in Santiago del Estero, Argentina, in 1984. A mother brought with her a five-year-old boy, paralyzed for two years. The child could not move. When his mother went to Communion, she left the paralyzed child sitting in his seat. She expected him to stay there.

It took a long time to distribute Communion to thirty thousand people. When the mother returned to her seat, her paralyzed son was not there. Convinced someone had abducted her child, the mother wept into the microphone at the end of Mass. Her son was missing! The "little lost one" was found playing with other children in the back of the stadium. God had cured the boy during the prayer for healing and he had run back to play with the other children.

Even people not physically healed still receive God's blessing. One man, a prisoner in a wheelchair, embittered for five years after a ghastly car accident, when suddenly at the stadium his attitude changed. Since the prayer rally, the crippled man feels like a useful person. He's begun to enjoy life.

"His soul was healed. His pessimism was cured. He does not feel the need to be healed of his paralysis."

Father Tardif: Babies from Heaven—I Pray and Jesus Heals

Sister Regina Catteeuw's brother, Lucas, and his wife, Maria Rosa, had been married since August 22, 1975. Their firstborn, Lucas, Jr., arrived on August 22, 1988, on their thirteenth wedding anniversary. Sister wrote to Father Tardif to remind him of a word of knowledge he received November 1987 at Ghent, Belgium. "A couple are here today who have been married for twelve years. They have not yet been able to conceive . . . A year from now they will hold their baby in their arms."

Cradling his son in his arms, the happy father said, "You have existed so long in our waiting and in our dreams. Every year spring and winter returned, but you did not come. That you did not arrive earlier is a secret between God alone and you."

"Do you work miracles?" asked a reporter in Colombia, South America.

"Father Tardif replied, 'No . . . I pray and Jesus heals.'"

When asked to describe healings that really impressed him, Father described a few that demonstrate God's sense of humor.

In 1984 in Monterrey, Mexico, the aisles were jammed at Communion time. As Father Tardif passed through the crowd, people tried to touch him and requested prayer. Father kept thinking, Jesus is the healer, why do they seek me? He saw a woman with tears in her eyes, carrying a child. For some reason, Father kissed the child. The next day, the woman testified that her two-year-old had been healed of deafness by Father Tardif's kiss. From then on, everyone wanted a kiss. Father Tardif told them that wives should receive kisses from their husbands.

At Monte Maria, a Charismatic community in rural Mexico, each Sunday over 50,000 people met for Mass. Father Gilberto Gomez prayed for the sick at that time. One Sunday, the pole of the Vatican flag fell and hit a crippled person who could only walk all doubled up.

"To the surprise of all, he rose up by himself. The falling pole had straightened his spine. Today he still walks normally."

Another healing that made Father Tardif laugh took place in Arequipa, Peru, in 1985. He announced the healing of a paralytic, signaled by mild heat in the legs and trembling. No one responded; the tense silence was upsetting. Father said that in a little while the person would be able to give his testimony and proceeded with other words of knowledge that were all confirmed, but the first one was like a bone stuck in his throat.

"The last word he received was, 'The Lord is opening the ears of a deaf person.'

"At that very moment, a person in a wheelchair stood up and shouted, 'Father, I can hear, I can hear! Until just now I heard nothing!'

"Father said, 'In fact, you are also the cripple the Lord has healed, but since you were also deaf, you did not hear that the Lord had cured you of paralysis. In the name of the Lord, walk.'"

The man started to walk to the applause and joyous laughter of the crowd. Father asked God from then on to begin by healing the deaf to avoid such situations. As a confirmation, when the author's husband, John Palmer, was healed through Father Tardif, he reported the deaf being healed first at the gathering.

Father Tardif: All God's Children

God heals Muslims, too. In October 1988, Father Tardif preached a week's retreat for 400 leaders of the Charismatic renewal in Burkina Faso, Africa. Many Muslims attended healing Masses celebrated in front of the cathedral each day. Zenabo, a forty-five-year-old Muslim woman, whose whole right side was paralyzed, was urged by friends to accompany them: "Tonight many sick people will be healed. Come with us."

Zenabo was healed. She testified at the closing Mass before thousands, "Open your hearts to Jesus. Jesus is alive. I am witness to this. I suffered from complete paralysis of my right side. I tried one hospital after another but they could not cure me . . . I am a Muslim, but I came and Jesus has saved me."

Maria Guadalupe Lopez de Preciado, whose husband Armando was a reporter for *El Occidental* daily newspaper in Guadalajara, Mexico, wrote Father Tardif witnessing to the healing of their daughter Claudia.

During a hernia operation on July 3, 1984, doctors suspected Claudia had cancer. Biopsy results would take a week. If as suspected cancer was present, a second operation would be required immediately.

On July 11, 1984, Dr. Barragan told the parents that their worst fears had been realized: Claudia had an inoperable third stage abdominal neuroblastoma. Two tumors had invaded most of her abdominal cavity. A miracle was their only hope. Claudia was taken to the oncology department of another hospital where Dr. Juan Arroyo confirmed the diagnosis.

The distraught parents brought Claudia to a healing Mass celebrated by Father Tardif on July 28. Many were healed, but Claudia was not. "After Mass . . . my daughter and I approached Father Tardif in tears and I told him, 'Father, my daughter suffers from an incurable cancer, and if she dies, I too want to die. She is my only daughter.'

"He said to me in a calm and soothing voice, 'Do not cry. In the name of the Lord, your daughter will be healed.' Having said this, he laid hands on Claudia's head and prayed for five seconds."

When Claudia's parents wrote, chemo and radiation had been completed, surprisingly without adverse reaction. Armando and Maria enclosed a copy of Claudia's records. One document dated November 12, 1984, says, "The tumors have disappeared. The patient can go home."

At the end of 1984, twenty thousand people filled the sports arena of a major seminary in Paraguay. One of the many testimonies televised live was that of Dr. Galeano Duarte from Caacupé. Dr. Duarte showed the crowd the crutches he no longer needed.

"According to medical opinion, I would have needed crutches for the rest of my life. I couldn't take a step without them."

"On Thursday . . . I found myself walking unaided in the streets of Asunción. I can feel my legs getting stronger. I am delighted to be able to walk well."

As Father Tardif said, he prayed and Jesus healed.

Father Tardif: Alcoholic Doctor and His Hunchbacked Child and Man in Coma Healed

Father Paul Pegeaud wrote from the Ivory Coast on December 23, 1987, witnessing to spectacular cures during and after Father Tardif's visit.

A four-year-old hunchback was carried to the service in the arms of his father, a doctor. When Father Tardif started praying for the sick, the child began to sweat profusely.

"He fell to the ground and thrashed about as if he had fallen into a tub of boiling water. Then he felt something pulling him up by the head and the arms and he straightened himself up on his own. He told his father, 'Dad, you are really a good doctor.'

"The father said, 'I'm not the one who has cured you. It is Jesus of Nazareth.'"

When the two arrived home, the father poured himself a stiff drink, "but his mouth spat it out, and he was thus liberated from alcoholism."

A great miracle, the healing of a man in a vegetative coma, took place at Santiago de los Caballeros, Dominican Republic, in autumn 1987: the healing of Oscar Lama. In a coma for two months after a car crash, Oscar was sent to a well-known hospital in Pittsburgh, Pennsylvania for a few weeks of treatment. Part of his brain had been removed. Specialists in Pittsburgh could do nothing for the man.

"If he ever came out of his coma, he would be like a vegetable deprived of normal human faculties."

During a healing Mass at Santa Cruz Cathedral in Valverde (Mao), Oscar's father asked Father Tardif to visit his son.

"We prayed to the Lord for his healing for five to eight minutes. The sight of this completely motionless human being was quite distressing. He had no reaction to any stimulant and could not make any voluntary movement."

Oscar had not spoken since the accident. The morning following Father Tardif's visit, the healed man called his parents on the telephone. The parents were overwhelmed. The next week, Oscar was watching television and was able to recall the names of players in sporting events he viewed. He regained his memory and all other mental faculties. Later he was able to rise from bed and exercise with physical therapists. Oscar Lama began to walk and now leads a normal professional life. His family and friends were all deeply affected spiritually by this miracle.

God heals by television, tape, telephone, whatever! A community Father Tardif began, Servants of the Living Christ, evangelizes by television. A childless woman watching one of their programs in her kitchen knelt and prayed for the baby longed for through ten years of marriage. She felt warmth as the Lord healed her sterility. A short time later, Emmanuel, a healthy boy, was conceived. The little family appeared on the Servants of the Living Christ television program.

One healing occurred in Santiago de los Caballeros, as someone listened to a tape of prayer for the sick. At the Servants of the Living Christ's House of the Annunciation, a telephone answering hotline runs all day for people in need who want to call. Some have been close to suicide. In person, on television, on tape, or by phone, our God reigns!

Father Tardif: We Get Letters. We Get Lots and Lots of Letters.

Mrs. Dolores S. De Reyes wrote from Guadalajara on February 21, 1983, thanking Father Tardif for praying for the healing of her daughter, Maria Guadalupe. In 1978, while in Guadalajara giving a priests' retreat, Father Tardif received a phone message asking prayer for Maria who had tumors in both breasts. Doctors had decided to remove her breasts.

The mother wrote, "She had just begun a four-day hormone treatment when I heard you were here and I became bold like the woman with an issue of blood. I asked you if you had a little time to meet us and pray for our daughter. You were very kind to agree. When my daughter spoke with you, she shed tears of joy. Less than a week after that meeting, we became aware that she no longer had any tumors. Five years have now passed and she no longer has any problem."

Father Tardif's mail was so copious that a nun took on the task of reading it. Sister told correspondents that Father was offering the Eucharist on the first Friday of each month for their intentions. A woman in Brazil wrote, "I was filled with joy by your letter in which you promised to pray during the Eucharist of the first Friday. Father, I want to tell you that it is precisely on that day that I was cured of my afflictions."

Father Tardif said, "I had not been able to read her letter, but the Lord had, and had looked after her."

"Saint Matthew summarizes the evangelical pedagogy of Jesus, 'Jesus toured all of Galilee. He taught in their synagogues, proclaimed the good news of the kingdom, and cured the people of every disease and illness.' (Matthew 4:23) . . . Jesus has not changed his method. We cannot invent a better one than his. To delete an element of the gospel is to believe that our methods are better than those of Jesus. To omit the healings is a betrayal of the gospel."

73

Father Emiliano Tardif died in 1999, but Jesus lives and heals forever.

Father Tardif: Prayer for Healing

This is Father Tardif's prayer for healing. Non-Catholics can adjust this to fit their beliefs. Father says to Catholics who are ill, "On February 8, 1984, we celebrated a Mass for the sick who are now reading these pages. Join us, in faith, in this prayer, placing your whole life in the hands of Jesus:

> Lord Jesus, we believe that you are alive and risen. We believe that you are really present in the Blessed Sacrament of the altar and in each one of us. We praise you and we adore you. We give you thanks, O Lord, for coming to us as living Bread from heaven.

> You are the fullness of life. You are the resurrection and the life. You are, O Lord, health for the sick. Today we want to present you to all the sick who read this book, because time and distance can never separate you from anyone. You are always present and you know every one of them.

> Now, O Lord, we ask you to have mercy on them. Reach out to them through your gospel, which we have proclaimed in this book, so that they may know that you are alive in your Church today: so that they may renew their faith and their confidence in you.

> We ask you, Lord Jesus, have mercy on those who suffer in their bodies, on those who suffer in their hearts, and on those who suffer in their souls, who are praying and reading the testimonies of what you are doing by way of your renewing spirit throughout the whole world. Have mercy on them, O Lord, we ask you, O Lord, from this moment on. Bless each one of them, grant that many of them may recover their health, that their

faith may grow and open them to the wonders of your love, so that they also may be witnesses of your power and your mercy.

We ask you, Jesus, by the power of your holy wounds, by your holy cross and by your precious blood: heal them Lord, heal them in their bodies, heal them in their hearts, heal them in their souls, give them life, and life in abundance.

We ask you through the intercession of the most holy Mary, your mother, Our Lady of Sorrows, who was present at the foot of the cross, she who was the first to contemplate your holy wounds, she whom you gave to us to be our mother.

You have shown us that you have taken all our sufferings on your shoulders and that by your holy wounds we have been healed.

Today, O Lord, we lift up to you, in faith, all the sick who have asked us to pray for them and we ask you to alleviate their illnesses and give them health. We ask you, for the glory of our heavenly Father that you heal the sick who are going to read this book. Grant that they may grow in faith and in hope, and that they may recover their health for the glory of your name, so that your kingdom may continue to spread through the hearts of all human beings, by way of the signs and wonders of your love.

All this we ask you, O Lord Jesus, because you are Jesus. You are the good Shepherd and we are all sheep in your flock. We are so certain of your love, that even before we know the results of our prayer, we say to you in faith:

Thank you, Jesus, for what you are going to do in each one of them. Thank you for the sick that you are healing at this moment, and that you are visiting with your mercy. Thank you, Jesus, for what you are going to do through this book.

From today, we place it in your hands and we ask that you dip it in your holy wounds. May you cover it with your holy blood, so that through his message the heart of the good Shepherd may speak to the hearts of the many sick who are going to read it. Glory and praise to you, O Lord."

≈≈

RND [*Notre Dame Magazine*], 8ᵗʰ issue, 5.

El Occidental, March 26, 1987, 9-11.

Emiliano Tardif, *Jesus Lives Today!* (South Bend, IN: Greenlawn Press, 1989), 8-9, 13-15,18-25, 28, 36-38, 40-43, 47-48, 50, 52-53, 59, 61-63, 67-70, 79, 101-103, 105, 111, 113-114, 117-118, 120-122, 125-126, 129, 132, 134, 136, 139-144, 146-148, 151.

Emiliano Tardif, *Jesus is the Messiah!* (South Bend, IN: Greenlawn Press, 1992), vii-viii, 8-11, 15, 17, 19, 21, 25-26, 29, 32, 39, 41-42, 44-45, 48, 75, 78, 80, 104-108, 112, 114, 117-118, 124, 126, 137, 147-149, 152, 154-155.

St. Paul's: Lourdes on Long Island, New York—The First Madonna Weeps

In March of 1960, Hempstead, New York was a modern-day Lourdes. St. Paul's Greek Orthodox Cathedral at 110 Cathedral Avenue was swamped by pilgrims eager to watch as one after the other, three lithographs of the Blessed Mother wept.

In 1960, the church was open day and night with lines reaching for blocks from the church down to Hempstead Turnpike. People of all faiths came seeking healing and reporters came speculating about the phenomenon. To this day, *Newsday*, the newspaper for Long Island, reports occasionally on the anniversary of the event.

The story began March 16, 1960 in Island Park, New York, where eighteen-year-old newly-married Pagona Catsounis was saying evening prayers at her family altar. A recent Greek immigrant who missed the family she left behind, Pagona poured out her heart to God before the Icon of the Mother of Sorrows.

Suddenly, Mrs. Catsounis noticed a tear form in the left eye of the Icon. It rolled down the cheek of the Madonna. As the picture wept, Pagona stared entranced for a long period of time. Then she called her husband, Peter. The Catsounises knelt in silence looking first at the tears on the Icon and then at each other as if to verify what they were seeing. Even though it was late, they called their relatives, who came over to watch with them. Soon a groundswell of relatives, friends, and neighbors of all beliefs formed lines outside their house and jammed their small apartment.

Finally on Friday, March 18, Pagona called the Pastor of St. Paul's to tell him the Icon was weeping. At 10 p.m., Father George Papadeas struggled through hundreds gathered outside the house.

"... many parked cars and ... people shoulder to shoulder ... filled the street, waiting . . . to walk up the stairs into the small apartment to view the Icon. Outside of the house were two police cars with the flashing red lights rotating."

Police supervised orderly movement of the crowd in and out of the incense-filled apartment. Father Papadeas stood motionless before the Icon watching a tear form, then gradually roll down the cheek of the Madonna onto her garment and down to the bottom edge of the lithographed Icon. The priest was deeply moved by this sign of the Presence of God.

On Monday evening, March 21, 1960, Father Papadeas returned with the spiritual head of the Greek Orthodox Church, Archbishop Iakovos, who was astonished to see the street overflowing with people. A police escort was needed to get into the apartment.

Unfortunately at this point, the weeping stopped. All that remained was a small bead from the last tear which crystallized, sparkling like a tiny diamond in the corner of the eye. The first Icon wept from March 16 to March 21, 1960.

But the Lord was not finished.

St. Paul's: A Trinity of White Birds

The *New York Journal-American* of Thursday, March 24, 1960, reported on the next remarkable events of March 23 when Father Papadeas brought the first Icon from Island Park to St. Paul's Cathedral in Hempstead. Wearing full vestments, the priest rode to the Catsounis' apartment in a borrowed chauffeured limousine leading a procession of cars.

When he stepped out of the door from the Catsounis' house, reverently carrying the flower-adorned Icon, three doves, unseen by Father Papadeas, formed a triangle high above. They remained above the limo for the half-hour trip to St. Paul's. The priest did not know the birds were flying in formation above the vehicle until the cars reached St. Paul's where hundreds of parishioners waited on the patio. When the limo stopped, before the door was opened, Father Papadeas was astonished to see three white birds that looked like doves swoop down over the waiting crowd, almost touching their heads while the parishioners gasped in unison like a choir.

The President of the Parish Council, who was following the lead car, rushed up to the priest. Bursting with excitement, he asked if Father Papadeas had seen the birds.

"From the very moment we departed from Island Park, they came out of nowhere, and were flying over the limousine like escorts all the way to the church."

Others had seen them over the Catsounis' house. As reported in the *New York Journal-American*, "A trinity of white sea gulls, soaring against the blue sky over Island Park, Long Island, have heralded the enshrinement of the 'Madonna of the Tears!'

"The gulls were spotted flying over the house and a woman in the crowd said excitedly, 'Look at the birds. It's a good omen!'

"The birds of good portent 'escorted' the procession of thirty cars to Hempstead and circled over the church while the service was being conducted inside."

Father Papadeas did not know that the birds remained in a triangular formation circling the dome above the church continually for the entire three-hour service until told by Italian workmen who had been cutting down a diseased tree outside the church. Their curiosity grew as they chopped away at the tree, stopping at times to watch. It wasn't natural for birds to be flying in formation for such a long time in a small area.

While the parishioners were exiting from the church, the workmen paused from their work and kept looking up at the birds.

Reluctant to come into the church in dirty clothes, the Italians waited for everyone to leave before entering. They were Roman Catholic, marginally fluent in English, and knew nothing of what was going on. After Father Papadeas explained, one worker said: "You know, Father, it had to be a sign from God because all during the three hours of the service, the birds kept circling the dome, and flew away after the last parishioners had left the church."

St. Paul's: The Second Madonna Weeps for Six Weeks

Early Tuesday morning during Holy Week, on April 12, 1960, Antonia Koulis of Oceanside, Pagona's aunt, called Father George Papadeas. She pleaded that he come quickly because another Icon was weeping profusely and hundreds of people were already converging on her home. This time the head of the Parish Council brought a ledger to collect signatures of witnesses.

When both men arrived at the Koulis' residence, hundreds of people had already gathered. A steady stream ascended the outside wooden stairs leading to the second-floor apartment. Visibly shaken, Mrs. Koulis led them to the family altar. Stricken with awe, Father felt chills running up his spine. Tears were forming in both of Mary's eyes in a lithographed print of an Icon of the Madonna and Child, a copy of the "Panagia Portaitissa," a famous Icon housed in the Iveron Orthodox Monastery, one of twenty large monasteries on Mount Athos in Greece.

Besieged by reporters from all the metropolitan New York newspapers, Father Papadeas removed the lithographed Icon from its glass frame to allow reporters to inspect the back of the print in an attempt to determine the source of the fluid. The back of the print was dry. The reporters were flabbergasted. By early evening, over two thousand signatures had been gathered from witnesses.

Determined not to miss the second phenomenon as he had the first, the Archbishop arrived from Brooklyn with his entourage after 11 p.m. His Eminence stood silently before the Icon, noticeably amazed. Then he announced that the Icon should be taken to St. Paul's on April 14, the afternoon of Holy Thursday. The following day, Wednesday of Holy Week, endless lines of people waited patiently for their turn to see the Icon at the Koulis' home.

On Holy Thursday, the Nassau County Police Department provided a large motorcycle escort from St. Paul's to Oceanside as the limo carrying Father Papadeas and Archbishop Iakovos led a caravan of cars to Oceanside for the transfer. Some motorcycle police edged ahead to stop all east-west traffic and others led the convoy non-stop to Oceanside.

At the Koulis' home, the clergymen held a brief service and then carried the Icon to the limo for the return trip to the cathedral. Every street in the area was filled with cars. Oceanside was an enormous parking lot; there were no open lanes for traffic. Gradually the limousine got underway, preceded by a police escort, squad car lights flashing, and sirens sounding. Police motorcycles blocked all east-west traffic until the last car had passed, a procession of 357 cars (topped in size only by the motorcade accompanying President Eisenhower on his visit to Nassau County).

When the Archbishop and Father Papadeas reached the church, the priests faced a battery of television cameras on tripods and behind them, calm and peaceful, were huge numbers of the faithful and forty priests who participated in the transfer service.

The congregants venerated the two Icons while the second Icon wept continuously. The Icon wept all through the magnificent ceremonies of Holy Week. Beginning Easter Monday morning, between 8,000 and 10,000 daily visitors formed an orderly line blocks long to see the Icons. Reporters noted how sweet a religious aura pervaded the crowd as people waited patiently for hours to see the weeping Madonna.

Rose Ann Palmer, Ph.D.

St. Paul's: Scientists Investigate the Weeping Icon

Feeling as though he were in a portable confessional, Father Papadeas adapted himself to the day and night crowds, seizing an opportunity to help people unburden themselves of their sins and concerns. The priest was touched by the patience of the interdenominational crowds, Orthodox, Catholic, Protestant, and Jewish, all waiting in endless lines for hours to experience the soul-stirring mystery of the Madonna who wept for six weeks, day and night, through many all-night vigils.

More than one hundred eleven organized pilgrimages visited the cathedral within three months. Some of the pilgrimages brought one, two, three, and four busloads of Orthodox pilgrims to the site from as far away as Chicago. The *New York World-Telegram and Sun* estimated that 500 pilgrims an hour filed into St. Paul's Cathedral.

Reporters from all the major newspapers camped at St. Paul's and conducted daily interviews with those filing past the Icon. Among witnesses to the phenomenon were four *Newsday* staff members: reporters Jim Hadjin and Bill Butler, and photographers Jim Nightingale and Dick Morseman. They had all gone to Oceanside in a skeptical frame of mind, but confirmed that they saw the tears.

The front page of the *New York Journal-American* of April 13, 1960, shows a large photo of the Icon taken by Mel Finklestein, staff photographer. Tears are clearly streaming. Although Mel was Jewish, he believed in what he had seen. Mel knelt when the Holy Icon was brought in procession to St. Paul's and said that this miraculous event had brought him back to his own religion.

When the *New York World-Telegram and Sun* asked permission to have the tears analyzed by a New York chemical laboratory, the Archdiocese gave permission for reporters to receive a specimen of the tears for a chemical lab analysis. Chemists arrived with syringes and took samples. Two days later, an analysis done by the New York Testing Laboratory revealed the tears to be of an oily nature, not classifiable among the known elements. They contained only a trace of

82

chloride, a major element of human tears, and contained no nitrogenous compounds, usually found in tears.

New York *Newsday* reported that scientists, engineers, and art experts could offer no natural explanation for the phenomenon. Reporters Bill Butler and Dave Kahn interviewed Dr. J. George Lutz, chairman of (Hempstead, Long Island) Hofstra University's Chemistry Department, who offered no explanation, although he initially advanced and then withdraw the theory that some pigment attracts water, a humectant (moisturizing agent) of sorts.

Reporters questioned Dr. Malcolm Preston, chairman of Hofstra's Fine Arts Department, who said the phenomenon was inexplicable. Anthony Giardina, president of the Nassau Chapter of the New York State Society of Professional Engineers, called it inexplicable from an engineering perspective. His predecessor, Clifford Dvorak, said there was an element of the spiritual at work. John Stamataky, a Bronx engineer who had viewed the first Icon, said that the phenomenon was beyond his powers to explain. Similar answers were given by Dr. Harold Clearman, chair of Hofstra's Physics Department, Caroline Keck, expert in the preservation of paintings, and by Dr. Joseph Rhine head of the Parapsychology Laboratory of Duke University.

Why did it happen? Were the tears for the twenty million Orthodox killed under Stalin's rule, or for the schism of 1054 that split Christendom? Or was it just God reassuring us that He's with us?

St. Paul's: The Third Icon Weeps for Twenty-Five Years

Because the Catsounis and Koulis families had donated their weeping Madonnas to St. Paul's, Father Papadeas reciprocated by giving a lithograph of his own to Peter and Antonia Koulis, Pagona's uncle and aunt. Bishop Athenagoras presented the Icon of Mary, Mother of Perpetual Help holding the Christ Child, to the Koulis family at the cathedral before a packed congregation.

Two weeks later on Saturday, May 7, 1960, Antonia called Father Papadeas to tell him that the Icon he had given her was weeping even more profusely than the one she had donated to St. Paul's. Grateful that she called him first, the priest pleaded with her not to tell anyone else because of the crowds it would attract.

When he saw the Icon weeping in the Koulis apartment, Father Papadeas froze. The manifestation was more powerful than either of the first two. Tears were forming rapidly and falling down Mary's cheeks onto her garment and to the bottom of the frame. When feelings of shock had passed, the priest opened the back of the Icon to see if it was as dry as had been the first and second ones; it was. Father Papadeas gazed at the picture with amazement and awe.

To avoid huge crowds, he carried the Icon to St. Paul's immediately without fanfare and placed the third Icon next to the other two. (Painted in Crete in the Fifteenth Century, the original of the third Icon can be seen today over the altar of the Church of St. Alphonsus Liguori in Rome.)

That day Father Papadeas gave a sermon after the regular service speaking by way of the public address system to the crowd outside the church. When he announced that there had been a third miracle, the crowd gasped. Everyone wondered why.

Dan Foley wrote in *Newsday*, Wednesday, May 11, 1960, that Father F. J. Andres, C.Ss.R., New York area director of the Redemptorists, a Roman Catholic order, felt that the weeping Madonnas were a sign that the Roman Catholic and Orthodox Churches should get together, healing a split separating the Eastern and Western Churches since 1054 A.D. (The Redemptorists promote devotion to the Mother of Perpetual Help.)

Then, for unfathomable reasons, the Archdiocese sent a telegram demanding that the three Icons be removed from St. Paul's and brought to Greek Orthodox Diocesan headquarters. Pagona and Peter Catsounis refused, insisting that the first Icon, the one they had donated to St. Paul's, remain in place. Antonia and Peter Koulis permitted the second

Icon to be taken to the Archdiocese, but requested that the Archbishop give them the third Icon, the gift thanking them for the donation of the second Icon. So the second Icon went to the Diocesan office while the first remained in St. Paul's and the third went back to Antonia and Peter Koulis. Still in the possession of the Koulis' daughter, the third Icon wept for about twenty-five years in the Koulis family home in Florida and stopped weeping only on the death of Antonia in 1990.

Thirty-six years later, at the time of his retirement in 1996, the Archbishop returned the second Icon to St. Paul's. The first and second Icons can be seen there today to the left of the main altar. Inside its shimmering gold mosaic interior, redolent with incense, St. Paul's surrounds the visitor with beauty, mystery, and extraordinary holiness.

St. Paul's: Who Nourished the Babies?

"When they're driving me crazy, I can use good guilt," said the young mother with a laugh, describing the shots and invasive procedures required to bring her children into the world. "You know, in vitro doesn't come with a guarantee," she continued, her voice serious. "It's oodles of money and many times people walk away without a baby."

After the Dimitris [not their real name] had tried to achieve a pregnancy for a year without result, Cynthia [not her real name] consulted a fertility specialist. Told her likelihood of conceiving was low, Cynthia used a fertility drug called Clomid for six months without success. Because fertility drugs may result in multiple births with associated health complications for the children, Cynthia chose in vitro as a safer alternative for the baby.

When in vitro failed at a fertility clinic near home, Cynthia went to the Colorado Center for Reproductive Medicine in Englewood, rated one of the best in the country. Fertility specialists there told the Dimitris that Cynthia had only a 30% chance of conceiving a baby through in vitro. Immediate treatment was impossible because Cynthia developed a cyst on her ovary and the second cycle of in vitro had to be cancelled.

Cynthia went from her home in Michigan back to New York to visit her mother. On Greek Easter, they knelt in the gold encrusted interior of St. Paul's in Hempstead before the weeping Icons of the Blessed Mother and asked God to give Cynthia a baby. While there, Father Nick blessed Cynthia and they all prayed. Cynthia took vials of blessed oil with her and while undergoing medical procedures anointed herself with it and prayed for a child.

The day after the complicated in vitro cycle began, Cynthia's grandfather died. Devastated, Cynthia wanted to go home for the funeral, but her family insisted she stay for the full cycle. After three weeks of taking one injection in the morning and another in the evening to stimulate egg production, Cynthia was notified that the eggs were ready to be retrieved. Five days later, two viable embryos were implanted. Two weeks later, Cynthia was pregnant. "When ultrasound at twelve weeks showed two babies and two sacks, identical twins, I was so excited that I hyperventilated and had to put my head in a paper bag to breath."

Delivered prematurely at thirty-one weeks, on January 18, 2006, Baby A weighed 3 lbs. 5 oz. and Baby B weighed 2 lbs. 14 oz. Baby A was on oxygen for 24 hours and then on a CPAP respiratory machine for a couple of days. "But they were feeders and growers. They had to stay in the hospital four weeks until they learned to suck, breathe, and swallow all at the same time which usually happens at thirty-four weeks in the womb. The doctors fed them through a feeding tube while the babies sucked on pacifiers and began to associate being full with sucking. It took them four weeks to do this."

Delivered at University of Michigan Hospital where doctors see millions of high-risk deliveries, the babies caused a stir. Their placenta was photographed for use in medical classes. One doctor said to Lisa, "This really is a miracle. We've never seen a placenta like this. The umbilical cords were hanging outside the placenta instead of being embedded in it and they were both too thin for the babies to have thrived. Baby B's was so thin that it seems impossible that she got any nourishment at all. Normally, umbilical cords have three vessels. The umbilical cords for both of the girls had only two, one artery and one vein. It was a miracle either of the girls got to be the size they were."

The grateful parents and two healthy little girls celebrated their first birthday January 18, 2007.

St. Paul's: The Tumor Vanished—Lilly

Prepped for breast surgery at New York Hospital Queens (formerly Flushing Hospital), Lilly had sent her husband home at eight o'clock in the morning. There was no point in his hanging around the hospital during her operation. He could see her later on in the day when she awakened from anesthesia.

Three doctors had confirmed the diagnosis of cancer and the necessity for surgery. Lilly had undergone an entire day of pre-admission tests on Good Friday, March 28, 1997. On the day of surgery, the following Friday, April 4, Lilly was given a final mammogram to pinpoint the exact location of the tumor. Markers were put on her breast, then she was wheeled into the holding area. As she lay on the table waiting for the surgeon to arrive, a nurse sped into the room.

"Somebody is going to be happy today," she said, waving some papers as she hurried toward the surgeon's office. The tumor had vanished. The nurse rushed back and took Lilly for a second mammogram using another machine, then wheeled Lilly back to her own hospital room. Eventually, the nurse, the doctor, and the radiologist hurried into her room together.

"Do you believe in miracles?" the radiologist asked Lilly.

"Yes, I do," she replied.

"I've been reading mammograms for twenty years and this has never happened to me before." He seemed angry. "Whatever was there is not there anymore. Go home. You don't need an operation. I just had time to pull on my pants and come over here and I came over here for nothing."

Lilly's doctor, Dr. R., smiled. "Would you want me to cut her when there was no reason?" He turned to Lilly, "Congratulations, Lilly."

"Never happened to me before," said the other doctor as he left the room.

Lilly called her husband, "They're finished. It's nothing at all. I can go home."

On March 29, 1997, Holy Saturday, the Saturday before her operation, Lilly had met her friend Thecla at Notre Dame Church in New Hyde Park. Thecla belongs to St. Paul's in Hempstead and suggested that Lilly and their friend Marie go with her to pray at the Shrine of the Weeping Madonna at St. Paul's. Lilly protested that she had a lot of cooking to do for Easter and couldn't spare the time, but Thecla insisted and they went.

Just as the three of them got to the shrine, a christening party arrived. There was a lot of noise and it was impossible to pray quietly at the Icon of the Blessed Mother. Thecla told Lilly to take some Holy Oil and apply it every day on the area of the tumor with the sign of the cross while saying, "I am applying this Holy Oil with the Blessed Mother's hand."

The night of April 2, two days before the operation, Lilly dreamed that she saw Jesus standing in a crystal box radiating powerful light. She felt comforted and healed by the dream.

A short time after the day scheduled for her operation, Lilly went to Milan on a business trip. While her husband saw clients, she visited the Church of St. Camilla, a church she had never entered before. She went upstairs to look at the sanctuary, saw some steps, went down them and gasped. There was the statue of Jesus in a crystal box radiating light, just as in her dream. Lilly exclaimed, "God, is it You? Are You really here?"

St. Paul's: Father Gregory's Funeral Cancelled

Beautiful, blond Marusia, called "Presbytera," the title given the wife of a Greek Orthodox priest, sat on one of the cordovan leather chairs in her husband, Father Luke's, wood paneled office at St. Paul's Greek Orthodox Cathedral. She told of packing dark clothes for her father's funeral, Ukrainian Orthodox priest Father Gregory—who sat beside her smiling and apologizing for his English.

At 3 p.m. on December 20, 2006, Marusia's mother, Helena, called from Millville, New Jersey, sobbing out a description of the increasingly serious progression of stroke symptoms suffered by Marusia's father, Father Gregory. Awakened by the sound of the priest bumping into walls at one in the morning, Presbytera Helena had gone back to sleep unaware of anything unusual until her husband awakened in the morning unable to smile.

He refused to call the doctor. By the time Presbytera Helena called their daughter Marusia in Hempstead, Father Gregory's face sagged on the right side, his right arm, hand, and leg were useless, and he couldn't move or speak. Marusia called the sheriff in Millville and an ambulance rushed her father to South Jersey Regional Medical Center in Vineland. Father Gregory arrived unconscious. His vitals were terrible; his blood pressure was 240/140. Late in the day, Marusia was told to come soon, her father was dying. The parishes in Hempstead and in Millville began a prayer vigil.

When Marusia arrived at the hospital, her father was still unconscious. The staff warned that death was imminent. Marusia had to stay at her parents' house with her two little girls during the day, then when her mother and sister returned from the hospital, Marusia could go to her father's bedside.

On the second day, Father Gregory was even closer to death. In the evening, His Eminence Archbishop Antony arrived from the Ukrainian Archdiocese in Bound Brook, New Jersey, bringing myrrh from the weeping Icon at the Philadelphia Church of Our Lady Joy of All Who Sorrow. The Archbishop, his monk assistant, and Marusia prayed together. Then the two clergymen anointed the priest's head and hands with myrrh.

As soon as he was anointed, Father Gregory lifted his head and turned it for more anointing. His daughter was surprised that her father heard them and could move his head. Two hours later, the priest shocked the hospital staff by sitting up and motioning that he wanted to go home. The next day, Father Gregory was sitting up and looking around as if puzzled about where he was. The sagging on the right side of his face was better, but his whole right side was still affected. Although amazed at his recovery, the doctors said he had a long period of rehabilitation before him. It would take six months to recover the ability to swallow and it was doubtful his right side would recover at all.

On the third day, Father Gregory ate a roast beef sandwich. The staff called it a miracle. Doctors administered a swallow test and declared he had no problem. Whispering by the third day and speaking on the fourth day, the priest was out of ICU in four days and out of the hospital in seven days. He spent only three weeks in rehab.

Father Gregory still speaks Ukrainian, Polish, German, and Russian fluently and English less fluently. Nothing about his appearance indicates he's had a stroke. He walks and drives as he did before his illness. The medical personnel at the hospital who watched his progress know that God worked a mighty miracle for Father Gregory.

St. Paul's: Tumor There, Tumor There, Tumor Gone—Matthew Bové

On April 21, 2007, the Johnsons sped to Boston, Massachusetts with Holy Oil for Matthew Bové, Mary Johnson's grandnephew.

About a year before, during a routine exam, the pediatrician had felt a mass in the sixteen-month-old's belly. In a few days, the mass was so large that it protruded from his belly like a little knob. At first doctors at Winthrop Hospital in Mineola, Long Island, New York thought the tumor was a mass of blood vessels, but the blood test for tumor markers indicated a rare form of liver cancer occurring in only 1 in 1.4 million children.

On February 28, 2006, after extensive, frenzied research, Ralph and Lauren Bové took their son to Boston Children's Hospital. In the six days between February 24 and March 2, Matthew's tumor markers went from 14,000 to 372,000. Normal tumor markers in the blood are below ten. A team of specialists began chemotherapy Saturday night at midnight; the tumor was too aggressive for delay. Matthew had four rounds of chemo. On May 18, 2006, he underwent a dangerous six-hour surgery to remove 65% of his liver.

Chemo had begun March 4 and ended August 4. Matthew's markers were not normal at that time, but doctors felt he would go into remission. The Bovés went back to Huntington Station, Long Island, in September 2006. In December 2006, Matthew's tumor markers were normal and the Bovés celebrated the long-awaited remission.

The child relapsed February 28, 2007. In addition to liver cancer, cancer was found in Matthew's brain. The day after the child's next cycle of chemo ended, a friend gave Mary Johnson Holy Oil for Matthew. Mary and her husband went to St. Paul's Greek Orthodox Cathedral to get more. The Cathedral was closed, but Mary noticed a man putting on a clerical collar as he got out of a car. Father Anastasios opened the Cathedral and gave them more oil.

The timing was bad. Mary was to be midwife for her daughter who was due shortly. Nervous about leaving town, Mary and her husband zoomed to Boston by noon to deliver the Holy Oil, left at five, and were home by nine. When Mary handed the oil to her niece, Lauren recognized the container. Someone had already sent her oil from St. Paul's, but Lauren hadn't known where it came from. She had just run out of oil after blessing the child with it each night for more than three weeks. Even the baby was in the act. Every night, the two-and-a-half-year-old blessed his parents with the oil, attempting a sign of the cross on their foreheads. Embarrassed by Matthew's oily hair, Lauren explained to doctors that Matthew was oily from constant blessing.

Two healing priests, Fathers McDonough and DiOrio, prayed over Matthew's picture. Members of the Order of St. Luke laid hands on the baby. A village in Zimbabwe, Africa prayed for Matthew. "Within the year and a half of diagnosis, we went from hundreds praying for my Matthew to thousands," says Lauren.

On June 4, 2007, at Boston Children's Hospital, Matthew was anesthetized. His skull was to be opened to remove the brain tumor. The surgeon used magic marker to note the site. One MRI view was missing and had to be redone. Two hours later, the surgeon told the Bovés the tumor was gone. Flabbergasted, the surgeon had called in heads of neurology, radiology, oncology, and neuro-oncology, most professors at Harvard Medical School next door to the hospital. The five doctors agreed there was no plausible medical explanation: the cause couldn't have been a blood clot, chemo, or swelling. Three MRI pictures of Matthew's brain from May 29, June 1, and June 4 showed tumor there, tumor there, tumor gone.

Fr. George Papadeas, *Why Did She Cry: The Story of the Weeping Madonna* (South Daytona, FL: Patmos Press, 2000), 33, 39-40, 45, 53, 95.

Joel's Mom, Dodie Osteen:
Healed of Liver Cancer

From her hospital bed, Dodie Osteen could hear her son Paul, a medical doctor, sobbing in the hallway. When diagnosed with liver cancer in November 1981, Mrs. Osteen, a registered nurse, knew as Paul did that the prognosis was death a few weeks to seven months after diagnosis.

Dodie's case was declared hopeless, no medical treatment was given, and she was sent home to die. To the amazement of the medical profession, the disease did not kill Dodie Osteen. She got better and better, and thirty-three years later still shows no signs of cancer. You can see her laughing and healthy in the audience at her son, Joel Osteen's, television services.

Mistaken diagnosis? Not according to St. Luke's Hospital in the Texas Medical Center at Houston where in 1981 Dodie underwent intensive testing for twenty days as the picture grew worse and worse. On the back cover of Dodie Osteen's *Healed of Cancer*, three medical doctors, Drs. Cherry, Walker, and Moore, testify to the correctness of the diagnosis and to the miraculous nature of Mrs. Osteen's healing.

As Dr. Moore wrote to Mrs. Osteen, "I must tell you that knowing all the players and having seen all the tests and X-rays has made a tremendous impact on me. It is one thing to read about miracles, but it is another to sit by and watch one happen."

Mrs. Osteen's husband of forty-four years, John Osteen, was pastor of Lakewood Church in Houston, Texas where their son Joel now presides. Focused on the prayer of agreement, "If two of you agree on earth about anything they ask, it will be done for them by My Father in heaven" (Matthew 18:19), Pastor John Osteen anointed her with oil, and John and Dodie both prayed face down on the floor.

That day, December 11, 1981, Dodie considers the first day of her healing, although she had many symptoms, felt ill, and was plagued by fear. Dodie felt God speak to her heart saying, "It's not your husband's faith . . . it is *your* faith that you must go on now."

To bolster her faith, Dodie carried on her routine as if already healed; despite feeling desperately sick, she got dressed every day and never took a nap. She laughed at symptoms and repeated God's promises to herself all day long. Joel's mom lists forty Scripture quotes that sustained her. When Dodie remembered the doctors' words and fear attacked her, she kept from drifting to the negative by quoting the promises of God to build her faith: "By the stripes of Jesus, I am healed" (1 Peter 2:24), "With long life will He satisfy me." (Psalm 91:16). In keeping with, "Pray for one another that you may be healed" (James 5:16), Dodie forced herself to go out to pray for others.

She pled her case with God (see Psalm 118:17). She kept a picture of herself in her wedding dress nearby and asked God to make her feel as she had on her wedding day. Dodie examined her heart to see what might block God's healing love and wrote letters asking forgiveness of seven people she might have offended. The whole Lakewood congregation prayed and fasted for her recovery.

Dodie Osteen says the tragedy is many people don't know it is God's will that they be healed. "And this information is the difference between life and death! . . . The fact that He healed me shows me He cares, and that He wants to heal you, too."

Prayer as Wart Remover

As a little boy, Joel Osteen's brother Paul had warts all over. Dodie Osteen tried every remedy imaginable, but nothing worked. One day it occurred to her that prayer was the one remedy not tried.

She lay hands on him and commanded the warts to leave in Jesus' Name. The warts remained. However, the child's family continued to pray, day after day. Although the warts still sat on the child's skin, very visible, the Osteen family rejoiced and praised God as if the warts had been cured.

"A week or two later our boy came in all excited. Several of the warts had disappeared. Soon all of them were gone."

›‹

Dodie Osteen, *Healed of Cancer* (Houston, TX: Lakewood Church Publications, 2003), 6, 15, 72-73.

John Osteen, *You Can Change Your Destiny* (Humble, TX: John Osteen Publications, 1978), 38.

John and Joel Osteen

In his book, *Become a Better You: 7 Keys to Improving Your Life Every Day*, Joel Osteen writes:

> Back in 1959, my father, John, was the pastor of a successful church with a thriving congregation. They had just built a beautiful new sanctuary and my father had a bright future. About that time, my sister Lisa was born with something like cerebral palsy.
>
> Hungry for a fresh touch from God, my dad went away for a while and got alone with God. He searched the Scriptures in a new way, and he began to see how God was a good God, a healing God, and that God could still perform miracles today. My dad went back to his church and he preached with a new fire, a new enthusiasm. He thought everybody would be thrilled, but the congregation's reaction was just the opposite. They didn't like his new message. It didn't fit in with their tradition. After suffering much persecution, heartache, and pain, my father knew the best thing for him to do was to leave that church.
>
> Naturally, my dad was disappointed. He didn't understand why such a thing should happen. But remember, out of rejection comes direction. When one door closes, God is about to open up a bigger and a better door.
>
> My father went down the street to an abandoned feed store. There, he and ninety other people formed Lakewood Church on Mother's Day, 1959. The critics said it would never last, but

today, nearly fifty years later, Lakewood Church has grown to become one of the largest churches in America and is still going strong.

I don't believe that my father would have enjoyed the ministry he had, and I don't believe he would have become all God created him to be, if he would have stayed in that limited environment. Here's a key: The dream in your heart may be bigger than the environment in which you find yourself. Sometimes you have to get out of that environment in order to see that dream fulfilled.

John Osteen: Scripture Can Change Your Destiny

The Osteens know about healing. Joel's mother was healed of liver cancer in 1981. Twenty years earlier, Joel's Aunt Mary was healed in what her brother Pastor John Osteen called one of the greatest miracles he ever witnessed.

After a very severe convulsion, Mary Giverns was diagnosed with epilepsy by a neurosurgeon and was given Dilantin. The year before, a slipped disc in her neck kept Mary home in traction in a neck brace on a hospital bed. After nine weeks on Dilantin, Mary was able to concentrate, study, and teach. Then things changed: Mary had horrible nightmares, blackouts, memory loss, and stumbled when walking. Further specialists were called in. Mary would spasmodically improve and then relapse. She suffered severe headaches and personality change. Supersensitive, Mary would argue and then apologize.

She said, "I remember the coma-like state, the torment, the cries, the inability to come back to reason, the barricade bed, fighting the nurse and my mother and the nights sitting in bed crying: 'Don't tell me there is no hell, this is it.'"

For two weeks during all this turmoil, Mary did not once open her eyes. For weeks she was unable to walk. Her coordination was gone. With arms around her mother, Mary cried she'd rather be dead than live like this. "The doctor said an infection had begun in my head and had brought on this seizure."

As Mary said she'd rather be dead, the voice of the Spirit of God told her to call her brother, John Osteen, whom she had not seen in two years. At the same time, while driving along the freeway, John had a vision of Mary, desperately sick. He told others in the car that Mary was sick, but that God said she would get well.

When John got home, his mother called and John started for Dallas. Opening his Bible for a word, Pastor Osteen pointed to, "Fear not, Mary, for thou has found favor with God."

A prayer companion and John arrived at his sister's sick room. Seeing Mary's condition, John shouted, "Do not tell me this is of God! God is love! God would not do this to my sister."

Mary heard someone say, "Get out of bed!" Immediately, she got out of bed, falling in every direction. They prayed that God heal her. They declared her healing done. They lay hands on her head and John prayed in tongues. A voice told her to walk. She ran.

"The nurse was frightened. Mother was jubilant! I walked, I talked, I ate, I told my husband about it, but in a sense I was shut up with God."

God healed her epilepsy that day. Many years later, Mary was still thanking God for her good health.

* * *

"More than likely you will be healed while reading this book, "said John Osteen boldly in *You Can Change Your Destiny*. The key to healing he felt is realizing that sickness is not God's Will. Get into agreement with God on this. Repeat His Promises given in healing Scriptures until you internalize them.

"You will never be healed as long as you think God wants you to be sick."

Memorize Scriptures to promote belief in God's Power and His Desire to heal you, His beloved child. Nothing is too hard for God, your Divine Daddy. He loves you more than your earthly parents and unlike them, He has unlimited Power to make you well. Receive His healing Love. He wants you healthy.

Joel Osteen, *Become a Better You: 7 Keys to Improving Your Life Every Day* (New York, NY: Free Press/Simon & Schuster, 2007), 15-16.

John Osteen, *You Can Change Your Destiny* (Humble, TX: John Osteen Publications, 1978), 13, 19, 52-53, 57.

Bridge for Peace: As They Prayed, I Could See More and More

Father Isaac Mensah, a young missionary priest from Ghana, lost his vision on the first Sunday of Advent in 2002 while saying the 7 a.m. Mass at St. Anne's Church in Garden City, New York. At the gospel, "The page turned white. The letters of the scriptures vanished." The priest worked from memory and rushed to the sermon.

Father had cataracts. On February 3, 2003, his ophthalmologist, Dr. A, removed the cataract on Father Isaac's right eye and inserted a corrective lens. Father had no problem after that operation. Vision in the right eye was fine.

Then during the first week of March 2003, Dr. B operated on Father Isaac's left eye. The priest had pain immediately after the operation and suffered pain and a red eye until April of 2004. Father Isaac went to see Doctors A and C every two weeks. Dr. C, a retina specialist, drained fluid from Father's eye and gave him drops. The priest suffered more and more pain.

Finally in 2004, Father John Gilmartin, pastor at St. Anne's, arranged a meeting at the rectory with his friend, an ophthalmologist, who referred Father Isaac to Dr. D. Father Isaac was in too much pain from his eye to attend the meeting.

When he was able to meet with the doctor, Dr. D said there was an infection behind the left eye where the lens had been inserted after the cataract operation on Father's left eye. Dr. D removed the old lens in

100

April 2005 and told him to let it heal. Father was without a lens in the left eye and had virtually no vision in that eye. There were still problems after that: the area behind the eye wasn't healing properly and there was leakage. Father went two times a month to meet with Dr. E, a glaucoma specialist, referred by Dr. D.

For a year, Father continued treatment with Dr. E. In January of 2006, Dr. E wanted to do a fourth surgery to rectify leakage behind the eye. After this surgery, doctors still couldn't insert a lens. Father couldn't see well enough to count the fingers on his hand. Even the big letters on the eye chart were unclear. However, Father's right eye compensated. He could drive during the day, although his night vision was bad.

Dr. E wanted to do a fifth surgery in August 2006. Meanwhile, Father had pain off and on in the left eye, especially in the morning. The priest had practically no vision in that eye, so when his right eye was covered, walking around was difficult. From October 2006 to February 2007, Dr. E insisted on further surgery to correct leakage of fluid. Until the leakage stopped, indicating no infection, doctors couldn't insert the lens. Father refused the fifth surgery, left Dr. E, and went back to Dr. A.

In February 2006 at St. Catherine of Sienna Roman Catholic Church in Franklin Square, New York, Father Isaac met Annette and Ed Eckart from Bridge for Peace, a group focused on healing through prayer. The couple prayed over Father Isaac. At first the priest couldn't read the large letters (2½ inches high) that said "Bible." Father Isaac said, "They gave me the Bible to read and each time they prayed over me, I could read a little more. They prayed three times and each time my vision was better. I went back to Dr. A. The leakage had stopped. Dr. A gave me a test and he was surprised. He was able to put the left lens in without further surgery. Now the vision in my left eye is perfect. No pain, no redness."

On March 4, 2008, Father went back to Dr. A, his ophthalmologist, for an annual checkup. The doctor said the priest's eyes are fine and expressed surprise at the healing of Father Isaac's eyes.

Bridge for Peace: Against All Odds, The Lump Vanished

The Taylors [not their real name] of Long Island, New York, had their first child in 1963 after a year of marriage. Then for twelve years, Linda [not her real name] had no other children. Hoping for another baby, she went from specialist to specialist, but none of their treatments worked.

In 1973, when a priest at a prayer group talked about Baptism in the Spirit, Linda didn't know what he meant. Some in the group were speaking in tongues. Linda felt the Presence of God. There was something there she wanted. When the priest asked who would like to be prayed over for Baptism in the Spirit, Linda rushed up, embarrassed that she was the only one. As the group prayed over her, they seemed to be waiting for something to happen, but nothing did. The only difference she felt was the desire to read Scripture all the time. A few days later while reading the Bible, Linda burst out joyfully speaking in tongues. Very excited, she called a friend in her prayer group. Linda says she had it before she knew what it was. "I came in the back door."

At that time, Linda felt God told her that she was going to have a son. In the joy of her born-again experience, Linda, who was not pregnant, told everyone she was going to have another baby, a boy.

They'd ask, "Are you pregnant?"

She'd say, "Not yet, but I will be. God is going to give me a son." And they'd look at her funny.

Three childless years later, Linda prayed, "I thought You told me I'm going to have a son." On a doctor's visit a short time later, Linda had God's answer. She was pregnant. After the birth of a healthy boy, at the new mother's six-week checkup, Linda got bad news. A big lump in her neck was a cold nodule near her thyroid. Dr. Francis [not his real name] had not told Linda before the birth, but she had to go into the hospital immediately. Ninety-five percent of the time, a growth in the neck of an adult is cancer.

A biopsy was impossible because if the tumor was cancer, it would spread throughout her body. Dr. Francis recommended an immediate operation to remove it. Prepared for surgery, Linda went to her prayer meeting where the topic was Numbers 14:28, "Say unto them, 'What you say in my ear, that I will do unto you.'" She felt God was saying, "Cancel the operation and wait for healing." All healers say do as the doctors recommend, but Linda had a strong feeling that she had nothing to worry about.

Linda had a long wait for healing. The lump got bigger. People commented so she wore turtlenecks to hide it. One day when their baby was a few months old, Linda looked in the mirror, saw the big lump, and overcome with fear ran out of the house, got in the car and drove. Near Waldbaum's grocery store, Linda recognized the woman driving in front of her and thought she might pray with her. In Waldbaum's vegetable department, Linda caught up with the other woman. They stood right there in front of the potatoes and prayed. "Need I say, we cleared out the vegetable department," she laughs. Only one lady stayed and stared. As they prayed, the fear left.

A year later, the growth was as big as a lemon. It stayed that way for three years.

Then one day, the lump was gone. Linda went back to Dr. Francis. She asked him to check her neck. When the doctor realized the nodule was gone, he said, "Do you know that's a miracle?"

Linda said, "Yes, but I wanted you to know it." Dr. Francis said it was the second miracle he had seen. The first was a man with a stroke who should have died but walked out of the hospital three days later. Linda Taylor is not recommending that anyone else ignore medical advice, but she must tell it as it was.

Bridge for Peace: God Specializes in Happy Endings

Nothing is worse than seeing your child suffer, but Sandy Martin's [not her real name] painful journey with her oldest had a happy ending.

Sandy witnessed Evan's [not his real name] triumph over Attention Deficit Disorder, alcoholism, and drug abuse.

Evan had trouble being accepted by other kids in the neighborhood. He entered school with low self-esteem, starved for friendship, needy. Behaviors meant to win other children drew negative attention from teachers. Sandy was on an emotional rollercoaster with him from first grade. He was on the wrong track through grade school.

In the sixth grade when Evan was twelve, he went to the youth group at St. Peter's [not the real name] Catholic Church. Members of the youth group accepted him. He was happy there. At the youth group summer camp, Evan did something wrong and was sent home from camp.

The pastor of St. Peter's, Monsignor Reilly [not his real name], does not garden and has never gardened since, but that day by the Grace of God, Father Reilly was gardening.

Evan walked home past the rectory and started talking to Father Reilly. They became best friends. He went back and forth to the rectory as if it were a second home. Evan now had a place to go and he was feeling better. Sandy's prayers had been answered. She is so grateful God put Father Reilly in Evan's life.

Around this time, Sandy experienced another miracle. She quit smoking. That doesn't sound like much of a miracle, but Sandy had tried many times before. Pregnant with her fourth child, the mother-to-be couldn't stop smoking. It was a big monkey on Sandy's back. Then, twenty years ago on Ash Wednesday, she asked God to take the cigarette addiction away and it left her just like that. God was answering prayer.

And there were other miracles. While pregnant with her fourth child, Sandy was unable to urinate because a fibroid was pressing on her bladder. Doctors told Sandy, an R.N., that she might have to catheterize herself.

Bridge for Peace prayed over her and the fibroid shrunk. She was able to urinate without the catheter.

Recently, Sandy had gall bladder symptoms and had gallstones. In pain and nauseous, Sandy asked the Bridge for Peace prayer team to pray over her, and all symptoms left. Ultrasound shows only gravel in the gall bladder. From experience in nursing, Sandy knows if she had gone into the emergency room with her pain, they would have operated.

As her son Evan grew older, he was hired as clean-up guy for the rectory, which was great because the job kept him in touch with Father Reilly. Despite that support, he fell in with a bad crowd.

Run by Franciscan friars, Youth 2000 gave a retreat for teens, intended to show the power of the Eucharist. Evan had a big conversion. He befriended Joe Campo, who runs the St. Francis House for boys in Brooklyn, the Bronx, and Yonkers. Evan went to the retreats every year. He'd bring with him kids who were emotionally needy and he was responsible for one boy being confirmed by Father Reilly.

Despite that success, Evan was involved with drugs and alcohol and changed high school several times. After high school, he became severely depressed. Joe asked Evan to go with him upstate to help out with work up there.

On the train to Buffalo, Joe Campo's guys told him they all liked him and wanted him to pull it together. Evan went to the retreat, then right into rehab.

At a retreat, he met his wife, the sister of one of the friars. Evan is now a drug and alcohol counselor and the happily married father of two. Sandy prayed twenty years for her son's amazing happy ending. God wins in the end.

Joyce Meyers: Ed Starrett, Firing up Your Prayer Power

Early Thanksgiving morning, November 22, 2007, on her national television program, the evangelist Joyce Meyers announced a special feature. A viewer had been healed by prayer from Stage 4 B-cell non-Hodgkin's lymphoma.

Film clips captured Ed Starrett's testimony. Ed, the slender mustached married father of four, was filmed in good health, back at work as a medical technician.

Clips showed Ed's doctor, Gary Vicik, M.D., a dermatologist, testifying about the case. Dr. Vicik diagnosed the disease in March of 2003 during a routine skin exam. Ed's symptoms were atypical and Dr. Vicik's diagnosis was astute.

Stage 4 B-cell non-Hodgkin's lymphoma is a highly aggressive cancer. Further testing showed the disease was already in Ed's lymph nodes and bones. Chemo was prescribed, but doctors did not hold out much hope.

Ed began chemo. As he lay there receiving infusions of chemicals, he looked around at the others in the facility getting similar treatment. Many were skin and bone, and he could envision himself eventually being emaciated and weak.

The picture was grim, but no matter what he saw and what the doctors said, Ed did not lose hope. He insisted God is bigger than this or any other disease. Ed was determined to do what he could to open himself so that God could get in and heal him.

Ed Starrett began a regimen of prayer intended to stoke up his faith. Like Dodie Osteen, he repeated over and over Scriptures in which God promised healing. Ed's friend, Mike Petrovich, prayed over Ed and helped fire up his faith from what the healed man calls a maintenance level to a power level.

Ed continually praised and thanked God as he repeated Scriptures promising healing to make himself believe in God's promises on a subconscious and unconscious level. Ed got a juicer and made vegetable juice and other healthful foods while asking God to heal him as he prayed and drank in the nourishment the Lord provides for our health.

After chemo ended, Ed and his wife were at one of the many, many prayer meetings they attended. Ed was being prayed over while his wife stood next to him. Suddenly, Mrs. Starrett felt a power touch Ed. At the same time, Ed felt a complete lifting of the burden of cancer.

When Ed returned to the doctor, tests showed no trace of cancer. The doctors are amazed at the outcome. Ed Starrett is enjoying the longest remission doctors have ever seen from Stage 4 B-cell non-Hodgkin's lymphoma.

1 Thessalonians 5:17-19: Pray without ceasing. In all circumstances give thanks, for this is the will of God for you in Christ Jesus. Do not quench the Spirit.

*   *   *

Psalm 30

. . . O Lord, my God, I cried out to you and you healed me . . .
Sing praise to the Lord, you faithful give thanks to God's holy name . . .
You changed my mourning into dancing;

You took off my sackcloth and clothed me with gladness.
With my whole being I sing endless praise to You.
O Lord, my God, forever will I give you thanks.

Sister Briege McKenna and the Kangaroo

"After all," said Sister Briege McKenna, internationally known healer, "I'm just a second grade teacher."

A charming woman with an Irish brogue, Sister was fresh from an interview on the *Oprah Winfrey Show* where she described her own healing from rheumatoid arthritis. "They (the staff at the *Oprah Winfrey Show*) kept trying to make it New Age, but I kept saying, 'It was Jesus. It was Jesus.'"

Sister entered the convent in 1961 at the age of fifteen. In 1964, she developed severe pain in her feet, diagnosed in 1965 as rheumatoid arthritis. Hospitalized in Belfast, Ireland, for many months, Briege painfully endured having her feet encased in plaster of Paris boots every night to prevent deformity.

After her profession to be a nun in 1967, Sister taught kindergarten in Tampa, Florida. The climate caused her arthritis to worsen. In 1968, Briege cried with pain. The doctor said her condition was hopeless and she would eventually be confined to a wheelchair. At that point, Sister could still walk, but slowly and painfully.

Spiritually dry, Briege didn't believe Jesus would heal her. "I believed that if I had gone to Lourdes . . . there might be a healing, but I did not believe that healing could happen in normal daily life."

In a wheelchair at an ecumenical retreat in Orlando, Florida, not asking God to heal her, but to give her a closer relationship with Him, she thought, "'There must be more to religious life and there must be more to Catholicism.' I had been good about 'getting my prayers in,' 'as a duty.' But there was no joy in talking to the Lord.'"

Then she thought that if the priest prayed for her, she'd get that closer relationship. "The Lord, as though he had read my mind, said to me, 'Don't look at him, look at me.' I remember looking at the clock as I closed my eyes. It was 9:15 a.m., December 9, 1970. The only prayer I said was, 'Jesus, please help me.'"

Sister gives a sketchy description of her healing in *Miracles Do Happen*, but on the air and in the green room at Telecare, the Long Island, New York, Catholic television station, Sister gave the full story. I've interspersed Sister Briege's words from her book with what I remember of our conversation.

While her eyes were closed, she thought the priest touched her on the forehead. Opening her eyes, she realized the priest was on the other side of the room. As she said in her charming Irish brogue, "He would have had to have been a kangaroo to have touched me on the forehead."

". . . there was a power going through my body . . . I felt like a banana being peeled."

In that instant, she was completely healed of rheumatoid arthritis.

"I looked down. My fingers had been stiff, but not deformed like my feet. There had been sores on my elbows. I looked at myself. My fingers were limber, the sores were gone, and I could see that my feet, in sandals, were no longer deformed. I jumped up screaming, 'Jesus! You're right here!'

"Since that day I have never had arthritis and have been completely free of pain."

Sister told me that she saw the doctor the next day, and he cried. He said he'd like to take credit for the cure, but had nothing to do with it. It was a complete miracle. He took her off all medication.

God Zaps Sister Briege with That Mysterious Electric Current

Fearful of sensationalism, Sister Briege kept her miracle a secret from the other nuns. She was afraid they'd think God had given her the gift of healing. Briege wanted none of that. "Besides, it's nobody's business. Why tell anybody?"

"I went from December of 1970 to June of 1971 having a marvelous experience of Pentecost. I would say, 'Jesus, you couldn't expect me to do any more. Here I am teaching forty-seven first graders, going to prayer meetings, leading a youth group, and going to a prison to minister.'

"In the back of my mind I was really saying that I was going to play it safe. I wanted the respect and approval of people."

She told us she was awakened in the middle of the night in June 1971 on the eve of Pentecost with a sense she should go to the chapel to make a Holy Hour [spend an hour with Jesus]. Fighting the call, she told herself to do the Holy Hour tomorrow, but finally went to the chapel. "So I sat there in our little oratory, saying, 'Jesus, here I am.'

"I had been in the chapel about five minutes when suddenly this extraordinary stillness descended on the chapel—it was like a cloud, like a fog. A voice said, 'Briege.'" (She told us a priest had told her, "If you get involved with those Charismatics, Briege, you'll be hearing voices," and that flashed through her head.)

"I turned to look toward the door because the voice was so clear it sounded as though someone had come into the chapel. No one was there, but I was very conscious that someone was present. The voice said to me as I turned back to the tabernacle, 'You have My gift of healing. Go and use it.'

"As soon as I heard this, a burning sensation went through my body. I remember looking at my hands. It felt as though I had touched an electrical outlet. This burning sensation went through my hands and out of them. And then the stillness lifted.

"I found myself kneeling, looking at the tabernacle, and saying, 'Jesus, I don't want any gift of healing. Keep it for yourself.' Then I made an act of contrition, not because I was sorry for what I had told Jesus, but for even thinking that Jesus would speak to me.

"Then I said to him, 'Jesus, I'll make you a promise. I'll never tell anybody about this.'

"That Pentecost was very special to me since I had experienced the Holy Spirit and had learned to pray to Him for all those gifts promised in Scripture and received in Confirmation. All this was more important to me now.

"I woke up on Pentecost morning and the voice was booming in my head, 'You have My gift of healing; go and use it.'"

Although nobody but the doctor knew about this experience, that day Sister was invited to pray for healing with a child at a prayer meeting at St. Joseph's Hospital in Tampa, Florida. Years later, she found out the child had been healed through that prayer.

In July and August 1971, Sister Briege went to study in Los Angeles, California. She had never told anyone in her convent about the gift of healing. She says, "The Lord Himself confirmed my gift of healing through two prophetic experiences.

"One evening at a prayer meeting in St. Angela Merici Parish, I found myself sitting beside an Episcopalian priest, an elderly man. At the end of the meeting, he said, 'Sister, I've never spoken to a Roman Catholic nun before, but I have a message for you. As we were praying, I got this very strong feeling that you have the gift of healing—and you know you have it because the Lord spoke to you in your chapel in Florida.'"

Sister Briege told us that she was horrified. She wondered who he was, a mind reader or what. "I told the minister, 'I really can't accept that. I belong to a strict congregation in Florida' and I went on to tell him all the reasons.

"He just looked at me and said, 'Tell me what happened in the chapel.'

"I said to myself, 'How does he know? I never told one single person.' I told him what had happened in the chapel, but said that I just couldn't accept it.

"He looked at me and said, 'Jesus will never force you. He reveals his will, but you are free to choose to follow him or not.' Then he turned and walked away.

"A few days later in church after Mass, I was talking with some people. A woman came up to me and said, 'Sister, I don't know you, but when you went to Communion, the Lord gave me a picture of you standing with a line of people coming to you. The Lord told me to tell you that you are being called into a great healing ministry.'

"In spite of the many people confirming what the Lord had said in our Tampa chapel, I still rejected his invitation to the ministry of healing."

Then one night Sister Briege dreamt that Jesus walked through her house with her. When he came to a locked door, Jesus asked Briege why He couldn't go in. She said that she wanted to keep something for herself.

Then Jesus showed her that inside that room was her reputation, what others thought of her. She didn't want Jesus in that room because she was preserving her good name. She didn't want to be thought a fool by other people. She realized that she couldn't be fully joyful as a religious until she had abandoned every part of her life and was willing to be a fool for him.

"That day on the plane I said to him, 'Jesus, You know I can't go back to Florida and tell people I have the gift of healing. I'll do the praying and you do the telling."

Sister went back to Florida and resumed her regular life. After two weeks, she went to a prayer meeting and a lady jumped up and said, "You have the gift of healing. You know about it, but you are more worried about the approval of people than you are about God's will."

The woman was a stranger, a freelance writer from Canada who had awakened with an image of Sister Briege's face on the wall and the knowledge that God had given her the gift of healing but that she was afraid of it.

The woman didn't know where this Sister was, but had been led by the Holy Spirit to the Franciscan Center in Tampa and that prayer meeting. She had told one of the sisters at the center that she was looking for a young Irish nun with the gift of healing.

The Franciscan nuns had told her that there were no Irish sisters there because Sister didn't live there and they didn't know that she was coming to the prayer meeting. But the woman had insisted that she would be there.

Sister Briege couldn't remember ever having seen the woman before. She made a joke of it and asked the writer if the Irish spirit had told her she was Irish. The woman had been present when Sister was healed at the retreat in Orlando. She kept insisting that God wanted Sister to work in the healing ministry, but Sister couldn't hear her, she was in a panic worrying about her first grade class, afraid that she'd be put into another ministry and taken away from her class.

Then a beautiful calmness descended on Sister and an inner voice told her not to be worried, that she was to be obedient to her superiors and that God would work through them.

Relieved, Sister Briege thought, now it's not my problem, it's my superior's problem. When she confided in her superior, her superior said exactly what Sister Briege wanted to hear: not to have anything to do with healing. It's too sensational.

Three weeks passed. Sister says she was pretending to worry about the welfare of the Church, but was really worried about being a fool for Jesus, about being called a "faith healer." Sister says she didn't consider that Jesus was a faith healer.

Two weeks later a woman who had been contemplating suicide said that she saw Sister Briege walk into her room in the middle of the night and stand beside her bed. She said that whether her eyes were opened or closed, she could see Sister Briege and if she turned away from her, there she was on the other side of the bed.

"As she told me this, I thought, 'Oh, Jesus, use me all You want during the day, but don't have me roaming through homes in the middle of the night. And I heard Jesus say to me, 'But I thought you said that if I'd do the telling, you'd do the praying.'"

The woman had been in despair, but her face lit up as she asked Sister Briege if God could help her. She was converted and came back into the Catholic Church.

"It was at this time that I said to myself, 'Briege, Mother Superior or no Mother Superior, what you have to do is seek the Lord and do his will.' She went to a priest who said that she must say Yes to God and let Him use her.

"I said, 'But Father, how can I know when to pray? I can't just go up to someone who is sick and tell them I can pray for them for physical healing.'"

He told her to go back to her community to live as before. "If this call is from Jesus, He will open up the way."

For six months after that, Sister Briege was skeptical. People were healed but she couldn't believe that Jesus was working through her. She thought someone God used would have to be perfect.

She prayed with a woman who was blind, paralyzed, angry, and had given up on the Lord. "When I put my hand on her, I said a little prayer with her and I felt the sensation of pins and needles, exactly as I had in the chapel when I had been given the gift of healing.

"As I was praying, I was saying to myself, 'Now Briege, don't go telling this woman she'll be healed. You know this is all psychological and she'll get disappointed. These tinglings in your hands are just your imagination.'"

The paralyzed woman thought Sister Briege had been sticking pins in her to make a good impression because she had felt something go through her arms. Then in the middle of the night, she got the power back into her arms. A few days later, she got her sight. But more importantly, she got a spiritual healing. Her attitude changed totally.

Sister went home to Ireland in 1972. She went to a hospital to pray for a woman who was dying of cancer and on the way out noticed a man suffering from shingles and she prayed with him. When both of them were healed, the town went into an uproar looking for the healing nun.

"People were phoning and coming to see me. Every time they saw a nun in a brown habit, they would run after her . . . People were shouting and whistling at my father as he worked in the fields, asking him where they could find Sister Briege. He said to me, 'My, Briege, you have a lot of friends.'"

I spent a lot of time with my Auntie Lizzie and sometimes there were as many as sixty cars parked outside her house. When I was home, she couldn't get any work done with all those people coming around looking for me and telling her all their sicknesses.

Shortly after that, she prayed in the cathedral in Newry. Worried that she was calling attention to herself and that she could get into trouble because the bishop didn't know anything about what she was doing, she asked God if it were His will that she be doing this on her holiday at home. Then she asked Him to teach her how to pray for people.

As she prayed, an old man came into the church and asked her to pray for him. He had fallen off his bicycle and hurt his wrist. She called him over and asked him if he had heard of her. He said no, he noticed she was a nun and thought she might say a prayer for him. She prayed for him and she could hear him praying the rosary.

In the middle of a decade, he looked over and said, "God, that was a powerful prayer. Could you write it out? The pain and the swelling are all gone."

"I heard the Lord say, 'You see, I brought in a man off the street. That's why I brought you home, to touch my people.'"

Next, the Lord showed Sister a picture of an enormous pink telephone over the tabernacle. Thinking it was a distraction, she wanted to get it out of her mind, but God told her that He wanted her to pray over the phone with people, that she didn't have to see them, that all she had to do was unite with them before Jesus. Time and space mean nothing to the Lord.

"When I went back to the motherhouse (in Florida), a sister said that a man from England wanted to come see me for prayer. He had a severe skin problem. I told the sister, 'He doesn't have to come here, I'll pray for him by phone.'

"'Does it work that way, too?'

"'I don't know but we'll have a go.' When the man phoned me and I prayed with him, he was completely healed."

While in Ireland, one of the sisters from the school said that a lady who worked there had a daughter in the hospital with a serious skin problem. "I couldn't go there, but I asked her to send the mother to me. I prayed with the mother and within a few days, the girl had been totally healed and had skin like a new baby."

Forty-four years later, Sister Briege has an international healing ministry. She has seen countless examples of the healing power of God.

117

If you would like Sister Briege to pray with you, more information and her schedule are available at www.sisterbriege.com.

Sister Briege and Jesus, Globetrotters

Only three women have ever been asked by the Pope to preach in Rome at the prestigious annual retreat for cardinals, bishops, and clergy. Sister Briege is one: has gift, will travel. All these years since God convinced Briege to use her healing gift, she may go from a huge rally in South America to a retreat in Korea and then right back to her classroom in Florida.

Inspired by the Scripture story of the centurion's servant, Briege reasons Jesus can give the order and no matter how close or distant the person, he or she will be healed. There is no distance with God.

When Sister was ministering to a large group of priests in Mexico, she said a brief prayer in the hospital with a priest who had cancer. The next day as Briege worked with a large group of priests, she heard the priest was dying. Instead of going to him, she and the priests prayed for the dying man where they were.

A year later, an article in a Mexican magazine reported the priest totally healed and back to college teaching. "Just because I am limited physically to one place, I should never limit the Lord."

At a healing service in Scotland, Sister Briege invited the congregation to intercede for loved ones not present. "Ask Jesus to reach out and touch them, just as the centurion begged Jesus to touch his servant . . ."

One woman's sister in Ireland was scheduled to have a cancerous growth removed the next day. Briege met the sick sister three weeks later. The growth was gone when she checked into the hospital. The woman had been healed in Ireland by prayer in Scotland.

Briege said she'd seen a lot of people healed, but "I still have to keep praying and many times I find myself thinking, 'Oh, that person's so sick' and wondering if healing is possible."

In Japan, an Irish priest told Briege, ". . . if only I could see somebody healed if they were blind or had bad legs, it would be very easy to believe."

Three days later, Briege prayed with twelve Jesuits, including an elderly French priest with a gangrenous leg scheduled for amputation after the retreat. The next morning, the French priest, who did not speak English, came up to Briege, who does not speak French, and made all kinds of signs to her. Briege thought him mad and walked away.

At breakfast, the same priest came running into the room with one of the legs of his trousers rolled up. His leg was completely healed.

Three seats away was her Irish friend. She said, "Father, there's your miracle."

The Irish priest said, "My God, it's awful hard to believe! Did he have gangrene at all?"

She said, "See, Father, it doesn't make it easier to believe."

Sister says, "The moral of this story, I suppose, is that people who have faith don't need to see." They know. God can do the unbelievable.

Sister Briege Says Persevere: Instant Coffee and Instant Miracles

"Jesus does answer us, but it may not be right away."

She gives as an example little David, who had a tumor on the brain and seven months to live. The parents were putting all their hopes on Sister Briege.

Sister told them they were God's partners in creating David and urged them to intercede with Jesus every night for the child's healing. The father thought maybe it was not God's Will.

Sister asked, "If Jesus were standing here, what would you ask Jesus to do for David? . . . Well," I said, "You ask Jesus to heal him. Ask him every day. Don't you be making up Jesus' will for Him. After all, miracles do happen! Just tell Him exactly how you feel and tell Jesus that you love little David and ask him to please heal him."

Briege urged them to gather David and their six children (some teenagers) around them to pray. "Just talk to Jesus. Even if it is only saying an Our Father and a Hail Mary slowly. Get the children to ask Jesus to heal little David and to tell Jesus they love him. As you pray, lay your hands on David."

As the months went on, the tumor grew. The father felt prayer was not working. The mother insisted they persist. Seven months passed and David had not died as predicted. The tumor grew, but David was not blind as predicted. After sixteen months of increased growth, the tumor began to grow smaller.

As they continued to pray, they saw the growth shrink and shrink until it finally disappeared. God had healed progressively rather than instantly. During those two years of nightly prayer, the children were transformed. After David's healing, the teens would not leave the house after supper until the family had prayed together. Prayer made them a close-knit family who loved God and one another. David was healed of his tumor and the family was blessed and strengthened.

Sister differentiates between miracles that happen instantly, and healings that may be progressive and may happen through medicine, through an operation, or through continued prayer.

At a retreat with Father Kevin Scanlon in Australia, Briege met a nun crippled by polio wearing braces on her back and legs. After Father Kevin anointed her, the nun sat in the chapel for eight hours praying in one position while her entire body shook. Sure she was experiencing the beginning of a progressive healing, Briege said, "Sister, God is healing you."

Sister Briege later read an article in a magazine reporting that daily for four months, the nun's whole body would begin shaking again as she rested. The doctor explained that her withered tissues and muscles were being brought back to life. She was in the process of being healed. The braces were removed.

"We live in an age of instant tea and instant coffee and instant photos: it seems everything is instant . . . We think that if God doesn't give us what we want right away, then he isn't giving it to us at all."

Sister Briege and an Under-the-Table Deal

Sister Briege urges that we come to Jesus with the same expectant faith as desperately poor people in the mountains of Latin America. Before an outdoor Mass said on an old table, Briege and the priest prayed for a little boy who had severe burns and sores on his body.

Briege thought, "My goodness, there's really nothing that can be done. It's so bad. We have no doctors or medicine here."

The priest told the old woman who carried the child to put the boy under the table during Mass. The priest had deep faith in Jesus and was excited about the celebration of the Eucharist. The people were enthusiastic.

At the Consecration, the congregation prostrated themselves on the ground and lifted their eyes to adore the Lord. "Then when I looked at the sacred Host, in my . . . imagination, I got the most beautiful image of Jesus with his two hands out . . . smiling with great love and compassion . . . embracing these poor people and saying, 'Come to me, all who are weary, and I will give you life and faith.'"

After Mass, Briege looked for the little boy. He wasn't under the table. In Spanish, she asked the woman who had brought him where he was. The old lady pointed to a group of children playing. "I looked at the child and he was fine. There wasn't a thing wrong with his little body."

She asked what happened to him.

"The old woman looked at me and said, 'What do you mean, "What happened?" Didn't Jesus come?'"

That same day before Mass, Sister saw a little boy who had a terrible facial deformity. "At the end of Mass, his mother came running up to me with her child in her arms and said, 'Sister, look at my little boy.' The boy's face was healed."

Briege was the only one surprised. The priest had communicated to the congregation that the Mass is a living experience with Jesus. They expected miracles.

That night, Briege felt God telling her that many are making false gods of people in healing ministries. ". . . tell people to take their eyes off Briege McKenna and fix their gaze on their . . . Lord, to put their faith in Me. You can disappoint them . . . as will any person who attracts people to themselves . . . if you point them to Me, then they will never be disappointed."

Briege knows she's to be a signpost, pointing to the healing power of God. People should intercede for themselves. God will listen to them. Briege says many say they talk to God, "But they haven't listened to Him."

Sister Briege Says, "Do It Yourself"

A young priest, ordained only six years, had cancer of the vocal chords and was scheduled to have his voice box removed in three weeks. He called Briege.

"I said, 'Father, I can pray with you now on the phone and I will, but this morning, didn't you meet Jesus? Don't you meet him every day?

The woman only touched the hem of Jesus' cloak, but . . . you receive him into your body. You have him in food. Do you realize that Jesus is actually going down through your throat? There is no better one to go to than Jesus. You ask Jesus to heal you.'"

Sister Briege heard him crying over the phone. When the priest went in for surgery three weeks later, the cancer was gone and he had brand new vocal chords.

In Sydney, Australia, a woman suffering with stomach cancer had an inoperable tumor that caused great swelling. The cancer had spread too extensively for doctors to operate. Briege prayed with her, but also told her to go to Mass and ask Jesus to heal her.

"That was early in the day, on a Saturday. That night, when we were having a rally, a woman came running up the aisle of the hall and she threw her arms around me saying, 'Sister, it happened! It happened!'

"I asked her, 'What happened?'

"She said, 'Look at me. I came to you this morning. I went to Mass as you said. When I was walking up to Communion, I said to myself, "In a few minutes, I am going to meet Jesus. I'm going to take him in my hand and I will ask him for his help" . . . I had no sooner put the Host on my tongue and swallowed it than I felt as though something was burning my throat and down into my stomach. I looked down at my stomach and the growth was gone.'"

Father Kevin Scanlon and Sister Briege give retreats for priests in Africa, Europe, North and South America, Australia, and the Far East. They were having dinner together in a restaurant in Dublin, Ireland.

Praying before the meal, Father Kevin said, "Let's ask Jesus to visit us now as he did on the road to Emmaus."

". . . as he said those words, I bowed my head and waited for him to continue the prayer, but he didn't say anything. I looked up to see what was keeping him. And sitting in the empty seat—I am sure it was in my spirit, but I saw clearly—was a beautiful image of Jesus smiling at me.

"Without saying anything he transmitted to me these words, 'I'm always present where I'm loved, revered, and welcomed.' Then the image faded.

"Father Kevin looked up at me. I could see that he was moved. He said, 'I just felt someone sit beside me.' His feeling confirmed what I had seen.'"

Sister Briege says He is the same Jesus, yesterday, today, and forever. "He is the Jesus who healed in the gospel. So he must be fulfilling his promises of answering his people's needs."

.

Sister Briege: Different Places (Hawaii, Ireland), Same Jesus

The Mormon girl asked Jesus to ease the pain in her hands. A Catholic in Hawaii had brought a Mormon friend with deformed hands for healing. Briege and Father Kevin were not laying on hands as usual, but told everyone to focus on Jesus as Father Kevin walked among the congregants holding up the monstrance, a large golden holder with the consecrated Communion Host in the center.

"As the girl looked at the Host, she felt something come from it and go through her body . . . the Mormon nudged her Catholic friend and said, 'Look.' She held out her hands . . . they were healed."

Sister Briege McKenna's Aunt Lizzie was her second mother. Briege lives in Florida and her beloved auntie lived in Ireland. Briege would say to Lizzie, "Don't you die before I come home."

Aunt Lizzie would reply, "I have no notion of dying. I'll be here when you come home."

In 1984 while Briege was in Brazil, a relative phoned that her Aunt Lizzie had a stroke and was dying so Sister was to come to Ireland immediately. Briege's superior in Florida arranged for plane tickets. Briege went to Mass before the flight. In her heart, Sister thought she'd be able to see Auntie Lizzie before she died.

On her way to Communion, Briege put out her hand to receive the Host and heard the Lord ask, "Briege, who is first in your life?"

"You are, Jesus."

"Then I don't want you to go home. I brought you here . . ."

"Oh, but Jesus, I have to go home because my aunt is dying and I'll never see her again and I promised to go and I have permission from my mother general."

"Briege, who is first in your life?"

"You are, Jesus."

"Well then, I do not want you to go home."

Briege realized leaving was selfish. Thousands of people all over Brazil had arranged to hear her. When she said "Yes" to Jesus, joy filled her spirit. God doesn't force us, says Briege.

"He simply asks. Almighty God stands before someone He created from nothing and humbly asks for love, for service, for obedience."

Several weeks later, thinking her aunt dead, Briege called Ireland. Her friend said, "You mean you haven't heard?" The day Briege decided to obey God the doctor stood over her aunt talking to a nurse. He said Lizzie was in a coma and would die soon.

The patient opened her eyes and said, "Well, doctor, how are you . . . ?" Shocked, the doctor ran out and sent in another nurse. As the nurse came in, Aunt Lizzie pointed to a No Smoking sign and said, "Now dearie, would you turn the sign around and get me . . . a cigarette?"

Ready to die, the aunt had been told, "No, Lizzie, I want you to wait for Briege . . . then I'll take you."

Sister heard Jesus whisper to her, "So Briege, did you really think you could outdo me in generosity?"

Sister Briege says we need to know how much Jesus loves us. Trust the Lord and abandon yourself to him.

෴

Briege McKenna, O.S.C. with Henry Libersat, *Miracles Do Happen* (Cincinnati, OH: Servant Books, 1987), 3-7, 12, 14-16, 44, 46, 52-53, 59-61, 66, 68, 93, 113, 126-128.

Sara and the Mysterious Electric Current

In 1972, Sara Hopkins O'Meara knew the prognosis. A single parent with two boys, aged six and ten, Sara would die within three months. Her body was full of cancer.

Kathryn Kuhlman's face flashed on television in Sara's hospital room after the operation. "I believe in miracles because I believe in God," the evangelist intoned dramatically. Then Kathryn pointed her bony finger right at Sara lying in bed and said, "Do you need a miracle? Be at the Shrine Auditorium this Sunday if you need a miracle."

Sara needed a miracle. She talked the doctor into releasing her from the hospital earlier than he advised. He warned her to stay in bed at home or bleed to death. Sunday, Sara got up, got dressed, and went to the Miracle Service.

She was too late. The doors were closed and every seat was taken. Banging on the door and pleading was useless. Crowds of people couldn't get in. Just as Sara and her friend Janice were about to leave, Sara saw someone she knew who had come out of the auditorium to get a sweater because the air conditioning was too cold. The woman told Sara to take her seat and told her husband to give his seat to Janice.

Sara walked in her own blood up the stairs to the balcony, dropped into the end seat in the last row, and was suddenly above the row looking down at her body. As Sara watched from above, she saw a pink cloud like cotton candy float toward her body and then surround it.

127

Kathryn Kuhlman stopped the service, turned, and pointed up at the balcony. The preacher said, "There's a girl up there, the girl in the red dress. The glory of God is all over her. She is being healed of cancer."

Sara wasn't sure she was the girl. She asked God for a sign that Kathryn was talking about her. Sara felt invisible hot oil pour over her. A thousand invisible hot needles pierced her. Then an electric shock knocked over all the people sitting in the row with her, and they fell like dominos.

Giving a talk in San Diego, Sara said, "To this day, Sister Mary Ignatius, who was at the other end of the row, talks about that electric shock from the Holy Spirit."

It was as if Sara had touched a live electric wire. The ushers came running. They urged Sara to go to the stage to testify, but she was reluctant because she was well known for her work with orphans.

Kathryn called out again, "There's a healing of the girl in the red dress in the last row in the balcony. She is being healed of cancer. Her body was full of cancer." Sara knew it was her, but still hesitated to go to the stage.

Then she heard a voice say, "You mean I would do this for you and you would deny Me?"

Sara leapt to her feet, totally energized. The pain vanished. The bleeding stopped. She walked down many steps to the stage and testified. Unbeknownst to her, there was an unexpected bonus. Sara received the gift of healing when her cancer was eradicated by the Power of the Holy Spirit.

Sara and the Melting Tumor

The doctor was dumfounded. Sara healed so totally that the next day skin had grown over the stitches. Surgery would be required to remove the clamps and the stitches.

Because medical evidence was vital to Kathryn Kuhlman's mission, Miss Kuhlman asked Sara to show copies of her X-rays while filming a segment on Kathryn's national television show. After the taping, Kathryn asked Sara to join her ministry.

Sara's job was calling out healings in the wheelchair section, before healings happened. Sara protested she couldn't do that. How would she know who God was going to heal? That was impossible. Sara feared she'd be wrong and people would lose faith in God. "Don't worry about a thing, dear," said Kathryn with a knowing smile.

Soon Sara understood why Kathryn seemed unconcerned. Before Kathryn called out a healing, Sara saw light around the person about to be healed. Amazed, she observed the phenomenon for months before daring to trust the light and call out the healing. When Sara confided her doubts to Kathryn, she laughed and told Sara God had great plans for her.

After Kathryn Kuhlman died on February 20, 1976, healing priest Father Ralph DiOrio requested that Danny Thomas, the actor, introduce him to Sara. The priest had read the chapter on Sara Hopkins' healing in Kathryn's book, *Nothing is Impossible with God*. Father DiOrio confirmed Kathryn's words: Sara had a healing gift. Father asked Sara to work in his ministry.

Presbyterian Sara and Roman Catholic Father DiOrio began doing healing services together. At a service for 3,000 in New York, Father surprised Sara by announcing to anyone not healed during the service that he would be laying on hands and praying on one side of the room and Sara would be doing the same on the other side.

Sara was embarrassed. She was an unknown without, as far as she knew, a healing gift. No one would go on her line.

She was right. There was one very long line snaking through the auditorium, the line for Father DiOrio. Sara stood alone, humiliated. Then she saw an unusually tall man at the end of the line talking to family members gathered around him. Sara could imagine the conversation. "It's too long to wait for Father DiOrio. Try that woman. What is there to lose? I'll hold your place. You can always come back on the line here."

The man walked toward her. Sara was horrified. She couldn't help him. He thought she could, but he'd be disappointed. He had a big tumor on his face. When she asked him what was wrong, he asked prayer for an inoperable cancerous tumor. Nervous, Sara closed her eyes and drew a blank. She couldn't think of a prayer to say, so she said, "Dear God, heal this man." His family began screaming and Sara opened her eyes. The tumor melted as they watched.

Sara was more shocked than the healed man. The commotion brought people from the end of Father DiOrio's line up to Sara's. The second healing was a lady with an incurable skin disease. The gauze fell off and new skin formed.

An eighty-year-old man, deaf for fifty years, claimed he could hear. These experiences convinced Sara that God had called her to be a healer. She prayed over people for two consecutive nights and many more amazing cures were reported. At present, Sara continues her healing ministry at a chapel near her home in Paradise Valley, Arizona.

Sara and the Throw-Away Children

Miracles come in small, medium, and large. It's anyone's guess what size miracle brought Sara and her roommate, Yvonne Fedderson, together with the throw-away children.

In 1959, Sara played Ricky's girlfriend on the weekly hit *Ozzie and Harriet* television series and Yvonne played David's girlfriend. The two young actresses tried out separately for a USO show in Japan. Miraculously, out of five hundred women auditioned, roommates Sara and Yvonne were selected for the show.

On a walk between storms in typhoon-ruined Tokyo, the two Hollywood starlets found eleven sobbing "throw-away children" ranging in age from ten to two. Starving, soaked, shoeless, and shivering with cold, the youngsters were huddled under a fallen awning trying to escape freezing rain. They were the half-Japanese, half-American foundlings of GIs on leave in Japan during the Korean War.

All the two women could understand from the Japanese dictionary was, "No mama sans. No papa sans." The girls opened their camel hair polo coats and huddled the children inside them. Then they shuffled them a mile back to the hotel.

Reprimanded by a colonel for bringing the kids to their room, Sara, Yvonne, and the children packed into a taxi van and went from orphanage to orphanage. The orphanages were all filled. It was getting dark and the girls refused to put the children back on the street for the night.

The women carried the children up their hotel fire escape after dark. Bribing maids with cashmere sweaters brought from home got blankets, towels, baby sitting, and promises to keep quiet about the children. The next day, the girls took the kids down the fire escape before dawn, packed them into the taxi van, and continued going from orphanage to orphanage.

The kids began crying when they approached the last one on the list. The driver explained the children had already been put out of there. Many people had died in the typhoons and there was only room for full-blooded Japanese orphans. The Japanese may have been too polite to say they felt American fathers and the American government had responsibility for the others. It was a political hot potato.

Enraged, the women went back to the colonel. He gave them a lead to Mama Kin, a Christian woman who had taken other mixed-blooded children into her home.

Mama Kin's dirt floor hovel had a doorway, but no door. It had windows, but no windowpanes. The roof leaked. Mama Kin had one hibachi for cooking and another for heat. The ten children she cared for in one room took turns wearing two jackets. She had just used up the last of her food. Out of shame, their families had turned the kids out to live on the streets until Mama Kin took them in. Sara and Yvonne left their eleven children with Mama Kin and promised to return the next day with provisions for all twenty-one kids.

That night, the girls stopped the USO show and asked the boys for money and help for the Amer-Asian orphans. The next day, a dozen young soldiers showed up with a truckload of supplies and repaired the hut. Mama Kin's orphanage grew to house one hundred throw-away children and became the first of four orphanages the girls built and maintained in Japan as "International Orphans, Inc." Moving "from obstacle to miracle, over and over," largely with private funding, Sara and Yvonne know God is always at their sides.

Sara, Just A Girl Who Can't Say "No"

By 1966, Sara and Yvonne had spent seven years in Sara's garage raising money for four orphanages in Japan. When Congress invited them to Washington, DC to honor their work, the two women were suspicious.

The Vietnam War was raging. Why honor them now? Would Congress dare ask them to do for throw-away children in Vietnam what they had done in Japan?

The answer to Congress would be "no." They both had their own children and were overwhelmed by the demands of the orphanages. On the flight from Los Angeles to Washington, the two young matrons wrote a gracious but definite refusal.

Sure enough, Congress made its pitch. General Wallace Green showed blow-up photographs of sick and starving Vietnamese-American children behind barbed wire, children without limbs from land mines, children sitting in beds that looked like cages.

With eyes full of tears, the women realized that God had spoken to their hearts again. They said, "We'd love to" at the same time; so much for the fancy refusal speech.

Shocked at the size of the job ahead, they barely spoke on the flight home. What would their board say? How could they raise even more money?

International Orphans Inc. met the challenge: from 1966 to 1975, Sara and Yvonne built five orphanages, a hospital, and a school for throw-away children in Vietnam. The orphanages were divided into Protestant, Catholic, and Buddhist sites.

The children's hospital had to be built because Seabees reported wounded Vietnamese-American children were left to die on battlefields since the Americans had no place to take them. Orphanages took the healthy ones, but there were few nurses, so children were not accepted in hospitals without someone to stay with them and take care of them. Soldiers offered to give part of their salaries to build a hospital for these kids.

The hospital project required fundraising, acquiring medical equipment, medicines and vitamins. Sara and Yvonne raised the money and sent the supplies while a general kept them abreast of progress by phone and photographs.

Miracle after miracle kept them inspired. When bombs damaged the roof of one of the orphanages, $17,000, a huge sum of money at that time, was needed to repair the roof before monsoon season, less than thirty days away.

The day before the deadline, they had raised only half. The general couldn't repair the roof. In a depressed frame of mind, Sara went to the post office on the way home. Curious about an envelope from Disneyland because International Orphans Inc. had no relationship with Disney, Sara opened it. Disneyland had no idea International Orphans Inc. needed money for roofs and no idea of the amount required to repair them, but the check they sent was exactly $17,000.

God had taken care of things. Sara says this happens all the time.

"Every time we've said, 'Yes, we'll do it,' God has provided. It's a test of faith to hang in there, not knowing until the last moment. And God knows we've had lots of those 'last moments' along the way. Reminding each other of this serves as a great boost to our faith, and the stronger our belief, the more we feel willing to take on."

✌✎

Sara O'Meara and Yvonne Fedderson, *Silence Broken: Moving from a Loss of Innocence to a World of Healing and Love* (San Diego, CA: Jodere Group, 2003), 7, 12, 26, 65.

Come, Holy Spirit: Drunken College Students and The Cross and the Switchblade

Like Moses on Sinai and the apostles on Pentecost, twenty-five college students near modern-day Pittsburgh, Pennsylvania had an encounter with the Living God on what is now called the "Duquesne Weekend." (February 1967)

During a retreat, without any warning, the Holy Spirit knocked them over, filled them with a powerful, life-changing ecstatic experience of His Love, and began the Charismatic renewal in the Catholic Church.

Why these kids? What primed the pump to allow the Living Water to rush into them and intoxicate them?

One of the books assigned to prepare the students for retreat was *The Cross and the Switchblade* by David Wilkerson.

How did the story of a small-town minister working with murderous New York City teenage gangs help open Duquesne students on retreat to the Holy Spirit?

Reverend Wilkerson talked to God and expected answers. When David was a candidate for pastor of a little church in Philipsburg, Pennsylvania, he and his wife, Gwen, were horrified by the condition of the cockroach-infested parsonage. Unsure of God's will for them, the young couple sat in the car with their infant daughter and prayed for a sign of God's will. Did God want them in that parish?

Taking as his model Gideon and his fleece (see Judges 6:36-40), the minister asked God for conditions—which the Church committee offered without being asked. David knew from this sign that the Lord wanted him to work in Philipsburg.

Reverend Wilkerson's mission to gangs in New York City really began on February 9, 1958 when the minister sold his television set. The only one in the family who watched TV, David felt the two hours spent viewing would be better spent praising and thanking God. Again he asked God for a sign. Conflicted about giving up his nightly entertainment, David asked God to show approval by having a buyer contact him within half an hour after the paper hit the streets carrying the ad for the sale of the TV. The minister's wife laughed at him. Twenty-nine minutes after the paper went into circulation, David had a buyer. God wanted His prayer time.

One night during his private two-hour prayer session, Reverend Wilkerson felt drawn to read *Life* magazine. Dismissing it as a distraction, David ignored the urge until it became so insistent that he realized it came from God. "Lord, is there something in there You want me to see?" he asked out loud.

With a pounding heart, the minister opened to a drawing of a courtroom scene that brought him to tears: seven boys on trial for a brutal murder for which they were undeniably accountable. Reverend Wilkerson knew God wanted him to go to New York and help those boys.

Accompanied by Miles, the Church's youth minister, David drove fearfully toward New York City with $75 given by his congregation in his pocket. As they drove, David asked Miles to pick a Bible passage at random as a sign from God that they were doing the right thing. Miles found Psalm 126, "They that sow in tears shall reap in joy."

*　　*　　*

The following stories show how New York City was transformed by Almighty God through Reverend Wilkerson's bungling. David talked to God, listened for His direction, and trusted that God would use him if he stepped out in faith.

David Wilkerson: Be Publicly Specific in Prayer and Learn Power

When the two small town hicks, Reverend Wilkerson and Miles, first hit big city nighttime traffic on the George Washington Bridge, David Wilkerson's misgivings grew to deep-seated fears. His fears were reinforced as he drove past Times Square, then center of the seedy sex industry, and saw everywhere dangerous gangs of lonely, angry, bored teenaged boys. Staying overnight at a hotel, David tried to contact the boys on trial to whom he felt called to minister. The District Attorney's office told him the only one qualified to give him access to the defendants was the judge.

Hoping for an interview with the judge, David went to court the next morning armed with his Bible. He and Miles skipped breakfast, adding a fast to prayer. If they had taken time to eat breakfast, the last two seats in the courtroom would have been taken.

Looked on as a newsworthy nut, David, his picture, and his story, hit the papers: a wide-eyed fanatic arrested while seeking to save the souls of the most hated kids in the city, the killers of a helpless polio victim. Reverend Wilkerson's reputation was ruined. He could lose his ordination as a minister and had embarrassed his family, and all to no avail. David needed the parents' permission to see and minister to the accused boys. How would he locate the parents? Shamed and defeated, he went back to Philipsburg, Pennsylvania, to face intense criticism. What was God doing?

In prayer, a Scripture verse kept popping into his mind, "All things work together for good to them that love God and are called according to his purpose." With it came a message so outrageous that David dismissed it each time it floated into his head, "Go back to New York."

The idea was so persistent that David asked his congregation for money for another trip. He collected exactly enough, $70, and he and Miles started off at 6 a.m. on the eight-hour trip. David prayed, "I do not ask to be shown Your purpose, only that You direct my steps."

David found Broadway, the only street he knew, and was driving slowly when he had an incredible feeling that he should get out of the car. He left Miles sitting there and had walked a half a block when a group of teens recognized him from the newspapers and called after him. They were part of "the Rebels." The kids thought of him as one of them, an outlaw like themselves. Part of God's perfect planning, the publicity nightmare had given David entrée to teen gangs. As he assured the teens that God was on their side and loved them just as they were, one of the members ran his open switchblade down the buttons of David's coat. This was dangerous business.

Within half an hour of returning to New York City, the minister met two street gangs and was invited to their clubhouses, nightmares of drugs, alcohol, sex, and brutal violence. God had answered his prayer said publicly and specifically before his Church.

David knew, "The day you learn to be publicly specific in your prayers, *that* is the day you will discover power."

Years earlier when he was twelve, his father, bleeding profusely from duodenal ulcers, was given two hours to live. While David's mother read over and over, "And all things whatsoever you shall ask in prayer, believing, ye shall receive." David laid hands on his dad and said, "Jesus, I believe what You said. Make Daddy well." Then publicly specifying, the boy called to the doctor, "I have prayed believing that Daddy will get better." The father got up from his bed healed. The doctor said, "I have just witnessed a miracle."

David Wilkerson: Gangs Bring Bibles to the Edward Street Police Station

For four months, March to June of 1958, Reverend Wilkerson took the eight-hour drive to New York City on his day off, arrived in early afternoon, walked the streets until early morning, then drove eight hours back home again. As the minister walked, he looked for the direction in which God wanted him to move.

David began his walk in the Bedford-Stuyvesant section of Brooklyn, at that time an area with more murders per square foot than anywhere else on the planet. The first night, snow, piles of garbage, and deep slush slowed his progress. He saw a drunk on the icy sidewalk. When David tried to help him, the man cursed him. Teen prostitutes solicited him. Leaving a huge housing project with broken windows and broken lights, David heard three shots. No one paid attention, but when a police car arrived, a few did stop to watch as police brought out a man dripping blood. "It took more than a shot in the shoulder to draw a crowd in Bedford-Stuyvesant."

Then David would get back in his car, pull up a car rug, and go to sleep. The minister knows now that he might have been killed by the "Little People," children ages eight, nine, and ten who had guns and knives and cultivated violence to show their manhood.

After four months of walking, David Wilkerson knew the biggest problem boys in the city had is loneliness. They felt no one loved them. From this sprang violence, sex, and drug addiction. Compounding the problem was the lack of drug treatment. Riverside Hospital could accommodate some addicts, but the only other public hospital in the country treating New York City addicts was a federal institution in Lexington, Kentucky.

The problem was so overwhelming that David was about to give up when the Holy Spirit gave him an idea. "They've got to start over again, and they've got to be surrounded by love."

Reverend Wilkerson saw in his mind's eye a nice house where kids could live any time they wanted to, be fed and clothed and loved. "Oh Lord," I said aloud, ". . . But it would take a . . . series of miracles such as I've never seen."

It did.

In one early miracle, David converted the murderous Chaplains and Mau Maus at the Fort Greene projects, where towering apartments housed thirty thousand people. The two gangs warred against the police. David and a trumpet player tooting "Onward Christian Soldiers" stood on a street corner. "I told them God loved them as they were, right then . . . some of them had committed murder. But God . . . saw what they were going to be in the future." Summoned to the Edward Street Precinct, the minister was congratulated by the police in front of six Mau Maus. They were there asking officers to autograph their Bibles. The gangs' war on the police was over.

Today Reverend Wilkerson's inner-city ministry offers residential and crisis counseling centers in more than 70 countries. In New York City, Times Square Church ministers to 7,000, among them hungry, destitute, addicted, and lonely people of all ages. Teen Challenge reaches out to troubled youngsters worldwide. Their Biblically-based program for the recovery of drug addicts is highly effective.

Like a trapeze artist with a trusted partner, Reverend Wilkerson took the leap, knowing God's hands would be there to catch him. It began when David sold his television set and turned viewing time into praying time. God took over his life. Give Him the time and He'll do it for you, too.

Dynamite

The Duquesne Weekend blasted the Catholic Church into Charismatic renewal. Ignited like holy wildfire, the Charismatic prayer movement in the Catholic Church spread from Pittsburgh around the country. Their experience lit the fire for millions.

On the Duquesne Weekend, God worked in a direct physical way. The Holy Spirit works in the same way today at Charismatic prayer meetings when people are slain in the Spirit: They fall flat on their backs in religious ecstasy.

Baptism in the Spirit blasts God's message: He loves us. All He expects in return is that we love Him and each other. Joy awaits you. Ask for it.

As a flabbergasted nurse friend of mine said, "What is happening to those people?"

The answer is astounding, "God is touching them." God is real.

Family Prays: Club Foot Healed at St. Frances Cabrini Shrine

John Boucher led the crowd in singing in English, French, and Spanish: "I say 'yes,' Lord," "Je dit 'oui,' L'Signeur," and "Yo digo 'si,' El Senor."

The crowd roared in fervor expressing deep desire to do the will of God. The man leading them in song is, as is Therese, his wife, the author of a number of books and a leader in the Charismatic renewal in the Catholic Church. John and Therese Boucher have offered their whole lives to God.

Sitting next to me in the audience was Therese, giving silent witness to God's touch.

In the first place, Therese's parent's considered her arrival a miracle; they had prayed for years that God send them a child. The little girl had a club foot, and although God had already performed one miracle, Therese Boucher's parents expected another one. Although they believed in the power of prayer, they did the sensible thing and also sought God's healing though medical treatment. The girl was fitted with a temporary cast and a date was set for surgery.

While the family waited for the scheduled surgery, they went to the Shrine of Mother Cabrini in New York City. There, before the body of Mother Cabrini displayed in a glass coffin under the altar, the little band of lay people prayed that God would heal Therese's foot. Several months later, the cast was removed prior to surgery. The operation was unnecessary. Therese had been healed through her family's expectant prayers. They knew God wants to say "Yes."

Father "Red" McDonough: A Child Rises from the Dead

"All I do is show up," said eighty-six-year-old Redemptorist, Father Edward McDonough, Boston's healing priest, nonchalantly dismissing amazing healings in his ministry. "God does the healing."

One of the more spectacular healings among thousands in Father McDonough's career was the resurrection of eleven-year-old Joseph Thornton [not his real name] at Massachusetts General Hospital in the 1970s. While playing near an abandoned factory, the child had touched a live wire and was electrocuted.

In a coma for over a month, Joseph was gone: his brain activity had stopped and his breathing was mechanically sustained. Doctors considered Joseph dead. They urged Mr. and Mrs. Thornton [not their real name] to pull the plug that kept life support machines forcing the semblance of life into their dead child.

The parents would not do that until every option had been explored. That included prayer. Madelyn Thornton [not her real name] asked Father McDonough, a renowned local healer, to come to the hospital to pray for her son. Father McDonough, from Our Lady of Perpetual Help Mission Church in Roxbury, Massachusetts, laid hands on Joseph in the Name of Jesus and prayed.

After twenty minutes of prayer, Joseph regained consciousness, opened his eyes, and looked Father Ed McDonough in the eye. Two days later, Joseph left intensive care.

News of the healing electrified the parish. Everyone knew about Joseph's miraculous recovery because the whole community had been praying for him. Father McDonough said the healing affected the neighborhood as powerfully as Lazarus' rising affected bystanders watching Jesus at work two thousand years ago. Because that same Jesus is at work today, Father urges that we put our faith in Jesus' healing power.

At the end of Father McDonough's last Sunday of the month healing service at Our Lady of Perpetual Help Mission Church, ushers collected names, addresses, and phone numbers of those claiming healing. Encouraged to get documentation from physicians, people filled two large file cabinets in Father McDonough's office with medically-documented reports of cures.

How did his mission begin? Father McDonough was introduced to the Charismatic renewal in 1967 at a prayer meeting in Maryland. Soon after that, baptized in the Holy Spirit, the priest started a prayer meeting in the Black parish where he was curate in Virginia.

When people were healed on a regular basis, the prayer meeting became a healing service. Although those healed would bring a friend and new people would come every week, in three years the group never grew beyond thirty, no matter how much Father tried to increase its size. Father McDonough said he learned from this experience that it's all in God's hands. Father is powerless: God will bring them and God will heal them.

In 1974, Father McDonough was sent back to Our Lady of Perpetual Help Mission Church with a history of a hundred-year-old healing ministry in the Roxbury parish where Father grew up. Ed McDonough was raised hearing about people he knew being healed through prayer, and as a ninth grader, had himself been healed of double lumbar pneumonia, responsible for the death of three other local kids. When he was healed, "Red" McDonough decided to become a Redemptorist priest. He died in February of 2008, still serving as a channel for the love of Jesus.

Peter and the Apostles Trip Out: Itinerant Healers

To show how powerfully God used St. Peter and the other Apostles, read these sections in the Acts of the Apostles showing their healing power. It was knowledge of God's Presence that gave Peter and the others the strength to give their lives testifying to their faith in Jesus, first at home in Jerusalem and then throughout the known world.

"Many signs and wonders were done among the people at the hands of the apostles. They were all together in Solomon's portico. None of the others dared to join them, but the people esteemed them. Yet more than ever, believers in the Lord, great numbers of men and women, were added to them. Thus they even carried the sick out into the streets and laid them on cots and mats so that when Peter came by, at least his shadow might fall on one or another of them. A large number of people from the towns in the vicinity of Jerusalem also gathered, bringing the sick and those disturbed by unclean spirits, and they were all cured." (Acts 5:12-16)

Even Peter's shadow healed in the Name of Jesus!

"As Peter was passing through every region, he went down to the holy ones living in Lydda. There he found a man named Aeneas, who had been confined to bed for eight years, for he was paralyzed. Peter said to him, 'Aeneas, Jesus Christ heals you. Get up and make your bed.' He got up at once. And all the inhabitants of Lydda and Sharon saw him, and they turned to the Lord." (Acts 9:32-35)

Healing is the best evangelism.

"Now in Joppa there was a disciple named Tabitha (which translated means Dorcas). She was completely occupied with good deeds and almsgiving. Now during those days she fell sick and died, so after washing her, they laid her out in a room upstairs. Since Lydda was near Joppa, the disciples, hearing that Peter was there, sent two men to him with the request, 'Please come to us without delay.' So Peter got up and went with them. When he arrived, they took him to the room upstairs where all the widows came to him weeping and showing him the tunics and cloaks that Dorcas had made while she was with them. Peter sent them all out and knelt down and prayed. Then he turned to her body and said, 'Tabitha, rise up.' She opened her eyes, saw Peter, and sat up. He gave her his hand and raised her up, and when he had called the holy ones and the widows, he presented her alive. This became known all over Joppa, and many came to believe in the Lord. And he stayed a long time in Joppa with Simon, a tanner." (Acts 9:36-43)

Anyone who can raise the dead and heal the sick can acquire wealth and power. However, the Apostles knew it was not their power, but Jesus' power that worked miracles. They did all in the name of Jesus. Humankind repaid them with cruelty: imprisonment, stoning, beatings, and finally death.

Twelve gutsy Jewish men on fire with the love of God heard Jesus' message, watched Jesus die, saw Him risen, and committed their lives covering the globe giving testimony. Our faith is based on their witness. They gave us Jesus.

All Were Healed: Whistle While You Work

The cathedrals of the Middle Ages were built in a fever of Charismatic renewal "that would sometimes grip whole towns, cities and regions. A good bit of the work was done by volunteers in an atmosphere of group Charismatic prayer."

The cathedral at Chartres, France, was begun in 1145 as part of a religious revival that started there and swept throughout Normandy. Ten thousand lived in Chartres at this time and of those, an astounding percentage, thousands, participated in constructing the cathedral.

Abbot Haimon was among them. "To join the voluntary organization that built the cathedral, Haimon says that men and women had to go to confession, put away grudges and make up with enemies." Notice the similarity to healers today urging those seeking healing to forgive all who have hurt them.

Nobles and common serfs worked together as equals, harnessing themselves to wagons, pulling loads of stone so heavy that sometimes a thousand people were needed to move them. By day, sounds of trumpets and flourishing of banners accompanied the work. Exhorted by priests, people burst into Charismatic prayer. They would "lift up their sobs and sighs from the inmost recesses of their hearts with the voice . . . of praise." Healers today teach that healing takes place in a climate of praise.

Overcome with God's Presence, workers would "fall to the ground with outstretched arms and kiss the earth again and again." Abbot Haimon reported innumerable healings as wagons stopped and workers prayed for the sick in wagons of their own.

At night, people rested, prayed spontaneously, and held healing services. Wagons were pulled up around the cathedral in progress, lights and torches were tied to the wagons, and the sick were put into groups. Singing psalms and hymns, people implored God to heal the sick. Charismatic worship healing services were continuous.

When the sick had not all been healed, people would become even more exuberant in their prayer, weeping and throwing themselves on the ground. Said Abbot Haimon, "Soon all the sick leap forth healed from wagon after wagon."

The crippled threw away their crutches and strode to the altar to give thanks. The blind could see and needed no one to lead them. After each healing, there was a procession to the high altar and bells were rung. The night resounded with hymns, praise, and thanks.

The glossolalic element was in their "sighs from the inmost recesses of their hearts," calling them, like "tongues," wordless vocalized prayers to express a deep love of God. "The spontaneous free-flowing movement of all their prayer is also obvious . . . Hymns and praises lasted late into the night."

The obvious connection between fervent expressive prayer and healing brings to mind praise-charged healing services today. Echoes of 1145 also ring as current healers encourage "saturation prayer urging that people continue to pray day after day until healing takes place." The same God heals today who healed all in 1145.

∾ひจ

David Wilkerson with John and Elizabeth Sherrill, *The Cross and the Switchblade* (Grand Rapids, MI: Chosen Books, 2000), 11, 13, 26-27, 45, 47-48, 55, 60, 69.

John J. Boucher, *Following Jesus: A Disciple's Guide to Discerning God's Will* (Pecos, NM: Dove Publications, 1995), 2.

Eddie Ensley, *Sounds of Wonder, A Popular History of Speaking in Tongues in the Catholic Tradition* (New York, NY: Paulist Press, 1977), 64-67.

Judith MacNutt and the Bibles

Prior to her marriage, psychiatric social worker, Judith MacNutt, then a Protestant evangelist, worked in Jerusalem, Israel, teaching English and religion to Palestinian girls. Short on funds, Judith and her associate, Lynn, told the girls to pray for a certain simply-written edition of the Bible that would make a perfect teaching tool.

Right before Christmas, an American sailor knocked on their door and asked for Judith and Lynn. Looking at the big sack slung over his shoulder, Judith teased in her rich Kentucky accent, "Well, you found them. Who are you, Santa Claus?"

"No, I'm from my ship, ma'am, and I've been looking for Judith and Lynn all over Jerusalem. Our prayer group on the ship asked God who we could help for Christmas and He told us to get these Bibles and bring them to Judith and Lynn in Jerusalem." The bag contained the exact number of Bibles the girls had been praying for in the exact edition Judith needed.

Mrs. MacNutt and her husband Francis are accustomed to miracles. In fact, one might say miracles are their business. A powerful healer from the early years of the Catholic Charismatic movement, Harvard-educated Francis MacNutt, Ph.D., a former Dominican priest, was laicized and married in the Church.

Cardinal Ratzinger (now Benedict XVI, pontiff emeritus) called the MacNutts, an internationally recognized healing team, to Rome for special recognition by Pope John Paul II.

At a workshop near their headquarters in Jacksonville, Florida, Judith described her accidental initiation into the healing ministry. At the first healing service Francis conducted after the MacNutts' marriage, Judith stood on the side watching a long line of people wait for Francis to lay hands on them, asking healing in the name of Jesus.

Wearing an ill-fitting wig, an emaciated woman, obviously undergoing chemo, approached Judith and horrified her by asking her to pray for her. "Oh, I'm so sorry. I don't do that. My husband does that. Look, right over there. And he's very good at it."

Across the front of the room, one after the other of those blessed by Francis were slain in the Spirit and fell into the arms of catchers. Their bodies covered the floor. People on line had to step carefully around and over the people who lay in ecstasy on the carpet.

"I can't wait on that long line, honey," said the pale, bony woman in the ill-fitting wig. "I'm exhausted and I have to go home. It's you or nobody."

Taking a deep breath, Judith put her hands on the woman, closed her eyes, and prayed every prayer she knew. Judith and the sick woman prayed together for a long time. The woman thanked Judith and left. When the cancer victim wrote saying her cancer had been cured, Judith knew God had called her to join Francis in the healing ministry.

Introduced to basic teachings on healing through Agnes Sanford and the Reverend Tommy Tyson, Francis McNutt helped bring the healing ministry to the Catholic Church in the late sixties. Author of *Healing*, a classic in the field, Francis with Judith promotes a simple but powerful message: "Let's not turn the Gospel 'Good News' that God wants us pain-free to the 'Bad News' that suffering is God's Will. He never once said, 'Go home and offer it up.' Jesus healed all who came to Him."

Francis MacNutt, Ph.D.: God Wants To Heal Us and God Has a Sense of Humor

Jesus "cured them all." Saying that Christianity is the power to heal, Francis MacNutt urges that we shed false humility and attempt healing prayer. He estimates that fifty percent of those who ask for prayer at any given session are healed of a physical sickness, especially when praying with a team or in a loving community.

"I say this as an encouragement for others to consider the possibility that God might use their prayers someday to heal the sick."

The first person Francis prayed for, a nun who had been through shock treatment for depression, had been helped as much as the best psychiatric science could help her. To Dr. MacNutt's surprise, despite the fact that the nun had been labeled incurable, she was healed.

"Somehow it was much easier to believe that God could heal the sick through prayer than to believe that He could heal through my prayer."

Francis says God has a sense of humor as illustrated in the unpredictable healing of Sister Avina Michels, O.S.F. Confined to a wheelchair as a result of a tragic automobile accident in which two other nuns had been killed, Sister sought healing prayer from a loving community. The prayer group had prayed for Sister Avina on a previous occasion and at that time her arm had been completely healed.

This experience had given Sister greater confidence in the healing power of prayer. Several months later, she asked the group to pray for the healing of her knees so that she could leave her wheelchair and walk. The retreat team gathered around her and placed their hands on her. Following the principle that it is good to be specific when asking for healing, they asked that God heal Sister's knees.

Suddenly Sister put her hands to her face. Her expression changed as she was healed of facial paralysis and neuralgia that she had not mentioned. The group was amazed: they had prayed for her knees and her face was healed. In subsequent sessions, she was completely healed through prayer and now walks without difficulty.

Dr. MacNutt tells of a retreat master who did not believe in faith healing and who staged a fake Miracle Service to teach college students on retreat that true faith means believing without signs and wonders.

The priest told the students he had the gift of healing and made a fake altar call. Thirty students came forward. The priest went along the altar rail imitating Oral Roberts on television. With no expectation that anything would happen, he prayed for each, put his hands on their heads and said loudly, "In the name of Jesus, be healed."

All the students were healed.

The healing of headaches the priest could explain as the power of suggestion, but there was a boy with his arm in a sling who waved his arm over his head and claimed he was cured. The only thing that made the priest feel better was a girl with a sprained ankle, who had claimed a healing, returning the next day to say the swelling had returned.

"Faith is important for healing, but if we, in our weakness, do all we can, God will bless us far beyond our own merits."

Having witnessed similar unanticipated cures a number of times, Francis concludes that God wants to make sure we have faith in Him alone and not in our own planned methods. The famed healer, Kathryn Kuhlman, agreed with Francis MacNutt.

In an interview with Francis, Kathryn Kuhlman said, "God is too big for us to confine."

Kathryn told Dr. MacNutt that she'd never written a method book on how to heal because she didn't know how, and if she did write one, the minute it was written, the Holy Spirit would do something contrary to what she said.

"I'm still learning the mysterious ways in which God moves." Then she agreed with Francis MacNutt, "I'll tell you one thing—I'm sure God has a sense of humor!"

Francis MacNutt: Faith Healing vs. Love Healing

Dr. MacNutt differentiates between two styles of healing: the power style and the love style. The power style stresses the faith of the sick person and sometimes makes those not healed feel they lack faith. The love style, preferred by Dr. MacNutt, dwells on God's willingness to heal those who come to Him with open and contrite hearts.

"I have seen extraordinary things happen when a climate of love was present. Sometimes there have been cures without explicit prayers for them."

Francis was asked by married couples to pray for an increase of their love for each other. As the retreat team prayed for Chuck and Alice for an increase of their love, a cyst on Alice's shoulder that had bothered her for some time disappeared with a sensation of heat.

Something similar happened in the summer of 1972. Francis and several others prayed for a Protestant missionary and his wife. Again their prayer request was for an increase of love between them.

After Francis and the team had finished praying, the man was shocked when he felt his abdomen. He kept saying, "It's gone. It's gone!" A hernia had been healed.

"Time after time we find people healed, not only through direct prayer, but simply because of their love for each other."

In 2001, a woman wrote Francis about being prayed for by a loving Church and family community:

". . . I'm forty years old and the mother of four children. Five years ago I had a mastectomy, and about a year and a half ago the doctors discovered that the cancer had spread to my liver . . . They shook their heads and sent me home after taking out my ovaries, saying in a few weeks I could start on chemotherapy . . .

"When I (am) . . . afraid . . . I . . . read (from MacNutt) 'God loves you, He wants to help you, have faith, He will heal you' . . . our parish was having prayer meetings. My husband took me . . . stood up, explained my situation and begged for help. The whole community prayed for me.

"My husband and children also laid hands on me at home and we prayed our heads off . . . we prayed that I wouldn't get sick from the chemotherapy; I didn't. Then that my hair wouldn't fall out; it didn't. And of course, praying all the time that Jesus would heal me . . . the doctor took another liver scan and . . . it showed the tumor to be much, much smaller."

As reported by Father John B. Healey, a loving community of priests prayed for him and other brother priests as described in "The Holy Spirit and Seventy Priests," (*Brooklyn Tablet*, September 13, 1973):

". . . a number of priests presented their physical ailments to Christ for healing through the ministering hands of brother-priests. In my own case I was healed of a severe difficulty in swallowing food which was due to a hiatal hernia in the esophagus, and which caused me to regurgitate a portion of every meal I have taken in the last few years. This difficulty disappeared immediately after the Mass. It has not returned. The Spirit of Christ is manifestly with us. Alleluia!"

". . . the minister is simply to pray as best he can and, above all, to love all the sick who come to him."

Francis MacNutt: Don't Scrutinize Your Doubts—Keep Your Eyes on God

Only God sees the full picture. Scrutinizing our own doubts makes us man-centered instead of God-centered. Stay focused on God.

". . . faith is not in my faith, but my faith is in God—in his goodness and wisdom—in his unfailing listening and answering my prayers."

Dr. MacNutt describes soaking prayer offered for a woman with a severe back problem. The doctor tested areas of the woman's back as the group prayed until the woman's pain was gone. To all but the doctor, the woman seemed cured because she was able to move pain-free. However, as the physician touched her back, one area was still tender enough to cause her to wince.

The doctor said, "This is amazing; I've never seen anything like this occur so fast. She's about ninety-five percent improved, but there's still an area that's not completely right."

The group prayed on until all tenderness was gone. Francis and the others had not been aware, as was the medical doctor, that the woman was still not fully healed and needed more prayer.

Dr. MacNutt cautions against telling people to claim a total healing because they have experienced some relief. He asks people to return for further prayer as a precaution until doctors verify the cure.

He cites the testimony of a polio victim healed in stages after having been wheelchair-bound for twenty years. When Francis and Sister Jeanne Hill prayed over her, the crippled woman's leg lengthened, but nothing else seemed to materialize. Then her husband took her to the May 1975 Rome Charismatic Conference.

"Monday at Mass in St. Peter's Basilica, a stranger came up to me . . . and said that the Lord was standing in the dome with his hands stretched over me and would heal me."

The woman in the wheelchair thought the lady was nutty, thanked her, and turned back to trying to see the altar from her spot in the wheelchair. The woman returned and told the handicapped lady to claim the healing power of the Eucharist when she received Communion.

". . . (when I took the host) I was enveloped in warmth, and wave after wave of something like electricity nearly knocked me out of my chair."

Her husband thought she was ill, but the polio victim realized she was being healed. The stranger reappeared and told her to claim the healing and not to doubt because it would not be all at once. Then she disappeared.

"But God continues to work with me and, day by day, I find myself . . . able to do things I haven't done in twenty years! My S-curvature is gone, my shoulders are even, and my body is in alignment. The left side of my face no longer sags . . . I can turn to both left and right in my chair to look behind me! I can eat without using the elbow for leverage! I can lift my left leg and hip off the chair! I can cross both legs. I can hold my left arm halfway up to praise the Lord. I can embrace my husband with that arm for the first time in twenty years. The hip muscles are getting stronger, as is the right leg, making lifting much easier. The right arm hasn't begun to move yet, but it will."

Francis says trust God. Sometimes more time and prayer are needed.

Francis MacNutt: Claiming Healings vs. Delayed and Progressive Healings

". . . for some, 'claiming their healing' . . . releases . . . the current of God's healing power. But to say . . . this method is for all sick persons leads, I believe, to grave pastoral harm."

Illustrating the concept of "claiming healing" successfully is the experience of a sister who claimed her healing as accomplished even though symptoms persisted and her condition, endometriosis, is usually healed only through surgery.

Three years after the healing, Sister wrote reporting freedom from pain for those three years. When first seeking prayer from then-Father

MacNutt's prayer group, Sister had intended to continue her medication every two weeks until it was depleted. Then she'd see if she were cured.

She said the Lord had other plans. He stopped the pain for three hours during the prayer service. Then He asked her quietly if she could prove her faith by stopping the shots that had given her great relief. She struggled with this while everyone was praying. The Lord had not made her think of stopping the shots until praying had started.

Finally she said, "Yes, Lord, I'll go all the way. Now you will be put to the test to really heal me."

Despite this example, Dr. MacNutt urges that we ask God to meet our needs, but not tell Him when or how to do it. Francis describes times he has seen intervals between prayer and healing.

On a Saturday night, a prayer group prayed for a woman whose arm was permanently immobilized through cancer and radiation. Physical therapy had not helped her. Several in the prayer group discerned that she had been healed, though there was no visible change. On the following Monday, she awakened with her arm restored to full mobility.

Saying one might be tempted to pray that his wealthy cousin help him in his financial need, Francis suggests simply naming the need and leaving the rest to God. He says three times he found this to be true. People he never expected to help him were prompted in prayer to put a check in the mail or to appear at the door and offer help.

Dr. MacNutt urges that we be open to healing in whatever fashion God chooses, describing how God cured Mrs. Robert Cavnar of Dallas, Texas, of a painful back condition in a manner she considered ridiculous—the "leg-lengthening" kind of prayer.

In "leg-lengthening," patients with orthopedic injury sit holding their legs out straight in front of them, heel against heel. Most people have an imbalance in leg length. As the group prays around the person, one holds the feet, and they watch while one leg moves out until both legs are the same length. (Dr. MacNutt claims 90% are healed or notably improved.)

Listening to an inner prompting, Mrs. Cavnar joined the praying group, asked for prayer, and was immediately and completely healed by the method she had rejected earlier.

If a person seems not to have been healed after we pray, we need not be anxious. Francis MacNutt has seen so many process healings (those taking place over a period of time) and so many delayed healings that he now just prays and entrusts the results to God.

Francis MacNutt: To Be Healed, Forgive

"Therefore I tell you, whatever you ask in prayer, believe that you have received it, and it will be yours. And when you stand praying, if you hold anything against anyone, forgive him, so that your Father in heaven may forgive you your sins." (Mark 11:24-25)

At one time, Dr. MacNutt thought this passage jumped from one subject to the other, but he now sees the vital connection between forgiveness and healing.

"If we deny forgiveness and healing to others, God's love can't flow into us."

Francis gives examples of the way forgiveness opened space in people's hearts so that God could pour in His healing love.

At a communal Penance Service conducted during a retreat at the Carmelite retreat house in Darien, Illinois, he stressed the need to forgive enemies. The retreat team of Mrs. Barbara Shlemon, Sister Jeanne Hill, O.P., and Francis MacNutt then gave two hundred people time to forgive anyone who had ever hurt them. Nowhere did then-Father MacNutt mention physical healing, yet two persons testified immediately that they had received physical healing.

One was a man who had endured constant chest pain as a result of undergoing open heart surgery. He was instantly healed of all chest pain when he said a prayer of forgiveness for his boss, a man he regarded as unjust.

Ironically, it was only because a lot of time had been given to the forgiveness meditation that the employee came to the point of forgiving his employer. At first he wasn't going to forgive the boss, but a lot of time had been allowed and he had a long time to think about it, and he finally decided to say a prayer of forgiveness. At that moment, all pain left him.

Dr. MacNutt reports the same thing to have happened when he conducted a repentance service at the West Virginia Camp Farthest Out in July of 1973. A young woman told Francis that a pylonidal cyst had been instantly healed at the moment she repented of a long-standing grudge.

A woman who requested prayer for inner healing had an unreasoning hatred of men including her husband because of harsh treatment and derision from her brothers. Before praying for that healing, Francis asked her to forgive her brothers. When she refused, he told her unforgiveness blocks healing.

The woman still refused, saying that even if she were destroyed by it she had to hang on to unforgiveness because forgiving her brothers would take away her last excuse for being the kind of person she was. If she could no longer blame her brothers, she would have to accept blame for herself. After praying a bit more, she realized this was contrary to her Christian commitment and to her desire to be whole.

"With tears she forgave her brothers as best she could. She then received the deep healing she was seeking."

Another problem he sees is misunderstanding the difference between one who does not have the gift of healing and prays a prayer of petition with a person who does have the gift of healing and prays a prayer of authority, standing in for God as his spokesperson. When one imitates the other, problems ensue.

It is only when praying in the name of Jesus that we can have absolute faith in our prayer. Praying in the name of Jesus means praying in the person of Jesus because the Hebrews thought the name of a person stood for the entire person.

He urges us all to pray for the sick but be aware of our limitations.

"Do not pretend to be better than you are! Develop your own style as the Spirit leads you. Moreover it is possible to grow in these gifts. Use what God gives you and you will see that God will use you more . . . Agnes Sanford recommends that beginners pray for the cure of minor ailments such as colds."

Although he agrees with Agnes Sanford, Francis says he has seen amazing healings through beginners in the healing ministry.

Francis MacNutt: Withered Leg Grows Six Inches through Days of Soaking Prayer

Francis advises that if healing is not immediate, try soaking prayer. While conducting a retreat in Rionegro, Colombia, in February 1975, then-Father MacNutt encountered the most remarkable example of healing through soaking prayer he has ever seen.

Around 4 p.m., Dr. MacNutt found Sister Jeanne Hill, Bishop Uribe, and others praying for a young woman with a withered leg. They told Francis the leg had grown an inch or more while they prayed. He joined them.

The nineteen-year-old Colombian, Teresa Patino, had suffered an untreated infection from stepping on a sharp object in a swamp when she was five years old. Osteomyelitis deformed her left leg from the knee down. The stunted and twisted leg was about six inches shorter than the other. The bad leg had a deep scar from an attempted bone graft.

As the group prayed gently for two hours, the leg seemed to grow another inch. About eight people prayed, taking turns holding her leg. They broke for dinner and then returned to pray for another two hours. Her leg grew another inch. The twisted leg was gradually straightening.

The next day, they gathered with Bishop Uribe at the house of Alberto Del Corral, the interpreter, and prayed two more hours in the morning and two in the afternoon. The leg had grown about three inches the day before and grew another inch so that by evening there was only a two-inch difference between the two legs.

Most remarkable was the correction of the right foot which had been flat and had no arch. It grew and changed shape until the arch matched the arch in the normal foot. Then the toes of the deformed foot grew from half the size of those on the left until they matched the size of those on her normal foot. They had doubled in size.

When growth stopped, the team decided unforgiveness might be blocking healing. After thought and discussion, Teresa decided that she needed to forgive her mother for a seeming childhood rejection. When Teresa was a little girl, her mother had been forced to board Teresa with people who could afford to get her medical treatment.

After Teresa forgave her mother, the group prayed for inner healing of her feelings of rejection. At that point, the leg again started straightening and growing.

Later in that afternoon, the leg seemed to have stopped growing a second time. This time Teresa shared that she had offered her crippled state to God if he would spare her brother's life when he was seriously injured some years before. She felt guilty because her healing seemed like going back on her promise to God. Bishop Uribe assured her that she was freed from the vow. Once again her leg began to lengthen.

As the day ended, they noticed the scar on her leg lessening and turning from purple to white. By now her right leg reached the ground and she no longer needed crutches.

Since then, with prayer from a local prayer team, her leg continued to grow until there was only half an inch difference. At one session her foot made a turn until the scar that had formed a spiral down her leg had become a straight line from knee to foot. After further prayer for welding of the broken bone, for the first time in fourteen years, Teresa walked again.

Francis MacNutt: Doctors in Awe in 1972 and in 2005

Francis MacNutt's healing ministry has covered forty years. In a letter dated May 1972, Mrs. Katherine Gould of Metairie, Louisiana, testified to her doctor's reactions to healing resulting from Francis and his prayer group's prayer for a number of Mrs. Gould's conditions, including a bladder hernia.

". . . You remember, we also prayed for an increase of my doctor's faith. (I'm enclosing his letter.) How I wish I could share the picture of his face after making his examination.

"He threw his arms up, saying, 'Thank you, Jesus,' because what had to happen was a lifting and restoring of all the organs in my pelvic region. According to him, this kind of thing is not successfully resolved without major surgery."

In a letter dated May 3, 1972, Mrs. Gould's doctor, James A. Seese of Metairie, described his awe at the results of praying for healing: "This is written to testify to the glorious and magnificent power and healing Grace of our Lord Jesus Christ. Mrs. Katherine Gould was seen by me, a gynecologist, for treatment of a bladder hernia—which can be corrected as far as medical science knows, only by surgery . . . This morning she returned to my office, entirely asymptomatic, without any discernible evidence of a bladder hernia. This precious Grace of Our Lord causes my heart and spirit to fill with joy."

Healing Line, the magazine of the MacNutts' Christian Healing Ministry in Jacksonville, Florida, describes current healings every issue. Testimony is given in the November/December 2005 issue by

Chris Freeman, whose husband is Administrator at Wolfson Children's Hospital in Jacksonville: "Thank you so much! An amazing thing happened today. I went in for my recheck because my platelets had dropped to 38,000 last week—not good (normal range is 150,000 to 450,000). When I found out on Friday that they were low, I asked for prayer from all of you. And lo and behold God did a miracle! My platelets today (Tuesday) are 279,000!!! This is the highest they have ever been and, needless to say, well into the normal range. My M.D. was in shock—had to do extra tests to be sure there was no mistake . . . it was no mistake. As I keep saying, God is Good! God is Good! (He's good whether they had been high or not, but it does make you realize the power in prayer. And thanks be to God!)"

The March/April edition of *Healing Line* described Dr. Erlig Larson's experience twenty years earlier. He had attended at an operation on a priest with fourth stage colon cancer. The surgeon removed what he could of malignant tissue, left the rest, and sewed up the priest. Subsequently, the priest claimed he had been healed during Mass. A second operation revealed no sign of malignancy. Dr. Larson, who had attended at both operations, said to Francis, "I saw that all the malignancy was gone! God had healed him."

Francis MacNutt: Was Christ a Faith Healer?

Jesus walking quietly among the throng gently touching and healing is in sharp contrast to Elmer Gantry (from the film of the same name) railing before hysterical crowds. The MacNutts feel prejudice against "faith healing" blocks access to the power of prayer for the sick.

Every issue of *Healing Line* includes joyful testimony.

In the November/December 2005 issue: "From a note handed to Judith: Fifteen years ago (July 1985) at the Shrine Auditorium in Los Angeles, you laid hands on me. Not only did I receive the Holy Spirit, but I was also immediately set free from alcoholism. Thank you so much and Praise God!"

"From a student at the School of Healing Prayer . . . (September 2005): (In June 2005) I had suffered from severe back pain for a very long time, with no medical relief. My back was hurting very badly during the school, and on the last day a Christian Healing Ministry prayer minister who saw that I was in pain stopped to pray over me. When she laid her hands on me and prayed, the pain left me. I have been free of back pain ever since that day."

"After listening to the tape series on 'Healing the Generations,' I prayed with my husband about my family issues related to my Irish roots and overeating. I no longer have the irrational fear that I will run out of food . . . I am eating more normally now and losing excess weight. Before this time, when I would diet and lose weight, I would become very panicked as I became thinner. Now I am looking forward to becoming healthier. Thank you for offering Godly wisdom to the Body of Christ, even to those who live far away from you."

"My husband and I attended the August Day of Healing Prayer, following which, after two very rocky days of anguish, my husband admitted to being an alcoholic and wanting to get better. That was a major milestone for him. We both appreciate the prayers on Monday that led to this revelation."

"During the last intergenerational healing session I received prayer about my daughter's alienation from the family. A miracle happened. The very next evening she called me and we had a long, pleasant talk . . . Plans are being made for family visits. I am praising the Lord for the healing that is taking place. I also am grateful to you for your help in showing me how to pray."

A retired internist, Erlig Larson, M.D., met one of his patients, an alcoholic, who had been alcohol-free for three years. Expecting the patient would give Alcoholics Anonymous the credit, Dr. Larson was surprised when the man said he had been healed through Christian Healing Ministries. The patient had gone to Christian Healing Ministries for prayer to break the habit and it had worked. Erlig shared the story in the March/April 2007 issue of *Healing Line*.

"I tell you the truth, my Father will give you whatever you ask in my name . . . Ask and you will receive, and your joy will be complete." (John 16:23b, 24b)

Francis MacNutt: Inch by Inch Legs Lengthened, Cancers Dried Up Without Asking

Francis advises to rely on God's light. Healing is a mystery. There are no formulas.

At a Charismatic conference in November 1973, Richard Appleby of Charleston, South Carolina, regained function without healing of his illness. Richard testified that fourteen years before his healing, he had developed a kink in his side accompanied by sharp pain that gradually worsened and kept him awake. X-rays revealed a deteriorating right hip. The specialist treating Richard diagnosed that the deterioration would progress, the pain intensify, and eventually he would be wheelchair-bound or in need of an operation with only a fifty percent success rate.

Richard spoke to then-Father MacNutt, who asked Richard to sit in the chair in front of the group. Francis lifted Richard's legs and noticed that one leg was about three inches shorter than the other.

"As he lowered my feet to the floor, he asked those close by to lay hands on me and pray. After a couple of minutes we stopped praying, and I heard a small gasp from a couple of people. Father McNutt said, 'Well, we've gained about an inch. Let's keep praying.' Suddenly I felt a tingling sensation in my right leg and in the right lower side of my stomach. Then I felt a great warmth come over my hip. We stopped praying, looked and Father MacNutt said, 'We've gained another inch. Let's keep praying.' By this time we were all praying as loudly as we could. Finally, Father McNutt said, 'Well it looks to me as though both legs are the same length.'

"Everyone in the hall praised God. I stood up and put my right foot on the floor perfectly for the first time in five years. I walked as steadily as I used to, completely free from pain. Everyone crowded around, congratulating me, and thanking God."

Richard Appleby went back to the same specialist who compared new X-rays with the old ones and said there was no difference in the bone structure. He found the lengthening of Richard's leg and his freedom from pain inexplicable.

Francis MacNutt observes that another way God heals is through arresting the sickness without full healing. He prayed with a friend who has multiple sclerosis. Two years later, the man had suffered no more attacks, a remarkable medical occurrence; however, the man still has arrested multiple sclerosis.

The last time Francis prayed with his friend, nothing seemed to happen related to the multiple sclerosis, but two small skin cancers on his face that Francis wasn't praying for dried up and fell off the next morning. His doctor had never seen anything like that before in his practice.

"Many marvelous spiritual developments have taken place, in his life and in his marriage . . . more important than the healing of the M.S . . . the cycle of M.S. attacks has been broken. Yet the M.S. lingers on . . . arrested."

Once Francis prayed and a tumor disappeared within an hour. A disbelieving doctor said Francis couldn't prove that prayer was the cause. All he could claim was that he prayed and after that the tumor disappeared. Francis agrees, saying, "For the believer, no argument is necessary; for the unbeliever, no argument will prove sufficient."

⋙⋘

Francis MacNutt, *Healing* (Notre Dame, IN: Ave Maria Press, 1974), 14, 34-36, 58, 125, 130, 132, 139-140, 145-146, 155, 173, 176, 311.

Francis MacNutt, *The Power to Heal* (Notre Dame, IN: Ave Maria Press, 1977), 30-32, 52, 58-61, 67.

Healing Line, March/April 2005, 4.

Healing Line, September/October 2005, 10-11.

Healing Line, November/December 2005, 4.

Agnes Sanford: My People Die for Lack of Knowledge

There was no doctor and there was no medicine.

"'Oh, little girl, little girl,' he murmured, 'if there was only something we could do for you.' This is the way Agnes Sanford, renowned healer, described the death of her year-old baby sister in China from amoebic dysentery while her missionary father sat by helplessly.

"There was (a way to heal the baby). For I have seen . . . such . . . illness healed almost instantly by the prayer of faith. If he had . . . known to give himself as a channel for God's power, laying both hands on the child, praying for her the prayer of command—the miracle-working prayer—she could have recovered as Peter's wife's mother recovered when Jesus rebuked the fever and it left her.

"The miracle working prayer: Lord, enter into this baby and destroy with Your might all germ and infection within her and fill her with new life. Thank You, Lord, for it will be so.

"A child can pray thus if he only believes! I have known a child to do it, and her baby brother to be instantly healed of polio. Or a woman can thus say the word of power, or a man—anyone wholly given to Jesus and believing that He lives and that the age of miracles is now . . . at the word of faith His power leaps into life and works through us as channels to create life . . . But my father did not know."

Agnes did not know either until she was a New Jersey mother of three, the wife of Reverend Ted Sanford. When her year-and-a-half-old son, Jack, developed a serious ear infection and was ill with a high fever for six weeks, she prayed continually, but always with fear and not with faith.

"'Oh, please make the baby well!' I would say, and then I would go and feel his forehead to see how much his temperature had risen."

When a young Episcopalian minister, Reverend Hollis Colwell, stopped by, Agnes told him about the child's sickness.

"'Well,' said he in his pleasant voice, quite casually, 'I'll go up and say a little prayer for him.'

"This surprised me . . . I believed in a . . . general way that God answered prayer for healing when He felt like it—unless for some reason He preferred for a person to remain ill. But why God would answer one person's prayer rather than another's, I could not imagine."

He strode upstairs. As she followed she knew he had some kind of power to get the job done.

"'Now shut your eyes and go to sleep,' he said to the baby. 'I'm going to ask God to come into your ears and make them well. And when you wake up, you'll be all right.' He laid his hands on the baby's ears and kept them there for several minutes.

"'Please, Lord Jesus,' he said, 'send your power right now into this baby's ears and take away all germs or infection and make them well. Thank You, Lord, for I believe that You are doing this, and I see these ears well as You made them to be.'" The child shut his eyes, went to sleep and woke up, his temperature normal and his ears well.

Agnes was perplexed. Why did God answer the minister's prayers and not hers? Lack of faith blocked her prayers. The child never had abscessed ears again, but whenever he had an earache he'd say, "Hurt. Pray." She'd do timidly what Reverend Hollis had done. It must have helped because the next time the child had an earache, he'd say again, "Hurt. Pray."

Agnes thought at first that the minister had the gift of healing, but says she knows now that he was not gifted, "but open to the life of God Himself. 'God's water of life could rush through him, for the pipeline between his spirit and God's spirit was intact.'"

Agnes Sanford: Do It Yourself

Agnes Sanford's do-it-yourself book, *The Healing Light*, teaches how to open the pipeline so that God's power can rush through you.

First, contact God. "Be still and know that I am God."

Second, connect with His life by a prayer, like: "Heavenly Father, please increase in me your life-giving power."

Third, believe the power is coming into you and to accept it by faith. Say: "Thank you that Your life is now coming into me and increasing life in my spirit and in my mind and in my body."

Fourth: decide on some easy, tangible thing to assess success.

For example, a working woman asked God to send her two pairs of rubbers for her sons to protect their feet from rain and slush. That night, the ground froze over solid and for two days the boys walked to school dry-shod. Upon the third day, a neighbor gave her two pairs of rubbers for her sons. If the rubbers had not arrived, and the experiment had failed, Agnes Sanford would have recommended examining what's wrong with us, what's clogging the pipeline.

God's will is that we be well. When our lights don't work, we know the problem is not in the flow of electricity in the universe, but in the wiring that connects us with that flow. Thomas Alva Edison tried six thousand times before producing steady light. That, Agnes says, is faith.

Agnes prayed for a nine-year-old with abscessed ears. Repeatedly he improved for twenty-four hours, then relapsed. Each relapse was worse than the last, and he was finally taken to the hospital for a mastoid operation. Infection began to invade the bones of his head and spinal meningitis threatened.

Agnes sought more power in prayer: she brought in a minister to pray with her, then two or three friends, hoping the right combination might provide God with the right kind of a wire for the inflowing of His power. The boy's condition grew steadily worse. In a darkened room on Good Friday, Agnes found him half-conscious, nearly blind, and close to death. If she had accepted death, the child would have died and the parents would have thought, "God's will be done."

Agnes phoned a more experienced prayer-worker for advice. "The parents are the barriers, dearie," she said. ". . . They must stop being afraid." . . . Agnes' prayer partner spoke to the parents and her assurance strengthened their faith. Then she told Agnes to go to the little boy at a certain time and place hands on him. "But don't try to do anything, dearie," she advised. "You've been trying too hard, and it's upset you. Just be still and know He is God and His power is flowing into you through me."

The child was unconscious. Agnes stood beside him with her hands on his brow, so conscious of a heavenly Presence that she returned home, giving thanks.

On Easter, (the child) was sitting up in bed singing at the top of his lungs. He went home within a week, swam all summer, and had no illness that winter. A year later, because he now lived in the Kingdom of Heaven, the child said, as Agnes had taught him to when sick, "I've got a fever now, but that's just the healing things in me doing what God and me told 'em to do and killing the germs. Tomorrow I'll be okay." And he was.

"Just as a whole world full of electricity will not light a house unless the house itself is prepared to receive that electricity, so the infinite and eternal life of God cannot help us unless we are prepared to receive that life within ourselves. Only the amount of God that we can get in us will work for us."

Agnes Sanford: Picture It Done

How long should we pray for healing?

"Until the healing is accomplished!

"Sometimes a prayer once or twice a day is sufficient, but sometimes we need to 'pray without ceasing,' to keep ourselves open to the continuous inflow of God's power.

"We do this, not by saying over and over again, 'Oh, please, Lord,' for that sounds as though we do not believe He is really working. It is much better to keep the power flowing by continually giving thanks for it.

"Every time we think of a condition within ourselves that needs healing we can say, 'Thank you, Lord, that your power is making me well.' And we can look ahead and see ourselves well and strong."

Agnes gives as an example a seven-year-old boy who had a leaky heart. Usually she had great success with healing a child's heart, and one prayer was all that was necessary, but Billy's heart was not healed with one prayer.

Deciding that she needed active cooperation from the child, she asked him what he knew about God.

"'I know all about God,' he replied serenely. 'God is in this room only you can't see Him, 'cause He's 'visible. And Jesus is in this room, only you can't see Him 'cause He's 'visible.'

"'Yes. Isn't that funny?'

"'Not to me, it isn't.'

"Thus I was reproved. Billy, I decided, knew about God with more profound simplicity than I did. His theology was quite sufficient for his seven years. It remained only for me to teach him how to make his knowledge of God work for the healing of his heart.

"'How about playing a little pretend-game with me?' I said to the small friend of God.

"'Pretend you're a big guy going to high school and you're on the football squad. Shut your eyes and see yourself holding the ball and running ahead of all the other fellows. 'Look at that guy!' the other kids will say. 'Just look at him run! Boy, he's strong! I bet he's got a strong heart!'

"Then you say, 'Thank you, God, because that's the way it's going to be.' Will you play that game every night, right after you say your going-to-bed prayers?"

"I left Billy grinning but noncommittal.

"A month later I returned. The mother had taken Billy to the doctor, as I had requested her to do. The doctor knew of his patient's experiments with faith and was delighted to pronounce the heart perfect.

"'Have you been playing my pretend-game, Billy?' I asked the small seeker after truth.

"The little boy's face lit up with a delighted grin. 'Sure have!' he cried.

"He had played the game. And upon playing it he had found therein a profound reality . . . The will of God for him was not a leaky heart, but health."

Agnes Sanford: Wired

The little girl had been in a cast for five months following infantile paralysis. Agnes placed her hands above the child's rigid knee and asked that the light of God shine through her into the small, stiff knee and make it well.

"'Oh, take your hand away!' cried the little girl. 'It's hot.'

"'That's God's power working in your knee, Sally,' Agnes replied. 'It's like electricity working in your lamp. I guess it has to be hot, so as to make the knee come back to life. So you just stand it now for a few minutes, while I tell you about Peter Rabbit.'

"When Agnes finished telling the story, she asked Sally to crawl to the edge of the bed and see if her leg would bend. The leg that had been rigid bent at an angle of forty-five degrees. Within two weeks, the child was walking.

"'How do you turn on God's electricity in your hands?' the child asked her.

"'I don't turn it on,' Agnes replied. 'I just forget everything else and think about God and about Jesus who is God's Son and our friend. And I believe that God can turn on that light in me because Jesus said He could. He turns it on, and when He is through with it, He turns it off.'"

Agnes Sanford sees God's life as a kind of light. While neither she nor the little girl could see it, the little girl could feel the heat from the light, and Agnes sensed in her hands and arms the flow of the invisible force that caused the heat.

At the crib side of a baby girl ill with pneumonia, Agnes knelt in silence, laid one hand upon the small, congested chest, slipped the other one beneath her back and asked God to come into her.

"Soon the waxy frame of the baby was filled with a visible inrushing of new life. Even the hands and feet vibrated as if an electric current were entering into her. A look of tension on the tiny face was smoothed away and she passed from a semi-conscious condition into a natural sleep.

"Two hours later her doctor came into the room. He stopped at the threshold, eyes staring, jaw dropped in surprise. For he had come to report his hospital arrangements for the child, and he beheld his small patient, bright-eyed and cheerful, sitting up in bed.

"'Mine doctor,' said she, 'can I have a cookie?'

"'My God!' exclaimed the doctor, startled out of his bedside manner. 'What's happened to her?'

"He was quite right. It was his God who had intervened—that was what had happened to her."

"Ye are the light of the world," said Jesus.

Agnes finds this Scripture quote to be literally true: "We are the electric light bulbs through whom the light of God reaches the world. Thus we are 'part God.' This does not belittle God, any more than it belittles the sun to know that a square of sunlight on the floor is part of its infinite and eternal shining."

Agnes Sanford: Undercover Healer at Fort Dix, New Jersey

During World War II, Agnes volunteered with the Red Cross at the Army hospital in Fort Dix. Violating the Red Cross rules, she prayed with patients and enjoyed close to 100% healing success even with nonbelievers.

One man, Sammy, had endured many bone grafts that did not take. After six months in traction, he was scheduled for another bone graft. In a month, doctors would take an X-ray and then insert two inches of bone.

Agnes told him there is healing energy in us that doctors call "nature," and she suggested asking God for more of it because God made nature. When the soldier protested that he didn't know anything about God, Agnes said he knew there's something outside of himself. He hadn't made the world. He agreed there must be something.

"Well, then, ask that Something to come into you. Just say, 'Whoever you are or Whatever you are, come into me now and help nature in my body to mend this bone, and do it quick. Thanks, I believe you're doing it.'

"Then make a picture in your mind of the leg well . . . See the bone all built in and the flesh strong and perfect around it. And play like you see a kind of light shining in it—a sort of a blue light, like one of these neon signs, shining and burning and flowing all up and down the leg . . . Then after you see the leg well, give a pep talk to all the healing forces in your body.

"Say, 'Look here, I'm boss inside of me and what I say goes. Now get busy and mend that leg.' And then congratulate them and tell them they're doing a good job, because they won't work for you, unless you encourage them.

"And after this, forget them and think of the life outside of you again, and say, 'Thank you, God. I believe it's going to be okay.' She told him to do this three times a day if it didn't get tiresome, always at the same time of day to build the habit. Agnes cautioned not to work too hard at it. She advised first getting comfortable and relaxing, then playing a game with it. He might imagine himself jumping over fences and so on.

"Three weeks later the boy was still in traction, but confided that he unfastened the traction device at night, got his leg out, and turned on his side all without pain. Horrified, Agnes cautioned him not to do anything without the doctors' permission.

"The following week he was in a wheelchair because the X-ray had been favorable and the doctors said he could get up. A month later she met him in the recreation hall walking with a cane. He told her he was still using her healing technique and was able to walk without the cane with a brace. 'Then you'll soon walk without a brace,' I told him.

"'I know it,' he grinned and a light flashed from his eyes to mine.

"I wondered as I went on my way to the PX how much he knew now about God. Certainly he knew something that made him very happy! . . . I saw him again, walking across the PX—without his cane— and very carefully not seeing me, like a little boy showing off."

To sum up her technique for nonbelievers:

1. Choose the same time and the same place every day. Make yourself comfortable and relax.

2. Remind yourself of a life outside yourself.

3. Ask that life to come in and increase life in your body.

4. Make a picture in your mind of your body well. Think especially of the part of the body that most needs to be well. See it well and perfect and shining with God's light. And give thanks that this is being accomplished.

Agnes Sanford: Thank, Don't Plead

Agnes defines prayer as our inner being that is part of God speaking to the framework of our flesh. She quotes Rufus Moseley, "As a sponge is in the ocean and the ocean is in a sponge, so we are in God and God is in us."

Agnes Sanford tells the parable of two little fishes who meet a frog. The frog warns the fishes they are in great danger.

"'No,' cried the fishes, much frightened.

"'Don't you know fishes can't live without water?' teased the cruel frog.

"The little fishes swam to their mother in great distress. 'Oh, Mother, Mother! The frog says if we don't find some water quickly we'll die! Mother, what's water?'

"'I don't know,' confessed the mother fish, who was an agnostic. 'I never heard anything about water. Let's go ask the otter.'

"'Water?' laughed the otter. 'Why, you live in water! That's what you breathe!'

"We live in God. That's what we breathe."

When a condition of her own required corrective surgery, Agnes decided to try to experiment with healing it through prayer. Her daily prayer removed the aching and weariness, but prayer did not correct the collapsed organ or remove the cysts.

She thought of having the operation, but because the condition was benign, there was no harm in waiting. Obviously her own prayers had not been enough, so she asked help from a distant prayer group and from friends nearby.

With additional prayer help, Agnes noticed as she was praying a drawing-up sensation, a distinct vibration, and warmth in the lower abdomen, increased vigor, and relief from pain. After some time she went back to the doctor.

"'I told you to come here twice a week for treatments,' he scolded. 'And I haven't seen you for a year.'

"'Well, I've been busy.'

"'You look good,' he admitted in a cold suspicious voice. 'What have you been doing?'

"'I haven't seen any other doctor,' I evaded.

"'You've certainly been doing something,' he insisted when he made his examination. 'You're a hundred percent better. *What have you been doing?*'

"I tried to tell him, but was obliged to desist when he began to exhibit symptoms of apoplexy."

Agnes points out that if she had given up on finding that her own prayers were not enough, the gradual healing would not have been finished. She cautions to make follow-up prayers, prayers of thanksgiving, not pleading:

"'Thank you Lord' we may say, 'your power is working in this person toward a perfect healing. Continue . . . to use my faith as a channel of power until the healing is completely accomplished.'"

Agnes urges that we pray keeping in our minds the picture of the person as completely healed until that picture becomes a reality.

Agnes Sanford: Life Saver, Be One Too

Breathless, Agnes Sanford's son ran into the house. The boy next door's father was dying "right now." Agnes knew Mr. Williams didn't believe in what he called "this healing business," but she knew her child expected her to help Fred's father.

The neighbor, a milkman, was so weak from a rheumatic heart that his children dragged him from his truck at night and helped him into the house. Just diagnosed with a second attack of rheumatic fever, Mr. Williams continued to work, afraid if he gave up he'd never work again.

When there was no answer at the door, Agnes walked in. Mr. Williams was slumped over a table, unconscious and breathing strangely, his face buried in his arms.

Agnes sat down on the arm of his chair, slid one hand under him, and placed her hands above and below his heart. His heart beat insistently, irregularly, terrifyingly, she says, like the kettle drums in Strauss' "Death and Transfiguration." Swollen to fill almost his whole chest, the heart's valves had burst and were leaking.

Forgetting the heart, Agnes fixed her mind on the Presence of God and invited Him to enter and use her. Then, because Mr. Williams could not hear her, she talked to the heart, assuring it that the power of God was at this moment remaking it and that it need not labor any more. Then she pictured the heart perfect, blessing it continually in the name of God, and giving thanks that it was being remade perfectly.

Soon the heart began to beat more quietly and regularly. Agnes felt the shifting that indicated the rebuilding of flesh and tissues. The heart seemed to beat normally and then it would begin its agitated pounding again. She talked to it in her mind as if quieting a frightened animal, "All right, now . . . Just take it easy. Easy now—easy does it. Just beat quietly and slowly. You don't need to labor. You're going to be all right. Easy now—easy."

Mr. Williams' heart quieted between her two hands. Agnes feared his reaction when he woke up and found her hands on him. When the neighbor came to, she told him she'd been saying a prayer for his heart. He thanked her and said he felt much better.

Mrs. Williams rushed back from telephoning the doctor at her neighbor's house to find her husband converted to "this healing business." By the time the doctor came, Mr. Williams had walked upstairs and was resting comfortably in bed.

"'Why, Williams!' cried the doctor two days later. 'Why, Williams! What has happened? Your heart has gone back to its normal size.'"

Prayer with laying on of hands had healed Fred's father, and if Agnes had not been there, Mr. Williams would have died. Agnes Sanford feels that despite good medical attention, many die for lack of a believer to lay hands on and project the healing Spirit of God into their bodies.

179

Saying that God has made ample provision for our every need, Agnes recommends two remedies for disease: science and healing prayer.

Agnes Sanford: Stopping Pain

Agnes slammed a very heavy door on her finger. The finger turned black. Very conscious of her power and authority as a child of God, she didn't say 'damn' and fight the pain. Instead, she held it up before God and blessed the pain, congratulating it as one of His healing agencies.

"The pain ceased instantly, as if I had somehow shifted my sensations over into the spiritual kingdom where there is no pain . . . a tiny hole appeared at the base of the mashed nail and all the black blood seeped out of it. The nail resumed its normal color and kept it, suffering no ill effects whatsoever."

When accidents happen, Agnes remembers that she is a child of God Whose light shines within her continuously. This declaration shifts something within her, as if a car motor were shifting into high gear. The results are amazing.

Agnes frequently spilled boiling fat on her hands while cooking. "If I do not lose my temper, the hand is not burned. One's reaction to boiling oil is exceedingly speedy. And if one gives way to temper first and allows it to burn, it is too late then to remove the burn by prayer, for by that time we are delivered to the judge of our own inner consciousness, which in faithful obedience to the thought-suggestion of fear and wrath has directed the hand to burn."

When Jesus gave the directive to "agree with thine adversary quickly," says Agnes, He knew the tremendous power of first-thought suggestion.

It's not necessary to stop frying potatoes and pray. Prayers have already requested the indwelling of God's Holy Spirit. The time of the accident, she says, is the time to assume dominion as children of God and assume it in any simple words that come to mind. She says things like: "I'm boss inside of me . . . And what I say goes. I say that my skin shall not be affected by that boiling fat, and that's all there is to it. I see my skin well, perfect, and whole, and I say it's to be so."

This is not prayer, but Agnes has already been charged that day with the power of God's indwelling life, so it is not necessary to ask for it again. Her remarks are a follow-up to prayer. The woman who controls a finger touched by boiling oil does so feeling God's power within.

As her prayers, her mental training, and acts of forgiveness fused into a higher consciousness of God's inner dwelling, Agnes became more and more aware of an inner source of power that she could tap at will. On the days when she is in harmony with God, Who is love, all things work together for her good. Her work is done easily and with power, and her decisions are quick and unerring. Everything clicks.

But when Agnes falls into annoyance and irritation, nothing clicks. She works slowly, makes careless decisions, and wastes time. She says, "God's light shines both within us and without us, and by learning to receive Him within, we begin to perceive Him without."

Agnes Sanford: Start Small

Anyone of normal intelligence can learn to read. Anyone of good will can learn to pray for healing. In fact, God tells us to do this. (1 Corinthians 12:31)

However, Agnes cautions: start small and don't pray if you are too emotionally involved. Agnes began by praying for minor illnesses. Her youngest would say, "Hurt, pray." Agnes touched the hurt and prayed, and the child would get better.

After Reverend Hollis Colwell healed Agnes' baby's ears, Agnes asked him how one acquires that power. His answer, dietary change, disappointed her so Agnes searched the Bible for clues. Inspired by "as a man thinketh in his heart, so is he" (Proverbs 23:7), Agnes decided to pray, "Lord Jesus Christ, Son of God, fill me with Thy Life" whenever her mind was free. She did this for a full year.

Her first attempt at major healing failed. Eager to heal a friend's son, eighteen-year-old Rhett on a home visit from a mental hospital, Agnes talked of her own healing from depression and prayed as Reverend Colwell had prayed for her. Nothing happened.

Agnes kept trying to learn healing prayer and grow stronger at it. Her first big success was prompted by a strong urge to pray for a child in the hospital who was in danger of death from strep. Prior to miracle drugs, the child's infection in the heart, the kidneys, and the bloodstream led to death.

Terrified at the prospect of praying for the child, Agnes asked permission of the weeping mother. As soon as Agnes sat down next to the bed and began talking to the three-year-old, she had no fear.

"'Larry, when you go to kindergarten, they teach you about Jesus, don't they?'

"The child nodded, his big blue eyes very solemn.

"'Did they ever give you a picture of Jesus?'

"He nodded again, his face brightening a bit . . .

"'Well, you remember when people were sick, Jesus put his hand on them and prayed for them to get well, and they did, didn't they?'

"This time Larry said, 'Yes,' in a small whisper.

"'He told us we were to do the same thing,' I said. 'Now, I'm not as big as Jesus, and I'm just starting to do this, but He said to, so, shall we try? He said He'd be there to help us, you know, even though we don't see Him.'

"The child nodded, completely understanding . . .

"I laid my hands on the region of the heart and simply asked Jesus to make him well, and then I thanked Jesus because I knew He was doing it. The next day, the child's bloodstream and heart were free of infection. The kidneys took one more day. But in three days, he was at home, completely recovered."

Because she had been used by God to save Larry, she tried and failed again with Rhett. "You fooled me," she muttered to the Almighty, and wouldn't pray for healing for three months after that. However, her second try cured a case of shingles within two days, proving she did have the gift of healing.

Start small, she says. Begin by praying for the healing of colds and minor illnesses. Also, don't pray if you are too emotionally involved with the patient as she was with Rhett. Ask for prayer help. God was telling her to learn how to help people like Rhett so they would not have to go to mental institutions. In obedience, she did that hundreds, perhaps thousands of times.

Also pray with others not emotionally involved with the patient. Our own love, if too emotional, may stand in the way of that great flow of God's love.

Why had she failed the first time? She had not prayed for the gift of wisdom. Wisdom would have told her not to begin with the most difficult cases. All things are possible with God, but not with Agnes.

In praying for the gift of healing, we are praying for the increase of the power of the Holy Spirit within us, directed toward healing. One day, years further advanced along the prayer journey, Agnes spilled a kettle of boiling water over her foot. Immediately claiming the power of the Spirit to heal the body through Jesus Christ, she stated by faith that the skin of her foot was not burned. When she took off the shoe and stocking, the foot was not even red.

Agnes Sanford: Love, the Wiring /Faith, the Switch

Agnes says that God's love heals, but our own blocks the flow of God's love, which is energy, not emotion. Fear accompanies human love, so if praying for a loved one, get someone further removed to help you pray.

In emergencies, Agnes mustered enough faith to overcome her fear for the well being of her child. Once during a polio epidemic, Agnes shut out love and fear and prayed successfully for her son, who was healed immediately of a very high fever, a symptom of polio.

During the first three or four years of her healing work, everyone she prayed for was healed with the single exception of Rhett. Blaming being too emotionally involved with Rhett as one of the reasons he was not healed, Agnes learned to put Christ between her and the person for whom she was praying. She sent her love to Christ and let Him do with it what He would. People felt the power of Christ's love, power rather than affection. Agnes was considered to be cold.

Among the wonderful healings of those early years were those attained by her Bible class members. One, a young mother, asked her to pray for Jimmie, her son, sick with pneumonia.

"'Why don't you do it, Peggy?' I replied. 'Just put your hands on his chest and ask the power of God through Jesus Christ to come in and heal him; I'll pray with you from a distance.'

"The young mother did and the little boy was well the next morning. Several days later he pointed out a lifelong condition and said to his mother, 'Let's ask Jesus to make that well, too.' The mother and son did and that also was healed."

On another occasion, the older sister of one of her son Jack's playmates was in bed with a very serious heart condition. Agnes "knelt by the bed and laid her hands above and below the heart and prayed for it to be healed, every valve opening and closing perfectly, the blood flowing in and out without difficulty of any kind. She felt the power entering in a flow that caused her hands to quiver in a way that she could not control." The child recovered and was able to walk downstairs the next day.

The Sanfords' on and off cleaning lady, Elizabeth, was dying of cancer. Elizabeth's son came to inform Agnes and bring her to see his mother on her death bed. The maid lay in a large bedroom with all her relatives surrounding her. Agnes prayed for healing, Elizabeth made a complete recovery almost immediately.

Agnes Sanford needed money, but refused to charge for healing. When her brother suggested she ask God for the money, Agnes was horrified, but her brother's suggestion changed her attitude. Paying jobs related to her healing work popped up.

Harpers requested she write *The Healing Light*. However, when the book was finished, Harpers and other publishers turned it down and it remained in a drawer, unpublished for two years. Finally the magazine *Sharing* printed excerpts and from that exposure the Macalester Park Publishing Company put the book in print.

The larger call drove Agnes on, "For Christian people must know that Jesus lives and heals today—they must!"

Agnes Sanford: Miracles in Wartime

During World War II, fear filled the minds of mothers of soldiers. Jeannie, one of the moms in the prayer group, had the gift of discernment. If a boy was missing in action, Agnes and she would pray together in the chapel, and Jeannie would see a picture of the soldier in her mind with which to reassure the parents.

"'I see him sitting on a wooden box in the corner of a barbed wire fence,' she said once. 'He looks thin and tired, but is not sick. He has on shorts and a T-shirt, so it must be in a tropical country.'" Her mental picture was accurate. Jeannie had the gift only when she and Agnes prayed together.

To do her part during the war, Agnes Sanford volunteered as a Red Cross Gray Lady in U.S. Army Tilton General Hospital at Fort Dix, New Jersey. As a volunteer, she was forbidden to talk about God. Agnes had every intention of following orders, but she could not stand to see a boy who looked like her son rotting with an infected bone that would not heal.

"'I know a power that could make you well,' I said.

"'Oh, yeah,' remarked the youth with something less than full enthusiasm.

"'Yeah,' I replied, for I find that without any intention of doing so, I fall into the manner of speech of the one with whom I talk. 'I don't guarantee anything, but it once got me out of a pretty bad jam, and it has helped a lot of other people. Want me to tell you about it?'

"'Okay, shoot.'

"'If I do, you've got to promise to keep it a secret,' I said, 'because I'm not supposed to talk like this.'

"'Okay,' remarked the boy again with a shade of relief on his face. He did not want to be the object of comment any more than I did.

"'Well, it's like this: there's a power in the air, sort of like electricity, and I've learned how to let it come through me into a person—and it does help him to get well. You know—sort of like X-rays.'

"The boy shrugged. 'May as well try it,' he muttered.

"'It's God's power. So I have to talk to God. Okay?'

"He nodded with a resigned and somewhat furtive look about him.

"'Don't worry! Nobody will know I'm talking to God. And look, we want the power to come right into that leg, so it will be better if I slide my hands under these comics and things. It's all right, I won't let anybody see me. You'll be able to feel the power come in.'

"I 'talked to God' with my eyes open, glancing at the boy in a friendly sort of way so as not to be seen by men to pray.

"'Feels hot,' he said.

"'Sure,' I said, 'it's like electricity.'

"I left him, and the next week the leg was much better. Within a month, during which we prayed each week, the leg was healed."

Agnes Sanford: More Wartime Miracles

Agnes Sanford prayed for healing as she went about the wards at Tilton General Hospital in Fort Dix. Only two of the hundreds of soldiers for whom Agnes prayed failed to receive a healing. This was a greater degree of success than she knew at any other time. She speculated that healing was facilitated because it had to be kept a secret, the boys did not waste energy in words, and she was free to follow God's guidance.

Before entering any ward, she would pray, "Lord, show me to whom I should speak." Then she would follow her hunch speaking to the one among the thirty-six to whom her compassion flowed the most freely.

"One soldier said, 'You don't remember me, do you?'

"'No, I don't,' I replied.

"'I was in Ward 16,' he said, 'and you came along and prayed for me. My leg was all full of osteo, see, and now it's well.'

"Praise the Lord! One prayer—no follow-up—the man forgotten. Yet he was healed!"

Soon she began teaching the men the prayer of faith. Strangely, the ones most hesitant about praying for healing were the good Christians. A Mennonite youth, lying for months with a third degree burn below the anklebone that would not heal, objected to healing. Was it God's will? Did Jesus heal today? Agnes knew Jesus walked the streets of New Jersey just as He walked the streets of Palestine, longing to heal wherever He finds a human body through whom to work.

Finally Agnes persuaded him to try it, assuring him that if his healing was not God's will, it would not happen. The next week, his ankle was completely healed. The young man glowed like a light. "I didn't know Christianity was like this," he said. "It's true, it's true."

There was a Catholic boy who objected, saying only saints can do miracles. Agnes remembered St. Paul's customary salutation, "To the saints which are at Ephesus." The soldier insisted, however, that you can't be a saint until you are dead.

Agnes went to the convent in her town and explained her problem with the Catholic soldiers. Mother Saint Eugene said, "We will pray for them . . . And we'll pray for the Protestant boys, too. Give us a list of those you see."

After meeting Mother Saint Eugene, Agnes was able to tell any Catholic man unwilling for her to pray for him to ask Jesus for healing when he received Communion at Mass.

Agnes would tell them to say the prayer of faith at that time, "Thank You, Lord, because Your Body and Blood that I have received is helping my bones to get well." Then she would ask if the boy wanted the nuns to pray for him.

Agnes Sanford: Frederick

One of the patients in Ward 17, an officers' ward, was an Army doctor healed by prayer. He believed in miracles because he'd seen three in Ward 17.

One was the miracle of Frederick. His death was imminent. Shriveled like an old monkey, with tubes in nostrils and wrists, he usually had a doctor or nurse with him. One day he was alone, and Agnes was able to go in to him.

"'You look like you're about washed up,' I said. (I had found that the men liked this direct, unvarnished approach.)

"'Yep,' he said.

"'What's the trouble?' I asked. I could see no wounds . . .

"'Blood clots,' he replied . . .

"This, thought I, should not be too difficult to heal. Therefore I told him of the power that might help him get well . . . he shut his eyes, a clear dismissal. But having got my teeth into this case, as it were, I was not moved to give up easily.

"'Listen,' I said at last, causing him by my forceful tone to open his eyes. 'If you'll just let me try, the way I told you, I promise I'll never mention the matter again, win or lose. Now, how about it?'

"'Okay,' he said wearily, and . . . drew back the sheet, and I saw to my horror that his abdomen looked like a pool of dark blood, barely covered by a thin membrane.

"'Guts torn out,' he said . . . 'They didn't want to carry me in from the battle field, but I told them they had to . . .'

"He had been kept alive for months by intravenous feeding, drugs and stimulants. If I had seen his abdomen at first, without stomach or any other digestive organ . . . I would not have spoken the word of faith . . .

"I laid my hands on the two sides of this red gaping pool of blood and visioned a stomach and all other organs perfect and called upon the Lord to bring this about."

When Agnes got home, she called the "Christian underground," every powerful prayer group she knew. Only a direct act of God through Jesus Christ could work this miracle.

The next week, Agnes passed his room, but he was asleep and she did not go in. Two weeks after their prayer, Agnes passed his room again. He was not in his bed, but the bed was rumpled and his name was still on the door.

Agnes went to the common room, but didn't see him. Then she saw a young, ruddy faced man who didn't bear the slightest resemblance to the wizened monkey she had prayed for. The young man gazed at her with a grin, and she noticed a tiny resemblance.

"'You can't be Frederick, can you?' I asked him.

"His grin broadened, 'Yes, ma'am, I am,' he said.

"Remembering my promise, I made no reference to his healing but simply said, 'What are you going to do now?'

"'Think I'll go to South America and get a job.'

"'That seems like a good idea,' said I . . . And I added, glancing at my cart, 'Have an apple.'" He ate the apple.

The next week he was discharged and at home. Three months later, she saw him again, tall, burly, handsome, looking like a lifeguard at Atlantic City.

Agnes Sanford: Rebuilding Five Inches of Bone

"What is this power that comes through you when you stand by a bed?" the man Agnes calls John Masterman asked her. Agnes urged him to learn to use the Light to heal his thigh, full of shrapnel and osteomyelitis, and to restore five inches of thigh bone that had been shot away. John Masterman is a character in her novel, *Oh, Watchman!,* written about Agnes' experiences at Tilton General Hospital. The book teaches ways of presenting prayer and healing through a series of parables.

John Masterman was drawn from life. A twenty-year-old soldier, he had been in the hospital two years and considered his life over. Instead, within six weeks of the prayer of faith, he was healed. Subsequently he became a clinical psychologist and in later years, Dr. John Masterman ran two miles every morning.

When Agnes questioned him in real life about some point of faith, he said, "How dumb can you get? Of course I believe it! . . . If even I, who know nothing and am nothing, could rebuild five inches of bone into my leg where there wasn't any bone, just by doing what He said, why shouldn't . . . He have raised His body from the dead?"

Healed, baptized, confirmed, thinking of Jesus every minute in keeping with the "game of minutes," John was living an exemplary life. However, he had a bad temper. After diagnosing and praying for depression and bad temper with no result, Agnes decided John's problem lay not in the conscious young man, but in the little boy within who had lived in the Gestapo regime.

She asked Jesus to enter him, go back in time, and heal memories of fear John had forgotten. Agnes asked the Lord to heal John as a baby in the cradle. It worked: John Masterman suddenly felt ridiculously happy from morning until night.

A clinical psychologist, John began to utilize this technique in his own practice, realizing as Agnes did that there are many who are not depressed or manic-depressive, but simply normal people carrying the chains of old memories.

Agnes learned to pinpoint prayer for healing by asking three questions: Were you happy as a child? When did you begin to be unhappy, and finally, why? Then she would ask Jesus to walk into the past through their memories and heal all the wounded places. Agnes pictured Him doing this. His love flowed around any old wound in the memory until the feeling associated with it was completely healed, so one can recall what once made him unhappy, yet feel the joy of new freedom.

"'Thank the Lord!' I imagine the person saying. 'That can't hurt me anymore.'"

Agnes puts the healing of memories under the heading of "the forgiveness of sins" for they come either from our sins or from sins against us, needing our forgiveness. She describes people freed from drug addiction by this technique.

Seeking publication of *Oh, Watchman!*, Agnes Sanford's literary agents put pieces of paper with the names of twelve possible publishers into a pot, prayed, closed their eyes, and drew out a paper marked, J.B. Lippincott. They were surprised at God's choice because the fiction editor there, Tay Hohoff, was disinterested in spiritual things.

To their amazement, Lippincott accepted it. Tay Hohoff had taught writing at Tilton General Hospital, knew the real-life John Masterman character, and recognized the descriptions of healings at the hospital and John's experience as true. God had given Agnes her heart's desire: the joy of being accepted as a creative writer.

Agnes Sanford: Fired

Caught praying for healing, Agnes was told to turn in her Red Cross uniform and leave. After two and a half years of service at Fort Dix, her strength drained by walking ten miles a day pushing a heavy cart while pouring out spiritual power, Agnes felt a lot of pain around the heart, but couldn't bear to stop until fired. Each week she would think about resigning, then a boy would look at her with wistful eyes, ask when she was coming back, and she couldn't quit.

Agnes struggled with anger. She had only one day to forgive the head of the Red Cross because someone was coming for healing prayer on Monday and Agnes knew if she remained angry, the person would not be healed. With the help of the Eucharist and determined prayer, she recovered in time.

After she left Tilton, an Army chaplain in a hospital on the West Coast asked her how to pray the prayer of faith for healing: eight men had requested it. She went to the coast, prayed with the chaplain for the eight men, and they were all healed.

After that, the chaplain learned to pray for healing on his own and became known throughout the hospital. Doctors would ask him to stand outside the operating room and pray for the success of difficult operations. Nurses would call for the chaplain when patients were in need of soothing.

"On one occasion the chaplain . . . prayed for healing for a soldier dying of cancer and the man recovered in six weeks, bought an old jalopy and disappeared."

Praying about what God wanted next, Agnes sensed the Lord telling her to write a novel about her experiences in Tilton General Hospital. She began *Oh, Watchman!*. Writing, her joy totally restored her strength, but lecturing and healing terrified and drained her.

One day while waiting for a bus after a meeting in New York City, Agnes absentmindedly stepped into a taxi. The cab driver had a bad cough. When they arrived at the Church of the Heavenly Rest, Agnes told him she could stop his cough. Both of them went into the church, and the man sat down in the back pew. Agnes told him she was going to put her hands on his chest and think in a way that she knew. After about three minutes of silent prayer, she removed her hands.

"'Gee!' said the taxi driver, 'I don't have to cough anymore.'

"'Sure,' I replied. 'Is the pain all gone?'

"He . . . waved his arm around in a . . . circle. 'When I do that it still hurts a little.'

"'Then don't do that,' I instructed him.

"He . . . took my hand and shook it fervently. 'You're a funny lady,' he said. 'I never met a lady like you before.'"

"Again, how wonderfully the Lord weaves together everything in the pattern of our lives. If we make a mistake in the human part of our weaving, He alters the pattern a little to accommodate the mistake and makes of it something even more beautiful and useful!"

The dismissal, the novel, and the cab driver all form part of such a pattern.

◦◦◦

Agnes Sanford, *Sealed Orders* (Plainfield, NJ: Logos International, 1972), 15, 96-98, 105, 107, 111, 118, 140, 142, 177, 179-183, 185-187, 194, 196, 199, 204, 211.

Agnes Sanford, *The Healing Light* (New York, NY: Ballantine, 1991), 3, 7, 12, 14-16, 19-24, 61-66, 86, 88, 105.

Agnes Sanford, *The Healing Gifts of the Spirit* (New York, NY: HarperOne, 1984), 73.

Babsie Bleasdell: Prophecy— Pulling Kleenex Out of a Box

In the early 1970s, when called on to speak at a retreat, Babsie Bleasdell had nothing prepared. Panicking at the lectern, Babsie prayed, "Lord, You have to help. I'm going to open this book and speak on whatever comes up."

The Bible fell open to John 4, the story of the Samaritan woman at the well. Babsie read the passage aloud, then began to speak. She heard herself saying things she had never thought of before; Babsie was a flute Someone Else was playing.

At the end of the talk, the priests and lay people were amazed at the wisdom revealed. Babsie was as surprised as everyone else. She now realizes God had not only rescued her from embarrassment, but He had also taught her how to yield.

At 2:30 that morning, Babsie dropped into bed. An hour later, she awakened, full of energy. She heard the Lord say, "Babsie, I want you to teach my people."

Startled, Babsie responded that she had nothing to teach. In a clear, clear conversation, God assured her that He would teach her and she would teach others. Then in a vision He showed people laying hands on others for the baptism of the Holy Spirit. When Babsie protested that the local contact with the Archbishop would not be happy with that, God replied, "If this is the way I choose to impart my Spirit, will you do it just because I say so? Yield, man, yield!"

Babsie had learned her first teaching, the meaning of yielding and coming into acceptance, when God used her as His instrument while speaking on retreat. She asked the Lord to teach her more. In visions, Babsie learned through infused knowledge. Then the Lord would lead her to a book or to a teacher to confirm the accuracy of what she had learned. Babsie finally knew God had definitely called her to the charism of teaching.

Babsie says the Lord calls and then enables each of us to obey His call by the overshadowing of the Holy Spirit. "Every moment God wants to talk to his people . . . one thing is certain, however: if God says something to me and I have not obeyed, when I come back for another word He will repeat the old word."

Babsie compares God to a mother telling a child to clean his room. "' . . . can I go to the picnic?'

"'Have you cleaned your room?'

"'No, Mommy.'

"'Clean your room.'

"Five hours later, 'What are we having for dinner?'

"'Have you cleaned your room?'"

Like a good mother God goes no further until we have obeyed.

Babsie calls prophecy lending one's tongue and voice to God. When prophesizing, Babsie first prays and then listens for the word of God. Usually God gives her a symbol. If Babsie got the symbol of a fox, it might lead her to think of Herod, a deceitful man. Then she would ask God what He is telling her and what He wants her to say. God might be warning against someone deceitful.

The first phrase Babsie uses is "The Lord says." What follows is like pulling a Kleenex out of the box, first one, then another. The prophecy is born on Babsie's tongue bypassing her mind. The Lord is saying, "Open your mouth and I will fill it."

Babsie does not prepare ahead of time. The gift of prophecy is the "now" word of God. Babsie Bleasdell says she is so conscious of the possibility of God speaking in the quiet time that if a mouse squeaks, Babsie pays attention to it because God uses everything.

Babsie Bleasdell: Woman Resurrected

A grandmother brought her six-year-old deaf-mute granddaughter to one of Babsie's prayer meetings for healing prayer. The child had never spoken.

Babsie wanted no part of it, but didn't want to hurt the woman's faith so she spoke silently to God. Babsie told Him she didn't have the faith to pray for the child. Babsie asked God to do for the child what He had done for the deaf and dumb in the Scriptures. Then she put her hands on the child's ear and asked in the name of Jesus that it be opened. Babsie placed her hands on the child's vocal chords and asked the Precious Blood to wash the chords and enervate them. Babsie spoke to the nerves in the ear. Then Babsie prayed in the Spirit and thanked Jesus for His healing power. Her next thought was to get out before they asked her to raise the dead. Babsie literally ran out of the room.

The following Sunday, the grandmother brought the child back saying that the child had spoken for the first time four days after Babsie prayed with her. Her first word was "Jesus" and now the girl talked incessantly. A year later, the child was succeeding in her schoolwork as if she had begun school on time with the rest of the children in her class.

A woman fell ill at a prayer meeting. Babsie asked people to pray with the sick woman. While the people were praying in another room, Babsie continued her talk. Then one of the group insisted Babsie pray with the woman. When Babsie located the sick woman, she was by herself, on the ground, lying flat on her back. The woman told Babsie the others had gone to call a doctor.

When Babsie laid hands on the woman and began to pray, the victim lost color, sweat so intensely that she seemed covered with water, and died. Babsie cried out to God telling him that He couldn't let that happen. Babsie reminded God that it was the beginning of the Charismatic renewal, that it was not highly regarded, and that the meeting was at an Anglican Church. Babsie called to God's attention what the Archbishop's position would be when he heard a Catholic woman was leading a prayer meeting in an Anglican Church and a woman died under her hand. For the sake of Your Own Name, Babsie told God, bring this woman back to life.

Then Babsie began to pray more seriously, hoping someone else would come along and pray with her. Babsie was relieved to see a seminarian walking towards them. She told Jesus that Ronnie, the seminarian, would help her, but Ronnie stopped, looked, and then walked backwards away from them.

Babsie cried out to God again, "Jesus, I am alone, just you and me! For the sake of your own name, give life to this woman!" Then she said, "In the name of Jesus, I impart life to you now. Come alive, in Jesus' name!"

To Babsie's relief, the woman's eyes opened. She told Babsie she felt very weak. Babsie told her God could change that. Babsie laid hands on the woman, praying that the strength of God invigorate her. The woman's face began to get back its natural color. The woman said she felt well. When Babsie saw the seminarian later, she asked him how he could have left her there to pray alone.

"Babsie, when I saw what was happening, I knew that woman was dead. I didn't have the courage to come and help. My thought was, 'Leave her alone. I will only be a drain on her faith. Let God work it out with her.' And as you see, he did."

Babsie Listens to the Lord and Quits Her Job

In the early days of the Charismatic renewal, Babsie worked for the dean of a medical college. One day, eight of twelve in the waiting room were there for Babsie, not for the dean. Babsie also monitored thirteen prayer meetings from home.

One Saturday, a pregnant hospital staff member, a Hindu, came into the office. She was losing her baby. While someone looked for an obstetrician, the expectant woman was left in Babsie's care. Each time Babsie tried to type, the woman spoke to her. Finally Babsie asked if the Hindu would like to pray with her, although Babsie only knew how to pray in the name of Jesus. The woman agreed. When Babsie finished praying, the doctor arrived. Later the woman brought her family to thank Babsie. The Hindu's baby was spared at the moment Babsie prayed with her.

Babsie toyed with the idea of leaving paid employment to work full time in the renewal. Since she had no money, the decision seemed irrational. Encouraged by Father Duffy, Babsie wrote a letter of resignation, but her boss refused to accept it and Babsie stayed on.

Finally, months later in July 1973, after two audible warnings from the Lord, Babsie quit her secular job. Determined to keep her word to God and at the same time keep her word to her boss to stay until replaced, Babsie worked without pay every day for the next three months. When given a small stipend, Babsie felt like a millionaire. God had taught her how to live without earning any money. The Lord provided.

Once free of a paying job, Babsie established Thursday as prayer day. On Thursday, people arrived at ten o'clock for midmorning prayer of the Liturgy of the Hours. That activity was followed by a prayer meeting. Then people came after work for another prayer meeting, counseling, and fellowship. This was followed by the evening prayer meeting.

God told her not to plan anything, but to be open to whatever He sent. Babsie began to pray the Holy Spirit prayer all day long and learned to wait on the Lord:

"O Holy Spirit, Soul of my soul, I adore Thee. Enlighten, guide, strengthen, and console me. Tell me what I ought to do and command me to do it! I promise to be submissive in everything Thou shalt ask of me and to accept all that Thou permittest to happen to me. Only show me what is Thy will."

One Friday, Babsie had no food, but decided to continue praying. She knelt down to pray and heard two children calling her. They brought chicken and rice and all the ingredients, except okra, needed for soup called callaloo. A friend showed up with okra a few minutes later. After the friend left, Babsie did what she had promised God she'd do. Evidently He wanted her to cook a big Sunday dinner even though it was Friday and she was alone with no one around to eat all that food.

Around midday, just as she finished cooking, she heard footsteps and then the doorbell. Six hungry people had been searching all over Arima, Trinidad looking for her. When they had eaten and left, a young man rang the bell. He was asking for money to return home after finding his relatives out of town. He ate the leftovers and Babsie gave him the last of her savings, a little box of emergency change.

She says, "That day the Lord delivered me from fear and brought me into trust."

Babsie Bleasdell: My God Rains—A Weather Miracle

A spectacular miracle was witnessed by a huge crowd at the first Caribbean Leaders' Conference and National Rally of Prayer Groups. Over five thousand lay people, thirty priests, and three Caribbean bishops watched a weather miracle.

People at an outdoor service ran when rain came down in torrents. Babsie took the mike and told the crowd Christians don't run. They stand because God gave us authority over the work of his hands. Babsie suggested they stand together and command the rain to cease in Jesus' name.

What a chance Babsie took. The group stopped and joined her in prayer, but the torrent increased and people ran away after all. Babsie was left standing alone with water filling her shoes. She turned, about to leave, when she saw three young men of three different races sitting with upturned faces, praying intently.

Babsie gathered her courage and said into the mike, "Lord, you held the sun for Joshua. You can do it for us. You who stilled the waves and the storm can still this storm for the sake of these three young men. For the sake of their faith, I stand in your Presence and command these clouds in the name of Jesus be sealed." Talk about putting your reputation on the line!

In that instant, the rain stopped and the sun came out. People returned, cheering the power of God.

At noontime, the clouds started to gather and Babsie began to feel discouraged. As she ascended the stage, a man congratulated her on what she had done that morning. Babsie said it's no use, it will rain again. Then the man spoke words Babsie never forgot, "Didn't you see what God did this morning? Hold on in faith. All is well."

And he was right. For the rest of the day, rain fell all around them, but not on them. They worshiped as if in a bowl surrounded by a curtain of water.

Miracles rain on Babsie. God healed her eyes without anyone asking Him. Babsie had worn spectacles for twenty-five years, but had never thought to pray for the healing of her vision because it was so easily corrected by putting on glasses. God healed her anyway. In May 1974 at a conference at Notre Dame in Indiana, Babsie realized that she could see perfectly. God healed Babsie's eyes behind her back.

Babsie takes God's Power for granted in a reverent way, using simple language to address her closest Friend. The result? Miracles! Reading about those miracles and the way Babsie talks to the Lord makes one think that we believers are not making full use of our prayer power, like homeowners shivering with cold because we don't know how to turn on the furnace in our Father's house.

Babsie Bleasdell: God Buys Babsie a Plane Ticket

A mother brought her twelve-year-old daughter to be prayed over by Babsie at a prayer meeting at the Cathedral in Trinidad. While the child screamed in the background, the woman told Babsie that her child did not speak. Babsie suggested the mother ask prayers of Mary Goddard, the healer featured at the prayer session. A renowned Protestant Pentecostal evangelist recommended by the bishops, Mary Goddard trailed miracles and signs wherever she went.

The woman insisted on Babsie. Feeling God would not be pleased by her refusal to pray, Babsie reluctantly laid hands on the child and prayed for her. Finally the screaming stopped, but Babsie had to leave the country the next day and heard nothing further.

At the Cathedral two months later, the mother of the mute child interrupted Babsie's prayers to report the girl had been healed. Amazed, Babsie reflected on her fear of praying for the child's healing. How wonderful, Babsie Bleasdell says, that God had used her halting prayers to heal the child.

Then God bought Babsie a plane ticket. Distressed because men in the Caribbean Charismatic renewal complained about women's predominance, Babsie declined to be an official representative of the group at the Second International Leaders' Conference in Dublin, Ireland in 1978. Although she yearned to go, Babsie Bleasdell insisted the Charismatic renewal send men from Trinidad with Father Duffy.

Because Trinidadians love the Irish missionaries who worked for their welfare, about twenty-six of Babsie's neighbors planned to attend the conference at their own expense. Babsie, too, felt deep kinship with the Irish whose priests and nuns had brought the faith to Trinidad, but she didn't have the money to go on her own.

More than love of the Irish drove Babsie to take the trip. She knew her less traveled neighbors were unfamiliar with modern conveniences. Most had never been on an elevator, an escalator, or an airplane. They needed a leader.

A week before the group was to leave, an acquaintance came to Babsie's house.

"She handed me an envelope saying, 'I don't know why the Lord told me to give you this. But you must have use for it.' And she turned and walked away. When I opened it, I found a check for $1,000.

"Two hours later, two younger women dropped in. I had been praying with one of them for her friend to be healed of cancer. 'Babsie,' she said, 'I wanted to tell you that my friend for whom you prayed has gone into remission. And we want to thank you for your prayers, and I brought you a little gift.'

"She handed me a check for $200. Her companion, joining in the act of thanksgiving, gave me two $20 notes. Here I was with $1,240 completely unsolicited. The airfare was $1,239. There was a $2 departure tax. So by investing $1 of my own, I was able to go. I took this as my confirmation that God wanted me to go and shepherd this group. But his purpose, as usual, reached far beyond that."

Babsie Bleasdell: God Writes a Speech—Babsie Thanks the Irish

Going to Ireland was like coming home. The sound of the brogue intoxicated Babsie. She heard herself as a child singing "Hail Glorious Saint Patrick" at the top of her lungs while waving a little green flag on March 17. Irish priests and nuns were spiritual parents to Babsie, ministering to her, teaching her, and nurturing her.

At the last minute, the Caribbean contingent was scheduled to present an evangelization workshop. Father Duffy proposed Babsie make the presentation. Babsie protested: she was not an official representative.

Father Duffy had nurtured the Catholic Charismatic Renewal in the Caribbean; he should make the presentation.

Father Duffy protested that he was Irish-American, not native. A Caribbean person must do this. He insisted on Babsie; she refused. After night prayer, Father Duffy reminded Babsie she was due to speak at nine o'clock the following morning. Babsie protested that she had nothing to tell the Irish people, except thanks for giving their sons and daughters for so many generations. The priest insisted she tell them that.

Babsie was downhearted. That night she sat on the side of the bed and prayed, "Lord, you see my predicament, I have not sought this. I don't want it . . . I have nothing to say . . . So I'm asking you to help me, if you can. I'm reminding you that when I stand there in the morning, if I can't open my mouth, your reputation will be at stake. My own reputation was shot long ago. So I have nothing to lose, but you, Lord, You! I would hate to bring dishonor to your Name. Therefore for the sake of your own Name, I am asking your help. Now I am going to bed." Babsie prepared nothing.

In sheer terror on awakening in the morning, Babsie opened the Scriptures to see whether in His Goodness He had given her a word. Babsie closed her eyes and opened to Psalms, "It is good to give thanks to the Lord, to sing praise to your name, Most High, to proclaim your kindness at dawn and your faithfulness throughout the night." (92:1-2) This was a confirmation. "Thanks" was the sum total of what Babsie had to say to the Irish people. God approved.

Three thousand gathered. The group from Trinidad sang a calypso "Gloria" that captivated the assembly. Then Father Duffy presented Babsie.

Her breath caught in her throat. With a great burst of emotion, Babsie expressed gratitude to Irish missionaries for what they had done for her individually and for the people of Trinidad as a whole. Babsie thanked them for schools from Pre-K through universities. Babsie thanked them for the Catholic faith they had fixed deeply in Trinidadian hearts. Babsie thanked Irish mothers and fathers for giving their sons and daughters to build the Kingdom. She elaborated on the missionaries' achievements among foreign peoples. A great act of thanksgiving flowed from the depths of Babsie's soul.

The crowd wept. Irish mothers, fathers, priests, and nuns crowded around her to thank her. An eighty-year-old Irish nun said Babsie had made her whole life seem worthwhile. The old nun had felt her life had been wasted in the missions. An old Irish missionary priest overflowed with emotion while thanking her. Babsie calls the speech in Ireland a firm rung in the ladder of her faith. Babsie Bleasdell had given her preparation to God and God had given her the words she needed.

Babsie Bleasdell: God Uses Babsie's Humiliation

Babsie and others formed a lay religious order. In May 1990, in Arima, Trinidad, in imitation of the early Christians, Babsie and other lay people publicly and formally committed themselves for one year as part of a new religious order. The purpose of the Word of Life Prayer Community: to serve the large number of Catholic Charismatic prayer groups that had grown and spread all over the Caribbean.

A Cistercian abbot from Australia, Father Gerald Hawkins (Dom Colamban), lived in the community with Babsie and other lay people for twelve months. In establishing the covenant lay community, Dom Colamban realized a dream that drove him from Australia to the United States to the Island of Grenada and then to Trinidad.

The abbot gave the community its name. Emerging from prayer aglow with God's inspiration, "He held out the Bible and pointed to Philippians (2:14-16): 'Do all that has to be done without complaining or arguing and then you will be innocent and genuine, perfect children of God . . . and you will shine in the world like bright stars because you are offering it the *word of life.*'"

The group flourished, but Babsie became depressed. When more people joined, it became necessary to build an extension. Not interested in being in the construction business, sinking money into buildings,

Babsie agonized over a series of questions. One was why Babsie had named the community dwelling "Ave Maria."

Suddenly, while Babsie was complaining to God, she felt a bridal veil fall on her head. It unfurled and wrapped itself around Babsie as she heard a voice say, "This house has been called 'Ave Maria' so that it might become the 'Womb of Mary,' bringing forth Christ. Nurture Him to full stature and give Him away to the whole world."

Filled with great joy, Babsie danced, crying out, "Lord, if you want it, you can have it. It's all for you."

Her determination to do all for God was highlighted in 1981 at a conference at Notre Dame in Indiana. A leader asked Babsie to sing "The Old Rugged Cross" in front of 25,000 people. When Babsie protested that she couldn't sing, the leader asked her to do it for Jesus. Because Babsie had promised never to deny God anything, she agreed, knowing it would be deeply humiliating.

Feeling like a raisin in a sponge cake in front of 25,000 white people, Babsie began to sing . . . One by one, the musicians put down their instruments in despair. Some of the audience tried vainly to support her. Babsie stumbled back to her seat feeling ridiculous. Knowing the deepest humiliation of her life, Babsie Bleasdell begged God to use her stupidity in some productive way. And God did.

Sister Ann Shields watched Babsie sing and wondered that Babsie was so surrendered to God that she could humiliate herself that way for Him. Sister decided to surrender completely to the Lord in the same way. Babsie was delighted. She had asked God to glorify His Name through her humiliation and He had.

The next day, Babsie gave a thirty-minute testimony before the same 25,000 people. To Babsie's surprise, her talk sold the largest number of tapes ever sold at that conference.

Babsie Bleasdell: God Plays Hide and Seek,
Then Cures Kids with Pinkeye

Sometimes Babsie has a powerful sense of the Presence of God and sometimes He seems to move away, leaving her desolate. She's learned this means God is calling to her: "Come up higher—there is more."

When this happens, Babsie prays, "Lord, I am so grateful that I have experienced You. Now I am missing You and I want You back. You promised that You would never leave me. Lord, I need You . . ." Then God returns and shows Himself to her more intensely and seems to be even more wonderful than before.

Babsie shares other experiences from her prayer life. ". . . if I promise myself that I will pray at four o'clock in the morning, I can be sure that at ten past four, the phone will ring . . . I have never been able to pray at the same time each day, yet God has given me the Grace of a good prayer life." Babsie Bleasdell has found that many times what seemed like a distraction was prompting her to pray about something or for something, so Babsie incorporates distractions into her prayers.

Babsie shares her approach to healing. She has twice seen the dead raised to life. She prays for all she's worth and leaves the healing up to Jesus, recognizing that the faith of Jesus is sufficient for any healing in the will of God to be effected.

She seeks that men change, transformed by the renewal of their minds and spirits into Christ Jesus.

In Jamaica, a priest insisted Babsie speak at a school where 650 young people were gathered outdoors in the blazing hot sun. Babsie felt it was mad to keep students outdoors unprotected from the sun, but agreed to speak, feeling she must obey all priests, even mad ones, as God's anointed. Because Babsie was under obedience to the priest, she felt God would have to honor her. Babsie whispered to some distant clouds, "Come on, come on." To her surprise, the clouds moved like birds. Babsie prayed, "God, you're not going to let me down. You can't let me down."

"Babsie Bleasdell asked the children if God was with them.

"They responded, 'Yes.'

"She said, 'Fine. The sun's hot, isn't it?'

"'Y-e-e-e-e-e-s!'

"'Now some of you have an unfair advantage. Umbrellas cover only some of you and some of you remain uncovered. God doesn't like that. He wants to give the same to all His children. So please, close your umbrellas.' Every umbrella went down. Under my breath I said, 'C'mon God, now it's your turn!' Then to the children, 'You see that cloud? God gave the Israelites a cloud in the desert.' . . . She prayed quietly, 'Okay God, you said where two or more agree and here we've got 650 agreeing.' . . . Then aloud she said, 'Come on, in the name of Jesus.' . . . The clouds covered the whole courtyard.

"Then Babsie noticed that many of the children had pinkeye. She asked them again, 'Do you believe God is here?'

"'Yes.' . . . .

"'God is going to heal those with pinkeye right away.' And before Babsie's eyes, they were healed. 'Then I thought, it's time to run. Amen. Let's go.'" God says, say it and it will happen. Babsie feels God wants you and me to use His Power as if it were ours.

Through miracles of God's arithmetic, Babsie established a halfway house for women in need and a home for abandoned children. She trusted God and God provided. Babsie says our prayer should be, "What do You want? What can I do for You? I have come to do Your Will."

Babsie assures us the Will of God is the safest place for us to be. *Babsie, Go Teach My People* closes with these words, "In the fullness of time, God called forth Babsie Bleasdell. In the fullness of time, God calls you."

꧁꧂

Babsie Bleasdell, *Babsie, Go Teach My People* (Steubenville, OH: Franciscan University Press, 1997), 27, 134-136, 142, 157, 163-164, 180-18182, 187-188, 228, 230, 232-233, 252-253, 279.

Father Peter Mary Rookey and the Firecracker

It was every mother's Fourth of July nightmare. Over eighty years ago in Superior, Wisconsin, two of Johanna Rookey's thirteen children, eight-year-old Peter and his little brother, Brendan, found a big firecracker in the gutter and rushed home with it as fast as they could. When it didn't go off after they lit it, Peter picked it up and blew on the smoldering fuse. There was a huge explosion. The firecracker blew up in his face. The child experienced searing pain and total blindness.

Dr. Barnsdahl insisted the boy would never see again, but Johanna Rookey knew better. God would heal her son. Every night, the family said the Rosary for the restoration of Peter's vision. Then in the spring, Mrs. Rookey set up a May altar in the attic and the Rookey family increased their prayers for the child's healing.

Peter Mary Rookey never doubted his mother's belief that if it were God's wish, Peter would see. The little boy promised God that if He gave him back his sight, he would become a priest. The doctor kept warning them their prayers were futile. The boy's case was hopeless.

After a year and a half, Peter's vision returned slowly and was finally restored. It was exactly what Johanna Rookey expected, a total miracle.

At the age of thirteen, true to his promise, Peter entered the Servite seminary in Chicago, five hundred miles from home. Full of fun and very homesick, Peter distracted himself with pranks like those his large, happy family played at home. Then, filled with compassion at the plight of sinners, Peter Rookey prayed at the gravesides of Al Capone, Diamond Jim Brady, and other gangsters buried nearby.

Ordained in 1941, Father Rookey didn't discover his healing gift until 1948 in Ireland while helping establish the Servite Order in Benburb, Ulster. People began talking about the young American priest whose prayers brought healings. Hundreds gathered at the new Servite Priory.

The chapel was too small to accommodate such a huge number of people, so healing services were held outdoors. Among those crowding to see the priest were Patrick and May Magee and their beautiful blind eight-month-old daughter, Patricia.

Patrick held the baby as he and his wife waited in a line two miles long. Then, because the little family had an appointment, they were led to the front. The couple watched as crowds thronged around Father Rookey in his black robe. He moved from one to the other holding his hands over their heads and blessing them with a crucifix.

Patricia had been born with detached retinas in both eyes. Operating would not help. She would be blind for life. When the priest finally reached the Magees, he put his hands on her head, touched her eyes, blessed her with the cross, and prayed over her. He told the parents to pray several times a day.

"Your child will see," he said. And then he moved on.

At home, the couple said the Rosary while grandma played with Patricia in a back room. When the child reached up to pull the window blind, her grandmother realized she could see.

As Patricia says today, "The sight . . . doctors said I would never have was given to me as a gift from God through the prayers of this priest." When a reporter asked if it were a miracle, she said, "All I know . . . was that I was blind and now I can see."

It's a Heat Wave: A Father Rookey Heat Wave

Ruth Allen was not in New Orleans praying for herself. She had accepted her fate. Two operations and drastic chemotherapy had not contained the cancer that was killing her. Ruth was there instead praying for her husband's recovery from a stroke. Tom needed the strength to raise their two children, fourteen and seventeen, without her. Ruth was a stand-in for Tom, a man angry at God for visiting so much tragedy on their family.

From her seat three rows from the front, Mrs. Allen expected to see what her friend had reported from Father Rookey's healing Masses in Chicago: People definitely healed. The friend also reported people "resting in the Spirit." When blessed, people fell back, were caught by ushers, and then lay on the floor as if sleeping while everyone else ignored them and continued the service.

At the Mass Ruth attended, people in wheelchairs slumped in front of the first row looking hopelessly sick. Mrs. Allen felt sick herself, but peaceful. After Mass, Father Rookey said it was possible for individuals to stand in as proxies for those who could not be there themselves for the laying on of hands and the anointing. Ruth felt reassured.

Row by row, people filed up to the altar rail for the healing part of the service.

"A woman . . . in a wheelchair stood up when Father Peter invited her to take a step in faith with the Lord. Then she walked across the front of the altar and returned to push away her wheelchair. I think it was her daughter who was with her, and she was both laughing and crying at the same time. Then a man stepped out of his wheelchair and also pushed it down the aisle of the church. The whole congregation clapped for him, and he looked so happy."

Father Rookey moved along the line at the altar rail to her right and as he did, Ruth looked at the Tabernacle and gave all Tom's ills to Jesus. When Father stopped in front of her, Mrs. Allen told him about her husband. The priest placed his hands on her head and made the sign of the cross on her forehead with Holy Oil. With his hands on her head, he asked God to heal Tom and to bless her for her love for her family.

"I'm not quite sure how to explain what happened next, but it was as if a wave of heat went right through my body, beginning at my head and going right down to my toes . . . And I felt myself moving back through the air, not really falling, but as if I was gently going down and I had neither the wish not the ability to stop myself . . . I felt an experience of total and utter peace . . . It really was a meeting with God . . . I felt loved and cared for and utterly peaceful and warm . . . without any inclination . . . to 'return' to the outer world." She was "out" fifteen minutes.

Tom began to get better and better every day. His anger vanished. His right arm gained strength and he could walk with a limp. At his checkup, doctors called it a good recovery. Ruth felt peaceful. Her prayers had been answered.

Surprisingly, she was feeling better, too. The doctors said it was a remission; enjoy it while it lasted. Two months later, hospital tests showed the cancer to be more contained. Puzzled, the doctors did more tests. These showed she was almost clear of cancer. The doctors said the chemo must have been more effective than they thought.

How come doctors had given her no hope? How come there was no sign of improvement after the last round of chemo? How come Tom had not improved until Ruth's trip to New Orleans? How come they both got better after the prayers of Father Peter Mary Rookey? As usual, God did it.

Ditching the Pilgrimage and Avoiding Father Rookey

A physical wreck, David Parks, Irish singer and big band leader, was unable to work. David had suffered with a severe bowel disease for twelve years. A professional footballer in his youth, by 1989 David was far from his old athletic self. Doctors had given up hope. Ten major operations had not helped.

David and his wife Anne attended a fundraising event at a Dublin hotel intended, his friends told Parks, to raise money for his family. Many of the country's leading entertainers would be there hoping to accumulate enough money for David's funeral expenses, although that is not what they told him.

David looked like a living skeleton. His stomach muscles had been cut, but he sang anyway. Then David's friends offered him a chance to travel to Medjugorje, Bosnia-Herzegovina with Father Peter Mary Rookey and 166 pilgrims.

David Parks wanted nothing to do with religious hysteria, but he and Anne had honeymooned in Yugoslavia, the tickets were a gift, and the couple might be able to slip away to Dubrovnik, Croatia, lose the pilgrims, and find a decent hotel. David managed to avoid Father Rookey at every turn, in the airport lounge, on the plane, and in Medjugorje.

Then, for appearance's sake, as Anne said, David agreed to attend just one of the healing services behind the Church of St. James. Anne kept pleading for David to get on line to be blessed. Finally David gave in, but told Anne he'd leave after that and go to Dubrovnik if he had to walk all the way.

Anne recorded the whole event on their borrowed video camera. First, an unknown priest blessed David, but he felt nothing. Then Father Rookey moved in front of David and asked what he wanted to pray for. David heard himself describing his poor health. Father Rookey blessed and anointed David with Holy Oil. The priest put an old worn crucifix in David's hands.

"David remembered Father Peter taking the cross from his hands as a strange sensation of heat ran through his entire body. And after that, nothing—until he found himself looking up from the red earth where he had lain, they later told him, for almost twenty minutes.

"There had been no thought of healing in his mind as somebody helped him to his feet. Only a sheepish feeling that he must have looked ridiculous lying there for so long. What had happened? He wasn't sure. The first thought in his mind, in fact, was had somebody hit him?"

Twenty-four hours later, his symptoms were gone. The nausea, pain, vomiting, and weakness had vanished. David was able to stand up straight and felt strong enough to climb the mountain.

Back home, the first tests showed a massive improvement and later tests found no symptoms. Although a huge part of his bowel was missing due to operations, he now experienced no signs of illness.

Back at his pre-sickness weight, a robust David Parks declared he owed both his physical and spiritual healing to Father Rookey. David spoke of the spiritual wilderness in which he had wandered. Where would he be if he had not been blessed by Father Peter Mary Rookey? God's Love expressed through the gift of friends and the prayers of his wife brought David Parks and Father Rookey together. Love saved David.

Father Rookey: The Miracle Prayer Lives Up to Its Name—Bridget Gormley's Twin

Bridget Gormley's twin brother Owen had a deep-rooted malignant growth in his brain. Originally considered too small to operate on, the "cyst" in Owen Gormley's brain had grown much larger in the two years since first detected. Doctors said without surgery, Owen would be confined to a wheelchair or worse.

After an operation on Wednesday, December 5, 1990, at Royal Hospital in Belfast, Ireland, Owen was told he needed further treatment at Beaver Park, Belfast's cancer hospital. On Thursday of the following week, the Gormleys still hadn't been given the full results of surgery. That day, Owen's doctor visited him with a leading specialist from the cancer hospital. The two doctors told Owen his growth was malignant and deep rooted, so deep rooted doctors couldn't assess the success of the operation. In chilling words, the physicians repeated that Owen would need further treatment at the cancer hospital.

". . . they would give no assurances for the future."

Then the doctors excused themselves for thirty minutes to examine the results of the most recent tests and X-rays. When they returned, Owen, braced for the worst, could not figure out what was going on. After an unnerving period of silence during which the doctors stared at Owen, they told him, "There is no need for any further treatment."

Owen thought they meant the situation was beyond hope, but there really was no need for further treatment; the physicians never explained why they had changed their minds. Owen was still in good health in 1994.

Bridget calls it a miracle and attributes the miracle to Father Rookey's "Miracle Prayer." When Owen was very ill, a cousin in America sent a prayer card with Father Rookey's picture on one side and the "Miracle Prayer" on the other. The card urged the prayer be said with feeling and belief. Bridget would sometimes say it ten times before saying it with what she considered proper focus and fervor.

Through the operation and the days that followed, the entire extended Gormley family prayed the "Miracle Prayer." When Bridget Gormley finally met Father Rookey in Northern Ireland in November 1993, she was too shy to talk to him, but put a letter about the experience into a box at the service.

*   *   *

Father Peter Mary Rookey's "Miracle Prayer"

Lord Jesus, I come before you, just as I am. I am sorry for my sins, I repent of my sins, please forgive me. In your name I forgive all others for what they have done against me. I renounce satan, the evil spirits and all their works. I give you my entire self, Lord Jesus, now and forever. I invite you into my life, Jesus. I accept you as my Lord, God and Savior. Heal me, change me, and strengthen me in body, soul and spirit.

Come, Lord Jesus, cover me with your precious blood, and fill me with your Holy Spirit. I love you, Lord Jesus. I praise you, Jesus. I thank you, Jesus. I shall follow you every day of my life. Amen.

Mary my mother, Queen of Peace, all the Angels and Saints, please help me. Amen.

Father Rookey: Trapped in a Wheelchair,
Nurse Healed in Spite of Herself

In 1985, Heather Duncan, a young nurse in Aberdeen, Scotland, irreparably damaged nerves at the base of her spine when she fell lifting a patient. Three operations failed. Nurse Duncan was left confined to a wheelchair, unable to walk. In case there is any doubt as to the seriousness of her condition, it was deemed worthy of a state disability pension.

Crippled for life, Heather saw her suffering as a gift from God. She prayed that He use her pain to benefit others. With friends, Mrs. Duncan went on pilgrimage to Medjugorje in Bosnia-Herzegovina. There she found deep spiritual renewal, but when her friends wanted her to attend a healing service with them, "I refused to go . . . I felt going to a healer was going against God's plan . . ."

Her friends were determined that Heather see Father Rookey. Trapped in her wheelchair, Heather had no choice. Annoyed and protesting, she was spun around and propelled rapidly toward the cemetery where crowds attended a healing ceremony.

While in the back of the crowd praying the rosary, Heather looked up to see what was going on. People were standing with hands raised praying over someone. When the crowd parted and a crying girl walked through pushing her wheelchair, Heather knew God had healed the girl and thanked Him for the miracle.

Heather's friends wanted to bring her up to Father Rookey, but Heather told them she felt her affliction was God's will and did not feel

God wanted to heal her. They ignored what she thought and pushed her through the crowd to a spot near Father Rookey.

When Father Peter stopped in front of Mrs. Duncan, he inquired about her problem and asked if there were a chance she might improve. Heather told him her case was hopeless.

"The priest then gave her his crucifix to hold and told her to look at Jesus." For fifteen minutes Mrs. Duncan stared at Jesus on the cross while intense heat filled her body. When Father Rookey tried to take his crucifix back, Heather fought him for it. She wanted to hold on to Jesus.

The priest asked the crippled nurse if she believed Jesus could heal her. Heather knew He could, but didn't believe He wanted to. Then Father Peter asked Mrs. Duncan if she wanted to take a step in faith. Heather said yes.

In a scene reminiscent of the Bible, Father Rookey said words Heather will never forget, "'Silver and gold have I not, but what I have, I give you. In the name of Jesus, stand up and walk.' And she did."

Heather stood up straight with no pain for the first time since her accident. She walked away from her chair with legs that felt normal. Heather had not walked in years. The only time she had left her third floor apartment was when ambulance men carried her down three floors for hospital visits.

"As a nurse, I knew that the years should have left my legs weak, the muscles wasted, but it was as if the accident had never happened."

Her X-rays are unchanged. Yet Heather is doing the medically impossible: walking, running, going up and down stairs carrying weights. Every day is a miracle.

Ninety-One-Year-Old Father Rookey
Prays as He Stands on His Head
[2007 interview]

Father starts his day with morning prayers and exercises. He does push-ups and stands on his head. "Yes, that's right, he stands on his head as he prays the Psalms!"

Regardless of the weather, Monday through Friday, ninety-one-year-old Father Peter Mary Rookey then prays as he drives an hour from the priory where he lives to the ministry office in Olympia Fields, Illinois. Father pops out of his car, rosary in hand, happy, energetic, and mischievous.

First, Father Rookey tries to sneak unseen into the busy office. When on occasion the priest's ploy works, the office breaks up with hilarity. Father loves to joke.

Then Father Peter begins his five or six hours a day on the telephone, listening to peoples' problems worldwide, and praying for healing. The phone rings so continuously that if it isn't ringing someone checks for a dial tone. Father Rookey takes two prayer breaks, one for private Mass at 12:30 p.m. and another for more prayer at 3 p.m. At these times, the healing priest prays for the intentions of those who have written or called asking for prayer. Then he leaves with homework, hundreds of letters, the daily mail.

"He reads and prays over each and every letter that you folks send him."

Results of Father Rookey's homework appear in the January 2008 newsletter (frrookeyicm.org): a lymphoma healed, fluid in the lung disappeared, a mass in the pancreas vanished, an aneurysm successfully treated, bacterial infection cured, persistent cough of five weeks gone two days after prayer, lost child located, emphysema dormant, heart condition improved, miraculous response to risky brain surgery, and rapid and complete healing after back surgery.

When I asked to interview some of those healed, Father suggested talking to the office staff. He said that each of them has been healed through prayer and will testify.

In 1988, Father Rookey caused a meltdown at Radio Telefis Eireann, Ireland's national radio and television station, when a scheduled six-minute interview stretched to forty minutes. The station switchboard lit up overwhelming the staff with calls. Father's progress through Ireland was followed with extended live reports of healings. Thousands attended his four-hour Masses.

The huge number of people slain in the Spirit and healed at Father's Masses scandalized conservative Catholics who might have stopped Father's visit to Ireland. Providentially, one of those slain was Father Tim Flynn, Irish Provincial of Father Rookey's order, the Servites. Father Flynn had known Father Rookey as a powerful healer in Ireland in the 1950s.

Although fearful of criticism, the provincial invited Father Peter anyway. At the end of Mass, Father Rookey began the healing service by saying, "Hate and be sick, love and be well, at peace."

Plenty of people were already lying on the floor slain. Heather Duncan invited Father Flynn to be blessed. Father Flynn, who considered himself too inhibited to be slain in the Spirit, went right out.

"I was deeply conscious of the Presence of God. I experienced a deep sense of peace and relaxation."

After half an hour, Father Flynn thought if he never got up again it didn't matter. He had been baptized in the Holy Spirit. Joy in life had returned. "In his will is our peace."

"The mercies of the Lord I shall sing forever."

Father Peter Mary Rookey Has Neither Silver
Nor Gold, But He Does Have a Gift

Like Peter and the early Apostles, Father Peter Mary Rookey follows the directive of Jesus, "Take nothing for the journey." (Luke 9:3)

A document certifying that Pope John Paul II honored Father Rookey as a Knight of the Holy Sepulchre, a few other documents, two habits, two pairs of shoes, underwear and a black bag containing prayer books constitute Father Rookey's possessions making all the more touching his words when praying for healing, "Silver and gold have I not, but what I have, I give to you. In the name of Jesus, get up and walk." The wording is two thousand years old and comes from the lips of Peter. (Acts 3:6)

On June 23, 1991, one hundred thousand pilgrims arrived at Medjugorje in Bosnia-Herzegovina. There on the journey, Father Rookey met wheelchair-bound Virginia Landy from Rhode Island. After two years, her puzzling symptoms had finally been diagnosed as multiple sclerosis. The medical world promised no cure, only a slowing of the progress of the illness. Born and raised Catholic, Virginia prayed, but was not a churchgoer. Everyone was surprised when she wanted to go on pilgrimage to Medjugorje.

Wheeled to a green tent set up behind the church, Virginia heard Father Rookey talk about God's healing power. When Peter Mary Rookey stopped in front of Virginia's wheelchair, the priest asked if she believed in the power of Jesus to heal her.

Virginia responded, "Yes."

Father said, "Silver and gold have I not, but what I have, I will give to you. In the name of Jesus, get up and walk."

Virginia walked. Not one or two shuffling steps as at home, but normal strides, her back straight. Later, Virginia Landy climbed the hill of Podrdo. At home in Rhode Island, her doctor was puzzled that

Virginia had no pain and was walking when three doctors had said she never would.

A young man in Balham, London, England, was healed of AIDS. The event made headlines on the front page of at least one newspaper. Those organizing the service had the boy's full name, but after his healing the youth decided to keep his identity secret to protect his family. Later, the healed man said he was willing to testify and to give his doctor permission to testify as well.

Father urges people to speak up. ". . . come forward and give honor and glory to God for the wonderful things He has done in their lives. 'Don't be like the nine lepers that walked away without thanking the Lord,' he says. 'Come and give praise and thanks to God.'"

Father Rookey: The Tumor Shrunk to the Size of a Pinhead

Kevin and Geraldine McIlwaine and their son Ryan lived on a farm in North Belfast, Ireland. Their little boy, Ryan, then two and a half, was not thriving. Medical tests were inconclusive. For the next three years, the McIlwaines brought their child to the hospital clinic every six months to be checked.

Finally in 1989, a brain scan showed what was wrong. A very rare massive tumor grew behind the child's right eye and probably had been there from the time of the boy's birth. "Geraldine and Kevin were told . . . . very little was known about (the tumor's) type in the western world."

Doctors removed as much of the tumor as they could, then referred the child to Beaver Park, the cancer hospital. There, Ryan received treatment daily for six weeks.

Geraldine, her mother, and aunt brought Ryan to a healing service at Holy Cross Chapel. In the front of the church with the seriously ill, Geraldine, holding Ryan, watched five priests process onto the altar.

Mrs. McIlwaine didn't know anything about Father Rookey, but she saw immediately there was something different about him.

The priest from Chicago told the congregation stories of people who had been healed by God, then invited those seeking healing to go up in lines for anointing with oil and laying on of hands. When Geraldine moved forward carrying Ryan, Father suddenly stopped in front of her. His assistant, Reggie Donnelly, tried to get the priest to move to the beginning of the line, but Father Rookey stayed put.

Peter Mary Rookey asked what was wrong. As Geraldine explained, she wept, her tears soaking the child's coat. Father Rookey said, "The beautiful tears of a mother." Then the priest blessed Ryan with Holy Oil and with the crucifix.

Father Rookey's sudden stop in front of Ryan McIlwaine indicated to the congregation that Father had received a word of knowledge concerning God's healing of the child. After that, everywhere Geraldine went, people stopped her to inquire expectantly about Ryan.

The child continued his treatment. Evidently doctors did not hold much hope for the efficacy of the radiotherapy. When a routine scan was done to see whether the treatment was having any effect at all, doctors were amazed.

". . . they'd never seen such results before, they said. The tumor had shrunk to the size of a pinhead and looked set to shrink even further."

As time passed, chances of the tumor recurring grew fainter and fainter. Ryan was taken off medicines doctors thought he'd need until the age of fourteen because the tumor was irritating the child's pituitary. Geraldine keeps looking at her strong, healthy-looking son and knows the child's healing is a total miracle.

*   *   *

Born in 1916 and still working, Father Rookey looks back at thousands of healings, some over the phone or by letter. The priest reads and prays over every letter.

Some healed through laying on of hands never contact Father Rookey to tell him so. Others don't want their names used. They are all part of an enormous unnamed mass of people healed.

Father Rookey stands in for Jesus when he reaches out obeying the Lord's command, ". . . lay hands on the sick and they shall recover." (Mark 16:18) God wants us well. Good health is His will for you.

ৰঙ্গ

Heather Parsons, *A Man of Miracles* (Oak Lawn, IL: CMJ Marian Publishers, 2005), 11, 25-26, 42-43, 67, 75, 77-78, 88-90, 142-143, 163-165.

Sabina Reyes, newsletter, International Compassion Ministry, Vol. XXIV, No. 1 (January/February 2008), 3.

Runaway Oral Roberts Expects a Miracle—Death Rides His Chest

Like Moses, Oral Roberts stuttered. When he was named, the boy's mother, Claudius Roberts, and her preacher husband, Ellis, did not know Oral means "spoken word." Before her son's birth in January 1918, his Cherokee mother crawled through barbed wire in a thunderstorm to pray for little Francis Engles, a child dying of pneumonia. Claudius Roberts promised God that if He healed Francis, she would give Him Oral, the unborn child she was carrying. Francis Engles recovered.

With tears running down her face, Oral's mother would hold him in her lap, tell the story, and say he'd be a preacher. When the child protested that he couldn't talk and definitely couldn't preach, his mother would kiss him and tell him that God would heal him and that Oral would talk to multitudes.

Sick of religion and poverty, Oral Roberts ran away from home at the age of sixteen. Despite what his parents told him God had planned for his life, Oral dreamt of becoming a lawyer and then governor of Oklahoma.

Because Oral was tall and a good athlete, his high school coach invited him to play basketball on a team in another town. There Oral fell into sinful ways, although family ideals haunted him and filled him with guilt. The teen's health was broken by work round the clock and four hours sleep a night. Oral collapsed playing basketball when making a driving lay-up and hit the gym floor with blood running out of his nose. He had tuberculosis.

Oral Roberts wound up back home. His mother had prayed every day that God bring him back, but not this way. The diagnosis was final stage tuberculosis. Claudius Roberts' father and her two sisters had died of TB. Medicines of the day were useless. Doctor after doctor confirmed the diagnosis. Oral and his family knew this was a death sentence.

Oral Roberts says, ". . . I thought only of blasted hopes, a life cut short, and death riding my chest."

Well-meaning people came to pray. When friends asked that Oral be healed if it were God's will, Mrs. Roberts asked them to leave. She insisted it was God's will that Oral be healed. Anyone around Oral had to buoy up his faith, not deflate it.

Six-feet one-inch tall, Oral Roberts slipped from 165 pounds to 120 pounds. For one hundred sixty-three days he lay flat on his back, despairing. Oral sobbed when he heard he was headed for the state sanitarium; few patients came out alive.

His sister Jewel felt God speak to her spirit. She said seven simple words that saved Oral Robert's life. Jewel's words gave him what he needed: hope. She said what God had put in her heart, "Oral, God is going to heal you!"

For the first time, Oral Roberts wanted God in his life. God became real and alive to him. As Oral's parents prayed for his soul, Oral saw the likeness of Jesus on his father's face and Oral called on Jesus to save his soul and his life.

His brother Elmer carried Oral on the mattress he was lying on to the back seat of his car and drove him to Reverend George Moncey's revival tent. On the way there, Oral Roberts heard the Voice say, "Son, I am going to heal you and you are to take My healing power to your generation."

His parents supported him on either side as Reverend Moncey prayed over Oral. The boy felt an electric shock go through his whole being. His lungs cleared, the pain and coughing left, and Oral was filled with energy. In an instant, Jesus of Nazareth had healed Oral Roberts of both tuberculosis and stuttering.

Oral Obeys God and Gets a Parsonage—Miracles Here and There

For years, Oral Roberts saw few signs or wonders. He ached to see God's power demonstrated in his life. One miracle happened when Oral was pastor at a Pentecostal Holiness Church in Toccoa, Georgia.

A deacon, Clyde Lawson, dropped a car motor on his foot. He called for prayer from Pastor Roberts and Deacon Bill Lee, who found Clyde on the ground screaming with pain, holding his right foot in his hands. His toes had been crushed and blood was running out of his shoe.

Sudden compassion came over Oral. He knelt down and touched the end of the shoe, prayed and got up. Clyde stopped screaming. He was able to move his toes and the pain was gone.

"Jumping to his feet, he stomped his foot on the floor and said, 'Brother Roberts, what did you do to me? . . . My foot is healed.'"

On the way home, Bill Lee asked Oral if he had that power all the time. When Oral said no, Bill Lee said power like that could bring a revival to the world.

The next miracle was financial. Married and the father of two, Oral Roberts was a student again. He didn't have a car and thumbed his way to and from revivals. Then in the fall of 1946, he was made pastor of the Pentecostal Holiness Church in Enid, Oklahoma. Oral was studying full-time, pastoring full-time, and trying to provide for his family on $55 dollars a week. He needed a place for his family to live.

A family in his Church invited the Roberts family into their home while living quarters were being arranged by the Church board. For a while it worked, but the host family had four children, the Roberts had two, and the house was small. Oral's wife Evelyn threatened to move back with her mother until the Church provided them with a proper home. Oral asked her for two more weeks to work on the Church board for better housing.

The board was unwilling to buy a parsonage. Oral felt the Spirit urging him to tell the board he would give his whole week's salary to start a fund to buy a parsonage.

Oral couldn't afford to give a penny, let alone $55. God was telling him to plant seeds of faith. Certain his wife and the board would not understand, Oral Roberts prayed it through until he felt peaceful about obeying God. Then Oral announced during a sermon at a Wednesday night prayer meeting that he was giving his paycheck to start the fund and invited the congregation to add to it.

"Remember, the greater the sacrifice, the greater the blessing. Give God your best, then expect His best," Oral said.

A German farmer gave $500. A couple gave $25. A widow gave $100. The largest building contractor in the Church gave $1,000.

When Oral told his wife he had given away their $55, Evelyn was horrified. What would they eat? Protesting that they had given their tithe of 10% and had to have something to live on, she went to bed. At four in the morning, a farmer knocked on the door and told Oral he had been unable to sleep because Oral had given his entire week's salary to God. He handed Oral four one hundred dollar bills saying the Lord had told him to dig the money up out of his yard and bring it to Oral as seed money. God had come through as promised. They had their parsonage.

Oral Hits a Neighbor's Car and Strikes Oil

Oral Roberts' old beat up Chevrolet's brakes failed and his car smashed into the back of a neighbor's car parked near the parsonage. No one was around. Oral was tempted to park elsewhere and evade responsibility for the damage, but he rang the doorbell of the house next door and told his neighbor he'd pay for repairs.

Gus was impressed that Oral was turning himself in and insisted no payment be made. A Buick dealer, the neighbor was shocked at the rundown condition of the pastor's car and gave Oral a high price for the old Chevy and a low price on a brand new Buick, Oral's dream car. Driving home from the dealer's, Evelyn made Oral stop the new car and get out. As other motorists gawked, they both put their hands on the Buick and gave thanks to God for the blessing of such a beautiful car.

Evelyn said, "Oral, this is more than just a new Buick. It represents what God will do when we obey and take Him at His Word. Let's just praise the Lord." They both felt God was still rewarding Oral for obeying His command to give Roberts' $55 weekly salary as seed money for the new parsonage.

As his twenty-ninth birthday neared, Oral Roberts was deeply dissatisfied. He had been healed twelve years before. At that time, the Voice had said, "Son, I am going to heal you and you are to take My healing power to your generation. You are to build Me a university and build it on My authority and the Holy Spirit."

His soul burned to heal in the name of Jesus. The Voice spoke to him once more, "Son, don't be like other men. Don't be like any denomination. Be like Jesus, and heal the people as He did."

How? He asked God how he could do this. The Voice told him to get on his knees and read through the four Gospels and the Book of Acts three times consecutively during the next thirty days. After that, God would show him Jesus and His healing ways.

Despite the demands of Church, school, and family, Oral read as God had told him. Through fasting, like St. Paul, Oral gained great inner strength. Through the reading exercise, Oral grew to know Jesus.

Oral says of Jesus, "He didn't come to talk about life; He is life!" The life of Jesus had flowed into Oral Roberts when Jesus healed his tubercular lungs and stuttering tongue. Oral realized he had been preaching to please the Church instead of burning inside to see the sick delivered. His outlook was changed by 3 John 1:2, "Beloved, I wish above all things that thou mayest prosper and be in health, even as thy soul prospereth."

Then God gave Oral the same dream night after night. In the dream, Oral saw everybody as sick in some way. Everyone has a problem, and God sees and hears that every moment of every day. The following Sunday as Oral preached, he saw people as if crying out to God for help. He preached out of compassion and faith that great healings were coming.

*   *   *

After many hours of lying face down on the floor, weeping and praying, Oral heard the Voice again. God said, "Stand on your feet!" Oral did so. "Go get in your car!" Oral obeyed. "Drive one block east, and turn right!" He did. Then Oral heard what he had hoped for, "From this hour you shall have My power to heal the sick . . ."

He rushed home hollering, "'Evelyn, Evelyn!'

"She said, 'What is it Oral?'

"'Cook me a meal, honey, I've heard from God!'"

God is Oral Roberts' Real Estate and Employment Agent

God had called. Oral Roberts quit his job and stepped out into the unknown. The Roberts family moved to Tulsa, Oklahoma. Centrally located in the United States, Tulsa had good air transportation, important for Roberts who trusted that he'd circle the world with God's healing message.

Oscar Moore, the preacher taking over Oral's former pastorate, invited the Roberts family to stay with him in Tulsa while they found a place to live. Every place the Roberts saw was too expensive. Oral had only $25 to his name.

Oscar Moore was in the process of selling his house. When Oscar told Oral the deal would close that night at six o'clock, Oral suddenly felt the house was his. He told himself this was absurd because the house had already been sold.

To work out this feeling, Oral drove to a city park and sat in the car, talking to God about his situation. Oral felt stranded. The unemployed preacher held on to the steering wheel and told God that if he were to begin his ministry he needed immediate help.

After intense praying, Oral became quiet before the Lord. Then he felt the Holy Spirit come on him. Oral drove to Oscar Moore's home, confident that the house would be his and help was on the way.

They ate dinner together. At 7:30 p.m., the buyer still had not shown up. While Oscar waited for the buyer, the Roberts went to a revival meeting under Reverend Steve Pringle's big tent. That night, Oral got the first job in his new ministry in Tulsa: Reverend Pringle asked him to preach a one-week crusade.

The next morning, Oscar gave his buyer until eight o'clock in the morning to show up. After eight, Oscar asked Oral if he and Evelyn would like to have the house. Oscar named a price and Oral said it was too much. Oral asked Oral what he would pay, they agreed, and Oral said sold. Evelyn did not know of Oral's experience of the Lord the night before and knew her husband had just agreed to buy a house when all he had was twenty-five dollars.

When Oscar handed Oral legal papers to sign, the size of the down payment took his breath away, but without a word, Oral agreed, trusting God. Then Oscar told them he didn't need the down payment right away. He said Oral could give him half the down payment in six months and the other half in twelve months. Oral never blinked an eye and said that was all right with him. Oscar didn't know until a year later that Oral Roberts had bought the house with no idea of how he was going to pay for it.

The first service of Oral Roberts' crusade opened in driving rain to a small group, but he preached with the power of God upon him. A few sick people felt they had been healed. The news spread throughout Tulsa.

"Three nights later, the tent was packed. On Sunday, the place was filled, and hundreds were standing around the edges of the one-thousand-seat tent. Steve said, 'Oral, you can't close this meeting. God is with you, and you must stay another week.' We continued the revival for nine straight weeks, with standing-room only for the people."

One night during the crusade, a man pulled out a revolver, pointed at Oral, and pulled the trigger. The bullet hit the canvas near Oral's head. News services featured the shooting, and within twenty-four hours Oral Roberts' name was known nationwide. Pastors extended invitations to preach around the country. Ironically through this event, masses of sick would receive the healings Jesus called "the children's bread."

The Hot Hand of Oral Roberts: There is a God and It is His Nature to Heal

Following the nine-week crusade in Tulsa, Oral gave a one-day service nearby. When he prayed over an eight-year-old deaf boy, Oral heard the Voice say, ". . . you have been faithful to this hour; and now you will feel My Presence in your right hand."

Oral placed a finger in each of the child's ears. In the right hand, Oral could feel the Presence of God, but not in the left. Oral placed the finger of his right hand in one ear at a time and prayed for healing.

"Instantly, the little fellow looked around. He put his hands over his ears, and he began to cry and look at his mother.

"I said to her, 'He is apparently hearing noise and voices for the first time, and it scares him.'"

When the mother spoke to her child and the boy tried to say her words back as best he could, the congregation and Oral Roberts were in awe. Oral knew it was as if Jesus Himself had touched the boy's ears.

Then someone carried up a woman who had trouble walking. Again, Oral "felt the Presence of God race down my elbow into my hand and into her being. She leaped up, raised her legs up and down a few times, looked around, and took off running through the crowd, praising God and crying."

Oral was astonished. It was unlike anything he had ever felt. "I had often felt His Presence flow through my whole being. It was something we had been accustomed to . . . an overpowering sense of God's personal Presence . . . Every Holy Spirit-baptized believer I knew had felt this anointing to some degree. It became what we all expected when we came together to pray . . . The main difference was . . . . God was telling me how I would feel His Presence directly in my right hand . . ."

Oral struggled to understand his new gift. The Presence of God coming to Oral's hand was not under Oral's control. He didn't feel it all the time and could not summon it at will. Oral kept it secret from everyone, even his wife.

A few days later, when Oral conducted services in Faith Tabernacle in Tulsa, he saw two acquaintances, Irma Morris, who sought healing from tuberculosis, and her sister Eve. That night God's Presence had come to Oral's right hand as he preached.

When Oral touched Irma, she stared and said, "'Your right hand. It felt on fire when it touched me.' Then as tears rolled down her cheeks, she said, 'Something in your right hand is causing a warmth to go through my lungs. My lungs are opening up. I believe I am being healed!'"

Oral stared at his right hand. It looked the same. However, he felt God's Presence charging through it during the entire healing service.

At home that night, Oral shared his experience with Evelyn. She asked him to pray for a condition that had bothered her for several weeks. As soon as his wife asked, Oral could feel the Presence of God running into his hand.

"When I laid my right hand on her, the vibration was going through it, and she cried, 'Oh, Oral, you are right. It is in your right hand. It is God!'"

Did she still have pain? "'Oh, no,' she said, weeping. 'It is totally gone . . . It's Your Presence, Lord Jesus. Help us to hold it precious and to give You praise for it.'"

Oral Roberts: Waiting for God

God told Oral to get the biggest tent he could and carry it to the cities. Oral ordered a tent that seated three thousand and used it for the first time in June 1948 in Durham, North Carolina. With the flaps raised, thousands more could stand five and ten deep outside all around the tent. By the last night of the twenty-one-day crusade, the crowd numbered nine thousand a night.

Every night of that crusade, six or seven deaf children from the local school for the deaf would show up in Oral's prayer line. "It was the most marvelous thing I had yet seen when one by one the children, without hearing and speech, felt their ears pop open. We taught them to say words, such as mother, daddy, Jesus, I can hear, and I can speak. It electrified the crowd—and me most of all."

The children would feel vibrating warmth from Oral's hand and believe God was healing them. Oral would feel it, his faith would leap, and he could pray boldly with confidence.

The hot vibrating hand of Oral Roberts caused major controversy. Skeptics suspected electric wires were hooked to Oral's right hand and they climbed under the stage looking for them.

Not everyone was healed when Oral felt the Presence of God in his right hand. This surprised him. Many were, but not all.

Quoting Romans 12:3, "God hath dealt to every man the measure of faith," Oral compares faith to oil in the ground that flows upward when drilled. Oral calls himself a faith releaser. "My touching the people with the Presence of God pulsating through my right hand became the point of contact for their faith *and* my faith to be loosed to God for their healing." Oral feels if faith is not released out of our hearts to God, our chance of receiving a miracle is slim.

By July 1950, Oral was ministering in a twelve-thousand-seat tent, the largest ever constructed at that time. After he preached to twelve thousand people, hundreds of very sick people filed by one by one as Oral prayed for their healing in the name of the living Christ.

What if the gift did not come? Oral developed a pre-service routine to prepare for the Presence: he rested and prayed from 5 p.m. until the crusade services began. The Presence would start coming into his hand a few minutes before Oral went in to minister.

In Philadelphia, Pennsylvania, it was time to leave, but the Presence had not come. Oral had vowed he would attempt nothing without this sign from God. He panicked. His stomach churned. He waited thirty minutes beyond his starting time. The driver knocked at the door. Oral still felt nothing.

He said, "'Okay, God . . . I am Your property. You told me I was to take Your healing power to my generation. You know it was not my idea, and I did not call myself. I cannot go without absolutely knowing the anointing, Your Presence, has come upon me.' I put my Bible down, took off my coat, and sat down . . . 'I am going to sit here until You let me feel Your Presence,' I said . . . Ten minutes passed . . . twenty . . . I still sat there . . . my associate . . . would do what he had to do.

"As I was thinking that, the Presence of God seized my right hand and began throbbing through it. I let out a yell, grabbed my Bible and coat, ran out of the room and hollered . . . 'Let's go. God's Presence is with me!'"

Oral Roberts: Waiting on the Lord

The Philadelphia crusade produced the most healings Oral had ever witnessed. Waiting for the Presence in Philadelphia taught him that God has His own timetable and if you follow it, the Lord will make up for what appears to be lost time.

A revelation came to Oral that ". . . the anointing is a time when God separates you from yourself and fills you with His glory so that when you speak it's like God speaking and when you act it's like God acting . . . It is an incomparable experience. God who is in you is now flowing up by His Spirit from your . . . inner being . . . I confess it is a driving force possessing me far beyond any powers of my own. My normal compassion is multiplied a thousand times . . . I have no control over when the anointing stops . . . the tangible Presence of God is not mine. It belongs to God."

Oral asks who is in charge: God or Oral Roberts? When the anointing in his right hand stopped, Oral found it best to stop abruptly and ask the audience to stand for the benediction. Oral says, "I must do my part and always trust God, but He alone does the miracle deed."

Oral Roberts faced a huge, hostile crowd of "show-me" types in a B-29 airplane hanger in Goldsboro, North Carolina. The congregants were Christians from Churches that did not believe in healing through prayer. They felt sickness was the will of God. On the fifth night of the crusade, as Oral prayed over Douglas Sutton, a boy on crutches because of Perthes' disease, Douglas felt the Presence of God flowing into him from Oral's hand. The boy's mother took his crutches and Douglas ran up and down the aisles. The crowd roared and wept. Many other healings followed. On the last day of the crusade, over twenty-five thousand gathered for the final service.

In September 1950, a terrible storm hit Amarillo, Texas, while Oral was conducting a service in a tent that seated seven thousand. With a mighty roar, winds swept off the Texas Panhandle and blasted the tent. As Oral told everyone to remain calm and trust God, men sitting near tent poles tried to hold them down.

The wind lifted Oral off the platform and like a miracle lay him down gently on the ground ten feet away. The huge canvas took off like a balloon and left everyone exposed to pounding rain. Oral rose, climbed back on the platform, and told people to go to their cars. In the parking lot, he laid hands on people and prayed with them. Over the wind and rain, a man in a wheelchair called to Oral to help him get out of the wheelchair. Oral put his right hand on the man's rain-soaked head and prayed. The man got up and was able to walk.

"He took off running, and that was the last I saw of him."

The next day, the Amarillo newspaper reported the fire department arriving at the scene expecting hundreds of casualties. Only three people had been injured and only one of those seriously enough to remain in the hospital. People who had been in the tent were interviewed and commented that the congregation kept singing hymns after the tent blew down. There was no panic among the seven thousand and only one serious injury. The firemen kept saying it's a miracle, it's a miracle.

As a replacement for the ruined tent, Ringling Brothers built a ten-thousand-seat tent and made it storm-proof. Evelyn and Oral emptied their little savings to guarantee no bill was left unpaid in Amarillo.

More Oral Roberts: Bruised but Not Broken

After the disaster in Amarillo, Oral and Evelyn had no tent and no money. Crusades had been scheduled for a year in advance, but Oral had no way of meeting those obligations until the new tent was finished. He was ready to quit.

Friends invited them to Tacoma, Washington, and helped pay their way. There, Oral met Billy Graham. Even though Oral was considered controversial because he believed in healing, Billy Graham asked Oral to lead the prayer at his meeting that night. Oral refused because he didn't want to cause trouble for Billy Graham. The evangelicals sponsored Billy Graham's crusades and the Pentecostals sponsored Oral's crusades. Oral's denomination believed in baptism of the Holy Spirit with speaking in tongues and healing as a confirmation of the Word when preached. Billy Graham's denomination did not.

That night, Billy Graham honored Oral by assigning him to pray before his sermon. After the service, Oral and Evelyn were stopped by a woman who asked Oral to pray for her healing. They were all under the edge of the tabernacle. Oral felt Graham's sponsors would not want prayer for the sick in the tabernacle.

The woman's husband was furious. "Oral Roberts," he said, "my wife is dying with cancer. God has called you to pray for the sick. If you refuse . . . God will hold you accountable."

Oral knew the man was right. The four of them moved out into the street. There Oral prayed for her healing away from the tabernacle. The pastor of a large Church in the area was watching. Impressed by Oral's piety, the pastor asked Oral to bring the new tent for a crusade the following year. God showed Oral Roberts he did have a future.

Six years later, in 1956, Oral shipped the tent accommodating ten thousand to Australia. In Sydney, the crusade went well, and it began well in Melbourne. However, the longshoremen were on strike and Communist agitators were in town. On the second night, several hundred longshoremen ran amuck in the tent, shouting obscenities at Oral and storming the stage to slap him around. The police could do nothing because Churches were not protected by law in Australia.

On the third night, it was even worse. A gang stormed in, cursing and laughing. Some intruders went on stage to hit and spit on Oral. The press joined the attack on him. "Oral Roberts, get out of Australia" became a slogan on the airways.

On the fourth night, a public figure officiated to keep order. The gang broke up the meeting once more. Hooligans surrounded the house where the Roberts were staying. They threatened Oral and his hosts. One insurance company withdrew insurance on the big tent and the U.S. government advised Oral to leave. It was not safe and the government could not protect him. Oral and Evelyn left Australia.

Oral Robert's team and his sponsoring pastors took out ads in Australian papers to explain why Oral Roberts left mid-crusade: Australia lacked a law to protect religious freedom. A prominent Presbyterian clergyman chided the media every day on his daily broadcasts. As a result of a change in public attitude, a law was instituted protecting even the despised little Pentecostal Churches. The following year, Billy Graham preached to ninety thousand in the soccer stadium without incident. Since then, Pentecostals have flourished in Australia.

In 1957 in America, Oral drew over two million people in twelve months, his largest crowds and his largest number of healings in any year. When he died in 2009, Oral Roberts had reached millions of people worldwide for over six decades.

৵৶৽

Oral Roberts, *Expect a Miracle: My Life and Ministry* (Nashville, TN: Thomas Nelson Inc., 1995), 24, 28, 32, 55, 59, 63, 67, 69, 77, 89, 91-92, 94-95, 98-99, 105-106, 108-109, 112, 123, 129.

Solanus Casey: Proxy for Jesus

Dead thirty years, Solanus Casey was fresh as a daisy! As part of the process moving Solanus toward possible canonization, experts opened Father Casey's grave. The coffin was full of water. Holes were punched to empty it. Doctors and twenty-five witnesses expected a mess.

Dr. Gordon Rose, head of mortuary science at Wayne State University in Detroit, Michigan, was amazed, ". . . the casket was brought into the friars' chapel . . . the body of Solanus was . . . almost 95% intact. The body had been embalmed, but the three doctors who officially examined it felt . . . the state of preservation . . . remarkable." The coffin was in shreds, but Solanus was in good condition. His hands and face were grey, but his body was pink and pliable.

Eight years later in 1995, after studying three volumes of testimony, the Vatican named Solanus Casey, Venerable. Included in the examination were the priest's notebooks with over six thousand entries up to 1956. Unfortunately, more than twenty-two years of "favors" from 1901 to November 1923 went unrecorded. However, the two miracles after death required for beatification and canonization have not as yet met the stringent requirements of the Catholic Church.

On the other hand, documentaries aired on both secular and religious networks are chock full of testimonies given by people healed through the prayers of Solanus Casey. Filmed testimonies aired both on the Eternal Word Television Network (EWTN), a religious broadcasting service, and on PBS in Detroit where Venerable Solanus Casey worked and is buried at St. Bonaventure's Monastery. Even *Unsolved Mysteries* ran a program on healings attributed to the prayers of Solanus Casey.

On EWTN, Tim Mulligan of Detroit said Father Solanus' healings were a family tradition. As a boy, Tim's grandfather, after a failed operation, had a high fever for sixteen days and went in and out of a coma. Doctors said the boy would die soon.

Tim's greatgrandma brought Solanus to Providence Hospital. Father Casey blessed the child and said the boy would be fine. An hour later, the fever dropped. Twenty-four hours later, Tim's grandfather came out of the coma.

At the age of twelve, Tim's father was completely paralyzed from polio as confirmed by spinal taps and other medical documentation. Tim's grandfather, now a doctor, called Father Solanus. As Solanus predicted, within three days the boy was able to move his arms and legs. In a week, Tim's father was completely healed. The cure was so effective that Mr. Mulligan's Army medical record in the late 1950's labeled him a hypochondriac, saying, "Thinks he had polio."

Edward C. Cortis of Detroit fought back tears as he relived the day doctors told his mother that his eight-year-old sister would die that night of meningitis. His dad brought Father Solanus to the house. They all knelt around her bed. Father Solanus touched her forehead and blessed her. He said everything would be fine. The next day, she was up playing. The doctors came in, saw the child and asked, "What did you do?"

On both religious and secular television, people testified joyfully to God's healing power at work through a monastery doorkeeper who stood in for Jesus the Carpenter, healer of all who ask. Venerable Solanus Casey was a proxy for Jesus.

Father Casey Keeps a Notebook: Doing What the Boss Told Him

Father Solanus Casey's prayers worked. Word spread like wildfire. In the days before antibiotics and Alcoholics Anonymous, people were even more desperate for healings and favors than we are today.

When people rang the bell, Father Casey did his job as doorkeeper at a Capuchin friary—he answered the door. It was assumed that people calling wanted to enroll in the Seraphic Mass Association, which linked the prayers said at Mass by hundreds of Capuchin priests. At most friaries, enrollment was not pushed and few came, but people flocked to Solanus' friary. As news spread from parish to parish, from layman to layman, the Christ-like Solanus' own personal healing gift was disguised by his enthusiasm for the Seraphic Mass Association.

Solanus' boss, the Father Provincial, heard about the amazing increase in enrollments at the friary in Harlem, New York. He heard too that enrollments were uncharacteristically resulting in "favors granted."

On a supervisory visit, the Father Provincial ordered Solanus to begin keeping a record of favors received. Following his superior's orders, Solanus immediately began recording miracles in a twelve-by-ten inch ledger-type book with heavy covers and ruled pages. The book was discovered nine years after Solanus' death on July 31, 1957, exactly fifty-three years after saying his first Mass.

The first entry in Solanus' notebook was made the day of the Provincial's visit, November 8, 1923. On that day, Margaret Quinn reported that her neighbor, Mr. M., had been healed of alcoholism and her sister, E. Remy of Philadelphia, Pennsylvania, of severe inflammatory rheumatism. A letter from E. Remy reported, "Thank God and the good prayer society. I'm feeling fine."

The variety of ills gave a cross-section of Solanus' followers. A woman asked prayer for two sons who were "drug fiends." Another woman reported her sixteen-year-old daughter missing for a week. One day after enrollment, the girl was found in Jamaica, New York. On December 9, a sister enrolled her brother who had been drinking heavily for five years. On December 14, she reported he had stopped drinking.

"Between November 8, 1923, and July 28, 1924, there are ninety-six memos. Forty-one mention petitions answered after enrollment in the S.M.A. by Father Solanus." Solanus Casey would pray with and for the petitioners as he signed them up. "... he prayed constantly for all those who brought their troubles to him."

An eighteen-year-old who had been keeping bad company, drinking, and staying out all night was enrolled on December 17 and "immediately gives up his wild life and returns to the sacraments." Doctors gave a woman with pneumonia three hours to live, but she recovered remarkably and was convinced it was due to her enrollment. Another recovered from a heart condition that doctors expected would kill her. Two days after enrollment, a woman regained her memory lost to concussion eight years previously.

Next to each miracle Solanus wrote in English, "Thanks be to God!" or in Latin, "Deo Gratias!" We say the same.

Solanus Casey: Did Barney Convert the Jesse James Gang?

In today's world, Solanus would have gotten straight A's. Born to Irish immigrants on November 25, 1870 in a Wisconsin log cabin on the banks of the Mississippi River, Barney (Bernard) Casey, Jr. was the sixth child in a family of sixteen children. The future Solanus was highly intelligent. "A quiet and thoughtful boy, he was forever working out ingenious ways to snare rabbits and prairie chickens—for game was important to the family larder."

A champion debater in grade school, Barney always got excellent marks in English. From childhood, he loved to read. There were plenty of books because his farmer father sold them to make extra money. The father bought books in the city and brought them back to the farm by train. He'd throw a heavy sack of books off the train on their property. His sons would pick up the sack and their father could then walk home from the station miles away unimpeded. Everybody in the family read the books carefully to avoid soiling them before sale.

The Casey parents read the classics and poetry aloud to their family at the dinner table, sang Irish folk songs, and told Irish folk tales. Each child chimed in. They were a cheerful, literary family. People loved visiting the Caseys. For one thing, there was always music. One of Barney's earliest memories was of his mother outside their home on the banks of the Mississippi hanging out wash and singing to her neighbor across the river. Young Barney taught himself to play the mouth organ and the accordion fairly well.

When crops failed, Barney, then a young teen, missed a lot of schooling helping out on the farm. He finally graduated from grammar school at seventeen. Nearby Stillwater, Minnesota was a logging town. His first job to help out financially was sorting logs on the river, dangerous especially for a skinny kid. In Stillwater he lived with his mother's brother, Pat Murphy. Meanwhile, Barney would go back and forth to his family on the farm. He was in demand as a fiddler at local barn dances.

When Barney was seventeen, his Uncle Pat, a guard at the Stillwater State Prison, got Barney a job as a part-time guard. There the future priest befriended one of the Jesse James gang, Cole Younger. Born to a wealthy family, Cole and his brother Jim were embittered during the Civil War when Union soldiers held a gun to their mother's head, forced her to burn down their home, then marched the family through waist-high snow for eight days. Their mother died as a result. The boys sought vengeance by turning to crime.

Barney may have been a player in Cole Younger's amazing conversion story. Cole was thirty-two when he met Barney Casey. Released from prison at the age of fifty-nine, Cole Younger went around the country on the lecture circuit speaking against turning to a life of crime. When Barney left from a visit to the prison, he treasured a wooden chest Cole made and gave to him; Barney brought his clothes to the seminary in that trunk.

Solanus Casey: Not Smart Enough to be a Priest

Always enterprising, Barney saw the opportunity presented by newly-installed electric streetcars. He became one of the first streetcar conductors in the Midwest. While working in Superior, Wisconsin,

Barney saw good prospects for the family and persuaded them to relocate there, near good jobs and higher education. A clever business man, he suggested the family tell real estate agents they would swap the farm for ten city lots.

At this point, Barney was a motorman and job trainer. Witnessing a murder on the streetcar tracks brought Barney back to thoughts of the priesthood, a dream he had entertained from the age of seven. A drunken sailor had stabbed a girl right in the path of the streetcar. Crowds of people surrounded the woman lying on the tracks. Barney stopped the car and jumped off. The sailor stood above the girl, brandishing a bloody knife. Police took the man into custody and medical people tried in vain to save the girl. Deeply affected by the sight of such violence, Barney prayed all night both for the victim and for her murderer. He thought again of offering his life to the service of God. Barney knew he had to do more to bring God's love and peace to the world.

His pastor recommended the Seminary of St. Francis de Sales in Milwaukee. Most of the classes were taught in German. Called the "German Seminary," this was the school Barney's brother Maurice had failed out of years before. Barney ignored the language problem looming menacingly in the distance. An additional problem was his age. At twenty-one, Barney had not even begun high school. He would be entering class with much younger men.

A prayer Barney used may have helped him then: "Do not pray for tasks equal to your powers. Pray for powers equal to your tasks—then the doing of your work shall be no miracle, but you shall be a miracle." (Anonymous, "Poem Prayer Used by Venerable Fr. Solanus" prayer card)

Today we know it takes five to seven years to master a foreign language well enough to study in it. Ignorant of that, the seminary expected non-German speaking Irish-Americans to study theology in German and Latin. Expelled after four years, Barney was devastated. He prayed through the summer and fall of 1896 asking God to show him His Will. The answer came on December 8, 1896. Praying intensely after Communion, Barney heard three words, "Go to Detroit." He knew God wanted him to join the Capuchin Order, the only religious order in Detroit.

Solanus Casey: Entire Wardrobe on Two Hooks

The Capuchins weren't Barney's first choice. He disliked the beards, the sandals, and the rigorous lifestyle. When contemplating the priesthood as a teen, Casey decided against the order. Nevertheless, as soon as the monks accepted his application, Barney left for Detroit. It was just before Christmas in 1896. A heavy snowstorm slowed the train to twelve miles an hour. Barney arrived at St. Bonaventure Monastery shortly before midnight on Christmas Eve. His cell, a 9' x 12' room, had a desk, a chair, and on the wall two clothes hooks to hold Barney's entire wardrobe after profession. Capuchin poverty is stark.

Although Barney had a happy Christmas, he was soon tortured by doubt, but all doubt left when Barney received his habit on January 14. Barney knew he was where he belonged. As a new man in Christ, Barney took the name Francis Solanus, after a violin-carrying Spanish nobleman-saint, a Capuchin who evangelized Chile, Argentina, and Peru in the seventeenth century. Although an intellectual, the first Francis Solanus had problems with foreign languages, too.

First assigned to Sacred Heart in Yonkers, New York in 1904, thirty-five-year-old Solanus was a Franciscan priest, simplex, that is, one who could say Mass, but, despite having studied canon law, theology, and philosophy for ten years in German and Latin, was not considered equal to giving doctrinal sermons or hearing confessions. Ironically, when permitted to give inspirational talks, Solanus was an eloquent and moving speaker.

Solanus was further humiliated when the pastors, puzzled about what to do with a priest who could neither preach nor absolve, assigned Solanus as sacristan, porter, and doorkeeper, jobs usually given brothers, not priests. Solanus Casey totally yielded to the Will of God and accepted his assignments with joy: they linked his love of Jesus in the Eucharist and his love of people.

Troubled parishioners from half a dozen ethnic groups poured out their sorrows to the kindly, nonjudgmental friar who answered the door and fed those in need. When there was trouble, people sent for "the Holy Priest," as the Italians called him.

Solanus' Italian interpreter was an eight-year-old child, Carmella Petrosina. In later years, Carmella gave an example of the power of Solanus' prayers. Carmella's mother, a midwife, attended a woman who had just delivered and was near death. Carmella was sent to get the Holy Priest.

"As soon as Father came in, he asked for holy water. But they had no holy water. Father Solanus said, 'Oh, poor, poor, poor.' I ran over to our house and got some. When I came back, he prayed over her, blessed her and from then on the woman got over her infection and lived a long time."

As early as 1901, three years before ordination, Solanus recorded circumstances of "prayers answered" in his mandated spiritual journal. As the years passed, miracles became routine, and word spread rapidly in Yonkers and beyond: This man's prayers had power.

Solanus Casey: Santa Claus is Disappointed

How did Solanus pray for healing? He chatted. As Solanus sat listening to visitors, he'd keep his eyes closed or look into space. After quiet discernment, the friar would look back into the eyes of the one in front of him, ask a few questions, pray, and then suggest the person thank God for past blessings and for those to be received in the future. Solanus would urge more frequent use of the sacraments and then suggest joining the Capuchins' Seraphic Mass Association.

People began to talk. Prayers offered at these chats were often answered. Soon Solanus was swamped with requests to visit sick people in the valleys below the monastery.

In July 1918, after fourteen years in Yonkers, Solanus was transferred to Our Lady of Sorrows at Pitt and Stanton Streets in Manhattan to direct altar boys and moderate the Young Ladies' Sodality. He filled his day with spiritual reading and prayer.

Three years later, Solanus was transferred to Our Lady of the Angels in Harlem as a full-time pastoral worker under the title of monastery porter. He'd answer the door and speak to people, first come, first served. Lines formed inside and outside his office.

"He radiated a sense that God cared about all those things. He often laid hands on those who were sick and prayed for a healing then and there. And his promises of prayer . . . were more than polite promises. He began to spend hours and hours in the chapel after office hours."

In the evening after Solanus mopped up the office, he'd go to the chapel where he'd pray for all who had come to the door that day. More and more people lined up to tell Solanus their prayers had been answered. Crowds were showing up every day.

There were reports of healings of mental illness. "A New Jersey man hospitalized in an asylum was healed and reported back to work within four months, his family told Solanus."

There were healings from gangrene. In February of 1924, Patrick McCue, a motorman, was told by doctors at Bellevue Hospital that his leg would have to be amputated because of diabetes and a gangrenous toe. After a friend asked Father Solanus to enroll Patrick in the Seraphic Mass Association, surgery was cancelled and the infection cleared up by itself. The motorman was back at work the end of March.

Crowds swamped Our Lady of Angels in Harlem. On July 30, 1924, Solanus' superiors decided to move him out of New York and back to headquarters, St. Bonaventure Monastery in Detroit.

Solanus was made assistant to the friary porter, Brother Spruck, who looked like Santa Claus. Brother Spruck needed help at the door so he could spend time as the Capuchins' tailor, making and mending habits for the order.

To Brother Spruck's distress, the bell rang constantly. Eighteen hours a day, lines of people formed inside and outside the monastery. Each hoped to speak to Solanus, the gentle, holy man whose prayers, Detroit soon learned, were often answered.

Solanus Casey: Chevrolet Gets a Blessing

You had to get up pretty early in the morning to beat Solanus Casey to the chapel. In fact, witnesses testified he sometimes prayed all night, on his knees, arms raised, deep in religious ecstasy. Sister Agrippina's brother was a novice assigned as sacristan. When he went into the chapel at 4:30 a.m., "Father Solanus was already there in the corner, praying." Solanus got little sleep, yet a co-worker, Brother Gabriel, said Solanus ". . . would be in the office from seven in the morning until ten at night . . . . He saw thousands of people."

Samples of the fruit of his prayer were found in his notebooks. On August 18, 1924, Solanus prayed with Mrs. Clara Kowalski, a twenty-three-year-old living in Detroit. Clara was anxious about taking an X-ray that might show the need for an operation on a dead bone in her ear. On August 30, Clara reported nothing had been found on the X-ray.

Then on September 1, Mrs. Kowalski told Solanus the danger was disappearing and good color was returning to the bone. On November 1, Solanus reported a complete cure. There were thousands of other similar happy resolutions.

In January of 1925, thirty-nine-year-old Earl Eagen and his wife rang the monastery doorbell. In so much pain that he looked seventy-five years old, Earl's greatest worry was who would take care of his family after he died of stomach cancer.

Solanus prayed with Earl and his wife. Eight days later, the couple drove sixty miles from Port Huron, Michigan to tell Solanus that Earl's pain was gone and he felt fine. The Eagen family and Solanus remained close friends until Solanus' death.

On February 4, 1925, a nine-year-old John Slyker was brought from the suburbs to see Solanus. His eye problem puzzled specialists. Blind in one eye, John had double vision in the other. On their way home, his parents noticed the child was reading street signs. Doctors called the immediate improvement of his vision "inexplicable."

In March 1925, John McKenna, a Chevrolet employee, told Solanus that an economic slump had reduced work at Chevrolet to a few hours a day. John McKenna couldn't support his family on reduced wages. He asked Solanus to enroll the company in the Seraphic Mass Association. "He winked at McKenna and reached for his pen. The wink said simply that God can answer prayer in any way he wishes."

"That same night the company received an astounding order. Two nights later McKenna waved triumphantly: 'Father! . . . we heard this afternoon that the company has an order for 45,000 machines, wanted in thirty days.'" All Chevrolet employees went back both full-time and overtime.

Thirty-year-old Anna Schram was operated on for gallstones on December 18, 1926. On January 20, 1927, doctors told her she had developed an abscess on her liver. They operated on her at Grace Hospital even though no one had ever survived such an operation. On February 17, Anna's sister, who had enrolled the woman in the Seraphic Mass Association before the second operation, phoned Solanus that her sister had survived the operation and was home and recovering.

These are just samples from thousands of cures associated with Solanus. In Detroit as in New York, Barney Casey, Jr. was a conduit for our Father's healing love. His success shows that God cares.

Maurus (510-584) and Solanus (1870-1957): Brothers Under the Skin

At St. Bonaventure's in Detroit, Wednesdays were super busy. Every Wednesday featured the "St. Maurus Blessing Over the Sick."

Allegedly, the Blessing derived from Maurus, a Benedictine monk, noted during his lifetime for the gift of healing. After Maurus died, the Benedictines continued to bless the sick. The Capuchin friars at St. Bonaventure's also used the blessing.

After Solanus arrived at the monastery, the number of people at the Wednesday blessing ceremony increased dramatically. The friary chronicle on February 19, 1928 said, "A very large crowd at the blessing at 3 p.m. Father Herman Buss acted as traffic cop, while Father Solanus offered the relic of the True Cross to the people."

Solanus gave a sermon at the blessing. He'd read stories of past healings from his "Notebook of Special Cases" or relate stories people had told him of their own experience of healings through the St. Maurus Blessing Over the Sick. His sermons revolved around trust in God, gratitude for past and future favors, and the need to come closer to God and to serve others.

Solanus was so focused on the sorrows of those he counseled that he would often be late for the ceremony. Bernadette Nowak was left waiting to talk to Solanus.

". . . before I could talk to him, he rose and said it was time to go to the church for the blessing. I was disappointed, but went to church. As he passed before the people kneeling, he passed before me, gently touched my cheek and said softly, 'Stop worrying now. You're going to be all right now,' or words to that effect. I had not seen him stop to talk to anyone else and was surprised. That night I had the first sound good night sleep in over a month. From then on I was better."

Many features of Solanus' ministry parallel those observed in other healers' services. Obviously, Father Solanus had received the word of knowledge concerning Ms. Nowak's problem.

Solanus used true stories of past healings to build the faith of those at the prayer service. His concept of gratitude for future favors is another characteristic of successful healing ministries. (See Oral Roberts' section) Solanus called it putting God on the spot. God has promised to give us what we ask in the name of Jesus and so when we ask, we thank Him, knowing God will live up to His Promise. Solanus' trust in the goodness of God was so great that Solanus knew when we ask that God wants to say "Yes" unless there is some drastic reason for Him not to. Strange isn't it, strange and wonderful that the loving God who created us gives to healers the same tools with which to bless us. Their hands become His Hands and their voices His Voice. God is good, all the time!

Father Solanus Casey: Skeptics

Wednesday healing services at St. Bonaventure's attracted Catholics, Protestants, Jews, and skeptics. One of the skeptics, Casimera Scott, went to the monastery for thirteen weeks "not believing that he (Solanus) could heal others."

"I saw a rabbi with his cap, long beard and heavy cane. He used to come every week, too. Now he had faith, and I was full of doubts. But when I saw him walk away *without* the use of his cane, then I believed."

A minister brought his seriously ill son to the Wednesday service every week. ". . . the minister said that he had hesitated coming in before because he didn't know whether Father Solanus would be willing to cure his son because he was not a Catholic. Father Solanus said, 'Only God can cure your son, but I will pray for him.'" Solanus always insisted that he was not the healer, God was.

Author Michael Crosby had access to the 1,300 page canonization document presented to the Vatican in 1995 on the cause for Solanus' canonization. In the testimony, Clare Ryan said she was diagnosed with cancer of the stomach. There was nothing doctors could do for her. Father Solanus blessed her and she was cured. After that Clare visited Father Solanus every two or three weeks for a year.

Clare didn't see much of him until 1941 when she came down with severe arthritis and was bedridden for nine months. Unable to get out of the car when her husband drove her to the monastery, Clare stayed in the vehicle. The priest put on his stole, got some holy water, and prayed over her in the car for about fifteen minutes. Then Solanus told Clare she would be all right.

That day, for the first time in nine months, Clare was able to walk up the stairs at home with her husband's help. Her condition improved and she could do her household chores and live a normal life. In 1984, forty-seven years later at the time of her testimony, Clare said her arthritis had begun to bother her again.

Marie O'Reilly testified to the Vatican that Dr. Kean, a dentist with staphylococcus septicemia, was not expected to live through the night. Father Solanus blessed him and told Mrs. Kean her husband would recover. The dentist was healed.

Marie O'Reilly also reported that a blind man, the father of a friend identified only as "Marion," was blessed by Solanus who prayed for the restoration of the man's sight; he regained his vision at the Consecration of the Mass.

Mrs. Martha Houlihan testified that Father Solanus healed her son James twice: once of whooping cough at the age of two weeks and then of life-threatening strep at the age of four.

Lawrence Kroha, M.D. testified that after graduating from medical school, he lay unconscious for sixteen days with a fever close to 106. "An hour after Father Solanus left me, my temperature was down to normal."

During the Depression, the Capuchin soup kitchen served up to three thousand people a day. One day Father Herman said, "'Father Solanus, we have no more bread and two or three hundred men are waiting for something to eat.'

"(Solanus) . . . told the men . . . 'Just wait and God will provide.'" He said an "Our Father" with the men in line. With that, a bakery man came in with a big basket full of food. He had a truck full and began to unload it. The men started to cry. Tears were running down their cheeks. Solanus said, 'See, God provides . . . put your confidence in God.'"

Solanus Casey: Too Many Cases to Include Here

Stories of the success of Solanus' prayers fill a number of books. A nurse, Sister Mary Joseph, while on duty at St. Joseph Mercy Hospital in Detroit in 1935, was struck down with a severe streptococcus infection of the right side of her throat. Her temperature spiked to 105 degrees and her neck became rigid.

"She began to slide into a coma with heavy choking spells." Her doctor told Sister Mary Philippa, the supervisor, the infection was spreading. He ordered preparations for a quick tracheotomy if needed. Sister Mary Philippa phoned Solanus, who came at once.

"When he entered the sick sister's room he went directly to a stand at her bedside, seemingly oblivious of others. Taking a book from his pocket, he started reading prayers slowly and quietly, though the sister was in the midst of a choking spell. Almost immediately, Sister Mary Joseph's choking stopped . . . for two hours he read and prayed, while three sisters, kneeling, joined their prayers to his. Then he closed the book and said, 'Sisters, it won't be necessary for me to return. Sister Mary Joseph will soon recover and join her community.'"

On the way out of the hospital in the company of the hospital chauffeur, Solanus met an acquaintance who requested a blessing for his wife who was recovering from a minor operation. Solanus blessed the woman and left the room.

In the hallway, out of hearing of the sick woman, Solanus told the man his wife would not recover. The chauffer witnessed the conversation.

The man was shocked. His wife's problem was a minor one. Solanus, who had the gift of prophecy, told the man to put his wife's soul in the arms of God and pray for the strength to accept his cross. The chauffer watched in the mirror as Solanus prayed all the way back to the monastery.

When the driver returned to the hospital, he rushed to see Sister Mary Philippa to find out what had happened. The man's wife had died shortly after Solanus and the driver left the hospital. Solanus had the gift and the curse of prophecy.

Father Solanus responded to people's requests in a particular pattern. Brother Ignatius Milne, who later worked with Solanus, said, "To those people for whom he gave . . . specific and detailed instructions, their problems were solved whatever they might have been. For those for whom Father merely said, 'I will pray for them,' they were not."

Marguerite Baker said, "One had a way of knowing by the way Father Solanus spoke whether he would promise a cure, or whether he just asked us to accept God's will."

Combined with the joy of witnessing healings was the pain of witnessing the lack of healing. Solanus was an instrument. He had no control over who was and was not healed. As he said over and over again, God did the healing, Solanus did the reporting.

❧

Brother Leo Wollenweber, O.F.M., Cap., *Meet Solanus Casey: Spiritual Counselor and Wonder Worker* (Ann Arbor, MI: Servant Publications, 2002), 116.

Rose Ann Palmer, Ph.D.

James Patrick Derum, *The Porter of Saint Bonaventure's: The Life of Father Solanus Casey, Capuchin* (Detroit, MI: The Fidelity Press, 1968), 26, 104-105, 112, 116.

Michael Crosby, O.F.M., Cap., *Solanus Casey: The Official Account of a Virtuous American Life* (New York, NY: The Crossroad Publishing Co., 2000), 56, 76-77, 79-85, 93, 271.

Catherine M. Odell, *Our Sunday Visitor's Father Solanus: The Story of Solanus Casey, O.F.M., Cap.,* (Huntington, IN: Our Sunday Visitor Publishing Division, 1995), 67-68, 83, 87-88, 93-94.

Padre Pio Wins Half a Golden Halo: Consiglia De Martino is Healed

A man on a galloping horse could see that Padre Pio was a saint. Pio had it all: the stigmata (wounds like Christ's that bled for years), extraordinary healings through prayer during his life, even verified reports of bilocation. However, part of the proof that one has won the golden halo of sainthood involves two miracles received through the intercession of the individual after his death. Talk about being worth more dead than alive! Miracles performed during a saint's lifetime don't count. To justify canonization, two miracles must spring from the intercession of the saint after his death. One miracle is required to be named Blessed (beatification). A second is required to be named Saint (canonization).

The high standard to which the Roman Catholic Church holds miracles used to prove the holiness of those raised to sainthood is well known (see Appendix). Healings are accepted as miraculous only after close medical scrutiny by a team of highly-qualified doctors.

The case of Consiglia De Martino of Salerno, Italy was judged to meet the medical board's rigorous standard and furthered the canonization process for Padre Pio. Mrs. De Martino, married and the mother of three children, fell ill on October 31, 1995. Despite extreme pain in her chest and stomach, "as though her insides were being torn away" Consiglia carried on her usual chores.

On November 1, the pain persisted, but she took her daughter to school anyway. Then on her way to Mass, feeling increasingly ill, Consiglia stopped in at her sister's house.

Alarmed to see a painful swelling the size of a grapefruit in Consiglia's neck, the two women rushed to Riuniti Hospital in Salerno. Two CAT scans revealed a "diffuse lymphatic spilling of approximately two liters caused by a rupture of the lymphatic canals."

Immediate surgery was advised, but Consiglia decided to wait and pray. No other treatment was given. A member of a Padre Pio prayer group, she had great devotion to the future Saint Pio and went on monthly pilgrimages to Padre Pio's tomb. From the hospital, Consiglia called San Giovanni Rotondo and spoke to Brother Modestino Fucci, a friend of Padre Pio's who had been in the monastery with him. Mrs. De Martino asked Brother Fucci to pray for her at the tomb. He rushed to the grave of Padre Pio and prayed there for Consiglia's rapid recovery. The saint had promised Brother Fucci that his requests would be heard by Pio after his death.

On November 2, the fluid deposit in her neck and the pain had both lessened. On November 3, the swelling had almost completely disappeared and an abdominal X-ray showed no evidence of the liquid. On November 6, a CAT scan confirmed the findings of the X-ray. The rupture had healed and the liquid deposits had disappeared. Consiglia was discharged in perfect health, and numerous examinations since then have proven that she had not suffered any adverse aftereffects from this illness.

On April 30, 1998, two and a half years later, the Medical Council of the Congregation for the Causes of the Saints, a committee of medical experts, judged her cure to be extraordinary and scientifically inexplicable. On May 7, 1999, the Venerable Padre Pio of Pietrelcina was beatified and proclaimed "Blessed" before a huge crowd in St. Peter's Square. The next hurdle, the second miracle, had yet to be jumped.

Padre Pio is Taken Off the Shelf: Dr.Wanda Półtawska

During Padre Pio's lifetime, books that dealt with his miracles were put on the Index of Forbidden Books or the "hell shelf," as Catholic students called it. In 1952 alone, eight books mentioning Padre Pio's miracles were banned in keeping with Canon 1399 of Canon Law.

Why? The Roman Catholic Church has a long history. They have seen a lot of tricksters. Only after an individual has been thoroughly investigated and stamped "saint" may his miracles be discussed. Ironically, after Pio's death, the banned books were used as historical sources by Church scholars proposing the saint's canonization.

Reports of healings through the intercession of Padre Pio hit the newspapers in Naples as early as June 21, 1919 when a government official was healed of a foot injury. Pasquale Di Chiara told a reporter, "I felt a strong burning sensation in my foot that soon spread throughout my body. I began to walk perfectly." The same article described Pasquale's daughter's healing from infantile paralysis. Padre Pio told her to take off her braces and she was able to walk without them from then on.

One of those convinced of Padre Pio's sanctity was the future Pope John Paul II who first met the friar in 1947. While on vacation from his theological studies in Rome, Karol Wojtyla went to confession to Pio at San Giovanni Rotondo. The Vatican has never denied the story circulating for years that Padre Pio prophesied then that the young Polish priest would become pope.

In 1962, when Karol Wojtyla, vicar of Krakow, attended the Second Vatican Council in Rome, he received a request for prayer for one of his closest friends, Dr. Wanda Półtawska. Back in Poland, Wanda was dying from a rapidly growing tumor in her throat. Doctors felt surgery would not help. A psychiatrist like her husband, Wanda was the mother of four children and a survivor of five years in a German concentration camp. She had been imprisoned by the Nazis for her promotion of a Catholic youth group for girls in Poland.

Karol Wojtyla wrote to Padre Pio asking prayer for Dr. Półtawska's healing. The letter was hand delivered immediately.

The messenger said, "As soon as I arrived at the monastery, Padre Pio told me to read the letter to him. He listened . . . to the brief message in Latin and said, 'I can't say no to that.' Then he added, 'Angelino, keep that letter on file because one day it will be important.'

"The next week I was given another letter to take to Padre Pio. This time Karol Wojtyla was informing him that Professor Półtawska had been completely healed. This miraculous event took place the day before they were going to attempt surgery on her."

Padre Pio and Matteo Colella: PlayStation in Intensive Care

The mother of little Matteo Colella sobbed as she knelt in prayer at Padre Pio's tomb. The doctors, including the child's own father, had given up hope. After working feverishly round the clock using all the technology available in 2000, physicians expected seven-year-old Matteo to die of meningitis.

In the House for the Relief of the Suffering, the hospital founded in San Giovanni Rotondo in 1956 by Padre Pio, the nurse wept as she bathed Matteo, thinking she'd be preparing him for the mortuary before the night was over.

While staff had labored frantically over a period of days to save the child, whose father worked at the hospital, everyone prayed. The mother enlisted prayer from all over Italy and even from Lourdes in France. She knew only God could save her son. Matteo's vital organs were failing, and he had fallen into an irreversible coma; death was inevitable.

Then, despite severe organ damage, the impossible happened: the child awakened and described a near-death experience which included an old bearded man in a long brown robe fitting the description of the deceased Padre Pio. The old man told Matteo not to worry, that he was going to be all right. The child was soon playing PlayStation in intensive care. The doctors declared his recovery a miracle.

There is a medical investigation instituted to examine alleged miracles: "First . . . two doctors carefully examine the miracle. Each one votes individually on the validity of the miracle. If they both agree, the miracle is then referred to a committee of five renowned doctors, who can be either believers or nonbelievers. Their task is to determine whether the miracle in question can be explained by medical science.

"If they establish that there is no logical explanation for the healing from a human or a scientific point of view, the whole matter is referred to a commission of cardinals. Their job is to determine whether the healing took place through divine intervention and through the intercession of the candidate. If they rule that it did, the case is sent to the Pope, who makes the final judgment."

Because the parents had intense, focused devotion to Padre Pio and had prayed for a cure with the whole monastery community near their home, at the tomb of Padre Pio, the healing was attributed to Padre Pio's intercession with God on Matteo's behalf. When Pope John Paul II accepted the healing as the final miracle needed to move Blessed Pio from beatification to canonization, Padre Pio became St. Pio of Pietrelcina.

Newspaper accounts of the canonization ceremony on June 16, 2002 estimated the crowd jammed into St. Peter's Square at 300,000, one of the largest gatherings in Vatican history. Large television screens provided a view of the scene in St. Peter's Square for those packed together on plazas and boulevards nearby. Hoses misted the crowd with cool water to provide relief from the 97 degree temperature. Volunteers distributed hundreds of thousands of bottles of water. Big white and yellow umbrellas shaded Cardinals near the altar.

In the crowd were Mrs. Consiglia De Martino, Dr. Wanda Półtawska, and Matteo Colella, three of many healed by God through the intercession of Padre Pio. Back at San Giovanni Rotondo, thousands of blue and yellow balloons were released as pilgrims cheered the canonization of St. Pio.

Padre Pio: *The Early Years—Pilgrimages, Bags of Chestnuts, and Lice A Poppin'*

In 1896, Padre Pio, then nine-year-old Francesco Forgione, went with his father sixteen miles by donkey from their home in Pietrelcina, Italy on a pilgrimage to the shrine of St. Pellegrino. When his father Grazio had finished praying, little Francesco pleaded with him to stay longer.

Next to Pio sat a woman holding a deformed child. She begged God to heal her son. Francesco wept and prayed with her. Finally, after a long period of weeping and praying, the woman threw the child on the altar, crying, "Why don't You want to heal him for me?"

"There was a moment of silence in the church, and then a cry of joy: the child stood up, completely healed. This event made a strong impression on little Francesco. Whenever he recalled it as an adult, tears would well up in his eyes."

In 1908, what biographers call Pio's first miracle occurred in his birthplace in Pietrelcina. Because of ill health, Pio spent most of his time studying for the priesthood at home in Pietrelcina, but in 1908 he was able to join his fellow seminarians in Montefusco, Italy.

There he collected chestnuts from trees in the forest surrounding the monastery and gave a bag of them to his Aunt Daria who lived in his hometown. She ate the nuts and saved the bag.

One day, using an oil lamp for light as she rummaged through a shed, Aunt Daria accidentally ignited gunpowder that exploded, severely burning her face. To relieve the pain, Daria wet the bag and applied it to her face. The pain disappeared and the burns left no scars.

The whole region witnessed a sensational miracle in April 1913. Lice had infested bean crops throughout the area, threatening ruin for local farmers. One of the farmers asked Padre Pio to pray in the fields.

"Padre Pio walked through his fields, praying over them and blessing them. All the while the lice fell from the beans with a popping noise. Then other people asked him to pray over their fields, and through Padre Pio's prayers, the insects were destroyed everywhere. Within a week, all the beans were free from infestation, and the harvest was particularly abundant that year."

An atheist, Freemason, and journalist from Bologna, Italy, Alberto Del Fante had written many vicious articles attacking Padre Pio throughout the years. In one, the journalist called Padre Pio, ". . . a fake . . . capable of duping people who were naïve, enthusiastic, and easy to sway."

When the journalist's grandson, Enrico, was diagnosed with a terminal illness, tuberculosis of the bones and lungs and abscesses on his kidney, his family asked Padre Pio to pray for the boy. Alberto's conversion took place when the atheist saw the child healed almost immediately right before his eyes after Padre Pio had been contacted.

Alberto Del Fante went to San Giovanni Rotondo, confessed his sins, and returned to Catholicism. Through an amazing change of heart and in thanksgiving for the miracle that saved his grandson, Alberto Del Fante wrote *Padre Pio of Pietrelcina, Herald of the Lord* describing thirty-six medically-documented miracles worked through Padre Pio prior to 1931.

Padre Pio: His Stigmata, An Embarrassment

In 1224, the sudden, mystical appearance of the wounds of Christ struck St. Francis of Assisi, the first of three hundred people to experience it. Two others lived in the twentieth century: Therese Neumann of Germany and Padre Pio, the only priest to receive the mystical wounds.

Padre Pio was deeply embarrassed by his stigmata. The first to see Pio's wounds was Father Pannullo, pastor of the church in Pietrelcina where Padre Pio spent years in study as a seminarian before continuing his education at the monastery in San Giovanni Rotondo. When Fr. Pannullo heard in 1918 that the stigmata had appeared on Pio's hands, he said, "You see them now. I saw them in 1910."

On September 7, 1910, Padre Pio had a vision while praying and received the wounds. Returning home, he told Fr. Pannullo what had happened.

"Then he added, 'Father do me a favor, ask Jesus to take them away. I want to suffer . . . but in secret.' They prayed together and God answered their prayer. The visible signs of the stigmata disappeared." [for eight more years]

In 1910, in a letter to his spiritual director, Padre Pio had said, "Yesterday evening something happened to me that I don't know how to explain or understand. In the middle of the palms of my hands red spots appeared, almost the size of a penny . . ."

In September of 1918, Pio received the visible stigmata again after Mass while praying for all the people dead and dying from war and the Spanish flu pandemic. Overcome by a deep repose and indescribable peace, he awakened to find himself bearing the wounds once more. Hoping to hide the stigmata from his fellow monks, Pio tried to stop the hemorrhaging by wrapping his hands and feet with bandages and by covering the wound in his side with handkerchiefs, but the stigmata was detected when blood dripped in the corridor.

"He prayed, ' . . . take away these signs that cause me so much embarrassment.' Jesus told him: 'You will bear them for fifty years, and then you will see me.'" Padre Pio called the wounds "these confusing things."

An avalanche of disapproval from Church officials followed. The major question: Were the wounds self-inflicted?

For fifty years, Pio was scrutinized by hostile Church officials and investigated by suspicious doctors. Physicians who examined the wounds wondered that they never festered, never became infected, and never healed.

Dr. Giorgio Festa observed the wounds while the priest was unconscious during hernia surgery. The incision from the operation healed naturally, but the stigmata wounds did not. He declared them scientifically inexplicable.

Especially interesting to Dr. Sala, who attended Padre Pio at his deathbed, was the condition of the skin after death where the stigmata had bled for fifty years. Like a baby's skin, it was unscarred and perfect, as if Padre Pio had never suffered an injury. Because Dr. Sala had described the bleeding and scabby wounds in detail for medical reports, he considered the unmarred skin more miraculous than the stigmata itself. Padre Pio died fifty years after receiving the stigmata at the age of 81 on September 23, 1968, as foretold in a vision he had years before he died.

Padre Pio: What a Neighbor!

The disabled in the area flocked to San Giovanni Rotondo. For the most part, Pio's followers could see him when he said Mass at 4 a.m. and when he heard confessions for many hours every day.

Among those healed in 1919 was sixty-two-year-old Pasquale Urbano from nearby Foggia whose disability had not been helped by medical treatment. Both his legs broke when he fell from a carriage and because they had not healed properly, Pasquale had for years used two canes for walking. During confession, Padre Pio told Pasquale, "Get up and go. But you have to throw away those canes." The crowd in the church was amazed when without canes Pasquale Urbano walked gracefully out of the confessional.

Another resident of Foggia, fourteen-year-old Antonio d'Onofrio, was healed in 1919. Stricken with typhoid at the age of four, Antonio had rickets and two large hideously deforming humps. In the confessional, Padre Pio touched the boy with his wounded hands. Antonio rose from his knees, the humps vanished, and he walked "straight as an arrow" out of the confessional.

Francesco Vicio was so deformed that he moved about on all fours with his chin almost touching the ground. A pious seventy-five-year-old, Francesco had been nicknamed "the little saint." His complete and miraculous healing caused a stir in the countryside around the monastery and beyond.

A worldly man, Emanuele Brunatto had a conversion experience through the saint, moved to San Giovanni Rotondo to live near Pio, and became a devoted and trusted friend.

While splitting logs in the monastery garden, Emanuele got a splinter in his thumb and several monks tried unsuccessfully to remove it. Then with a smile, Padre Pio pulled it out gently, painlessly, and effortlessly.

On another occasion, Emanuele had an infection in his toe. Because he couldn't walk, he rode a mule to the monastery for Sunday Mass. Much to his surprise, Padre Pio insisted that he walk home. As Emanuele walked home, the pain gradually abated and by the time he arrived at his destination, the pain had gone. When he took off the dressing, the gauze was soaked through with pus and blood, but the infection was gone and only a white scar remained. Emanuele's toe had been completely healed.

A well known Italian comedy writer, Luigi Antonelli, had cancer extending from his ear to his back. Saying that medicine at that time had not progressed far in two thousand years, Luigi quoted the old motto: "Opium et mentiri" or "Drug the patient and lie to him" as being as true for cancer patients in his era as it had been in ancient times.

He asked his doctor to tell him the truth. The doctor told him that he would live six months if operated on and just three months if not. When Luigi Antonelli decided to have the operation, someone suggested he visit Padre Pio. The saint prayed for Luigi, his cancer was arrested, and he enjoyed many more years writing newspaper articles, going hunting, and working on comedies.

Padre Pio: Tracer of Lost Persons

While World War II raged, many lost track of loved ones and sought help from Padre Pio. When Pio heard their heartrending stories, he'd weep and then a mysterious strength seemed to surge from his soul, "accompanied by a miracle."

One of the miracles benefited a relative of Cleonice Marcaldi, the aunt of the Mayor of San Giovanni Rotondo. In future years, Cleonice would be administrator of the hospital Padre Pio would found in 1956, Casa Sollievo della Sofferenza or the House for the Relief of the Suffering.

Cleonice's nephew, Giovannino, a soldier in the Italian army, was a prisoner of war. His parents had not heard from him, feared him dead, and were crazed with grief.

"One day his mother flung herself at Padre Pio's feet . . . in the confessional. 'Tell me if my son is alive,' she said. 'I won't let go of your feet until you tell me.' Padre Pio was deeply touched and with tears streaming down his face said, 'Get up and go in peace.'"

Although relieved because she knew her son was alive, the woman still had no idea where he was. A few days later, Cleonice decided to ask Padre Pio for a miracle. She told the priest she was going to write a letter to her nephew with only his name on the envelope because she had no idea where to send it. The aunt said she was leaving it up to Padre Pio and his guardian angel to get it to her nephew. Pio didn't say anything.

That night, Cleonice wrote the letter and set it on her nightstand. The next morning, the letter was gone. Sure there had been a miracle, the aunt thanked Padre Pio. He said, "Thank the Virgin Mary." Two weeks later, the nephew wrote saying he was replying to Cleonice's unaddressed letter.

Another miracle benefited a rich socialite, Luisa Vario, who, bored with life, at first sought Padre Pio out of curiosity. When she first approached the confessional, Pio told her he would hear her confession later. When her turn came, Luisa told the priest she didn't know what to say.

Padre Pio told her life's story as if reading it from a book. All her sins were described in detail except for one major sin Pio had not mentioned. The priest waited in silence. The socialite knew her confession would not be valid unless she told all. Finally Luisa gathered the courage to confess the missing sin.

"'That's the one I was waiting for,' Padre Pio said. 'You've won the victory. Don't get discouraged.'"

Luisa, half-Italian and half-British, had a son who was a British naval officer. Reading English newspapers brought by tourists to San Giovanni Rotondo, Luisa learned her son's ship had been sunk.

Certain her son was dead, Luisa Vario ran in tears to Padre Pio. The saint comforted her by telling Luisa that her son had escaped shipwreck. Then the monk gave her the exact name and address of the hotel in England where she could contact her boy.

Padre Pio: The 1950s—Healed by a Dream

Before an incurable illness changed his perspective, Savino Grieco would not permit his wife to go to Church or to teach their children about God. An atheist in Puglia, Italy, notorious for fighting religion, Savino disbelieved as strongly as his wife believed. The conflict broke his wife's heart.

Then in 1950, Savino was diagnosed with a terminal brain tumor and another tumor behind his ear. Fear of dying had overwhelmed him at the time of diagnosis. Facing death while under treatment in the hospital in Bari stirred up a powerful need to turn to God. This desire for connection with the Lord continued as Savino was moved from Bari to Milan to undergo surgery the doctors doubted would be effective.

In the hospital in Milan, Savino Grieco dreamed of Padre Pio. In his dream, Savino saw the saint touch him on the head and say reassuringly, "Watch, you'll get well with time."

Savino recovered rapidly after his healing dream of Padre Pio. However, despite the improvement in his condition, the doctors were insistent on operating. Finally, certain the operation was a mistake, the sick man fled the hospital and went to relatives in Milan just before the procedure was to take place.

However, the pain returned, worse than before, and Savino Grieco was forced to humiliate himself by returning to the hospital. Although the doctors were furious that he had fled, ethics prevailed and the staff resumed treatment. Preparations for the operation began once more.

During pre-op tests, Savino was startled by the fragrance of violets, a scent reported to announce the presence of Padre Pio. To the physicians' amazement, when the final pre-op test was given, it showed that tumors targeted for excision had disappeared on their own.

On leaving the hospital, when Savino asked for the bill, he was told he owed nothing ". . . since we didn't do anything to save you."

Savino Grieco went to San Giovanni Rotondo to thank Padre Pio for his prayers. When the grateful man arrived, the pain returned with such force that he fainted. Two men carried him to the priest's confessional. When he regained consciousness, Savino said to Padre Pio, "I have five children and I'm very sick. Save me, Father, save my life."

"'I'm not God,' he answered, 'nor am I Jesus Christ. I'm a priest like any other priest, not more and perhaps even less. I don't perform miracles.'

"Crying, I implored him, 'Please, Father, save me.'

"Padre Pio remained silent for a while. He lifted his eyes toward heaven, and I noted that his lips were moving in prayer. At this point I once again smelled an intense fragrance of violets. Padre Pio told me, 'Go home and pray. I'll pray for you. You'll get well.' I went home and since then every symptom of the illness has disappeared.'" [He was symptom-free for fifty years.]

Padre Pio: A Cure for the Incurable—Giuseppe Canaponi Testifies Thirty-Five Years Later

Doctors had tried unsuccessfully to heal Giuseppe Canaponi's leg, damaged when a truck hit his motorcycle as he headed for work in 1945.

Fruitlessly searching for medical help in Italy, Giuseppe went from hospital to hospital: to Sarteano, Chiusi, and Montepulciano.

In Siena, Dr. Leopoldo Giuntini at the Orthopedic Clinic treated Giuseppe for a year and a half. Finally, in Bologna at Rizzoli Hospital, after the first few operations, Giuseppe's leg was partially repaired, but it remained rigid and the wounds never did heal.

Doctors at the Orthopedic Clinic in Siena decided to forcibly flex the knee using a Zuppinger device. Surgeons hoped for the added benefit of general anesthesia as a relaxant during the procedure to improve the flexibility of Giuseppe's knee. Tragically, the femur broke again during the procedure. Dr. Giuntini declared Giuseppe incurable on his discharge from the Orthopedic Clinic in Siena. "I was going to have a stiff leg for the rest of my life," Giuseppe said.

Thirty-five-year-old Giuseppe was unwilling to accept this. Back at Rizzoli Hospital in Bologna, doctors agreed to attempt another operation which might or might not result in partial improvement. Giuseppe decided against it.

Raging and suicidal, he took his anger out on his wife. Crutches were useless because his stiff leg had open wounds and was painful. When he tried to walk alone, he'd fall, scream and curse. Giuseppe, a nonbeliever, scoffed at his wife for attending Church. He'd curse and she'd cry. When she told her husband about Padre Pio, Giuseppe laughed and cursed the saint. Despite this, Mrs. Canaponi wrote to Padre Pio. Finally, when dramatically failing health brought the prospect of imminent death, Giuseppe agreed out of desperation to go to see the saint.

In December 1948, despite terrible pain, Giuseppe lay on a stretcher for the train ride to Foggia where they were to change to the bus for San Giovanni Rotondo the next morning. After the bus trip the next day and a walk on unpaved roads to the church, Guiseppe lay on a bench in the church half conscious from exhaustion. From where he lay, he could see Padre Pio in his confessional. Padre Pio stared at Giuseppe and his body began to shake as though he had been given a powerful electric shock.

At 4 p.m., Giuseppe and his son went on line to go to confession. Propping himself on his crutches, Giuseppe struggled up to Padre Pio. The priest told Giuseppe his whole life's story, as if Pio had lived with him for years. Speaking softly and not scolding, the priest helped Giuseppe see how ridiculous his behavior had been. Giuseppe was so enthralled that he forgot about his leg.

When the friar raised his hand to give absolution, Giuseppe's body shook again as if he'd been struck by lightning. He knelt, made the sign of the cross, got up, took his crutches in his hands, and walked away unaware of the healing.

"'Guiseppe, you're walking!' his wife said. The Canaponis wept with joy: Guiseppe's knee flexed painlessly and his wounds had healed. When thanked the next day, Padre Pio said, 'I didn't do the miracle. I only prayed for you. The Lord healed you.'"

Padre Pio and Gemma di Giorgi: School Closed—No Pupils

Gemma di Giorgi was born without pupils on Christmas day in 1939 in Ribera, Sicily.

"When I was three months old, (my mother) . . . began to suspect that I would not be able to see . . . a doctor in Ribera, unable to determine the gravity of my condition . . . had her (Gemma's mother) take me to Palermo to ophthalmologists named Dr. Cucco and Dr. Contino. They said that I was blind because I didn't have any pupils.

"My family was desperate . . . My parents told me that they often took me in front of Mary's altar in the church because it would take a miracle to heal my eyes."

One day in 1946, when Gemma was about seven, a religious sister advised Gemma's parents to seek out Padre Pio. Gemma's grandmother asked the nun to write Padre Pio requesting prayers for the little girl. One night after sending the letter, the nun saw Pio in a dream.

"Padre Pio asked her, 'Where is this Gemma for whom so many prayers are being offered that they are almost deafening?' Still dreaming, she introduced me (Gemma) to him. Padre Pio made the sign of the cross on my eyes and disappeared. The next day this nun received a letter from Padre Pio in which he wrote: 'Dear daughter, I assure you that I prayed for the child. I send you my best wishes.'"

Struck by the coincidental arrival of the letter the day after the dream, the sister urged the di Giorgis to go at once to San Giovanni Rotondo. Although travel was difficult because it was just after World War II, the family left the same day with some other people from their area. Gemma reported that she could see something as the train followed the tracks by the seaside. Her grandmother didn't believe her because Gemma's eyes had no pupils.

In San Giovanni Rotondo, Gemma made her first confession to Padre Pio. Her grandmother told her to ask for healing. The child forgot, but Padre Pio touched her eyes with the wounded part of his hand and traced the sign of the cross.

Crying because the child had forgotten to ask for a cure, her grandmother waited all day to go to confession to Padre Pio and ask a blessing for Gemma. "Have faith, my daughter," Padre Pio told her, "The child shouldn't cry, and neither should you be worried. Gemma sees and you know it."

When Gemma received her First Communion from Padre Pio, he traced a second sign of the cross on her eyes.

On the train ride home, Gemma thought the shadows she'd seen during the earlier train trip had become clearer. In Cosenza, her grandmother asked the hospital eye specialist to examine Gemma. He said, "There's no explanation for this. Without pupils, a person should not be able to see. I don't understand why this child sees."

Four months later, Dr. Caramazza in Perugia examined Gemma's eyes carefully and declared vision impossible, but Gemma's sight got better and better. She went to school, learned to read and write, and grew up living a normal life in Ribera. In addition to traveling around the world telling her story, Gemma has been featured in a documentary film about doing the impossible: Eye doctors still insist a woman without pupils can't see.

Padre Pio: Dead But Still Working—Alice Jones

In 1973, five years after Padre Pio's death, an accident left Mrs. Alice Jones, an English Protestant elementary school teacher, in piercing pain throughout her body. Rest was prescribed, but her condition worsened. At Broadgreen Hospital in Liverpool, England in 1974, doctors detected spinal deformity and a tumor causing paralysis in her left leg.

Several years later at St. Helens Hospital, doctors inserted steel supports in her spinal column. Confined to bed for twelve months with a cast on her arms and chest, she was unable to bend her body. A lift moved her every four hours so that nurses could change her position. Despite all this care, the operation was a failure.

Worse than ever, Alice walked (when she could bear the pain) using a brace. An orthopedic shoe with a spring moved her foot back to its normal position. A steel brace supported her chest and she used two crutches. In indescribable pain, Alice huddled on the floor all day fearful of breathing because motion triggered excruciating back spasms. Unable to move and unwilling to be carried, Alice Jones was borderline suicidal, trying to kill the pain with tranquilizers and whiskey. Alice lost her faith and could no longer pray.

An Anglican priest, Reverend Eric Fisher, visited her on May 27, 1980. Embittered by seven years of paralysis, Alice poured out her anger and confided her decision to commit suicide.

When Reverend Fisher laid hands on her back, Mrs. Jones felt tingling warmth that remained all night. Leslie Jones, Alice's daughter, noticed a fragrance of violets in the room after the priest left, but Alice didn't smell anything.

The next day at 11 a.m., Reverend Fisher returned to tell Alice he had been assured in prayer that she'd be healed.

"He said: 'Take off the brace on your leg and throw it away.' I felt my paralyzed leg, and I felt a piercing pain . . . as if my leg was pierced by a hot iron. With much difficulty, I got up off the floor and sat in a chair. Reverend Fisher insisted, 'Try to walk.'"

"Suddenly Alice saw superimposed on his face the image of an old man with a beard, dressed like a monk. The old man talked to her in a foreign language, but she understood. He said, 'Jesus, Jesus.' Then he lifted up his hand and added in a whisper, 'Your foot is strong now and your leg is healed. Get up and walk.'

"I hesitated. For seven years I hadn't taken a step without any help. The old monk insisted . . . 'In the name of Jesus, walk!' I followed his orders, and without any help I walked across the room. The monk disappeared. Her daughter and son-in-law didn't see the monk, but they noticed a strong fragrance in the air, which Alice couldn't detect. All pain disappeared. Reverend Fisher blessed her and left saying, 'Now you no longer need me.'"

Alice stood a while in shock, then put on an old pair of high heels and danced around the house with her grandson in her arms. Later, when Reverend Fisher, a follower of Padre Pio, gave her a holy card picturing the saint, Alice recognized him from her vision.

On August 9, 1980, Alice Jones had X-rays taken on the advice of Dr. Francis Mooney, a fervent Catholic and a famous pathologist. They showed no change in her deformed backbone, yet she is pain-free and functions as if healed.

Padre Pio: Getting God's Opinion

The Church wants God's opinion in the canonization process and requires two posthumous miracles attributable to the intercession of the candidate as a sign of God's approval. In the process of selecting two, an overwhelming number of miracle stories are accumulated and some are filed at San Giovanni Rotondo.

From Cuneo, Italy, a mother described her son Mauro's healing. Diagnosed with a tumor a couple of years earlier, Mauro went from hospital to hospital seeking help. All the specialists said there was no hope. Desperate, the family asked the intercession of Padre Pio. The mother vowed she would go on a pilgrimage with Mauro to San Giovanni Rotondo if the boy were healed. Medical tests showed the tumor had vanished.

From Boscoreale, Naples, Antonio Carotenuto writes: "On May 17 (no year given), I came down with a form of paralysis that left me immobile for five months. It was the result of a hernia to a disk in my back. I was admitted several times to the hospital and finally Dr. Giuseppe Giuda told me that I needed to have surgery right away. Before the operation, I prayed to Padre Pio. The night before the operation,

I had a dream. I saw Padre Pio smiling at me. He reached out to me with his hand and said, 'Don't be afraid. Nothing's wrong with you. You're fine.'

"I woke up crying with joy. Nurses from the hospital came running to my room. I told them what had happened. In the morning the doctor examined me before operating and discovered I was healed. The hernia to my disk had disappeared."

From Turin, Mrs. Giuseppina Sireci Chimento writes: "One morning in October of 1980, after having suffered from indescribable pain in my right hand because of a form of arthritis, I turned to Padre Pio and asked him to take away the pain. Nothing happened. That night I went to bed and forgot about my prayer. Contrary to how I usually slept, that night I slept fine. In the morning, I didn't have any pain. The fingers on my hand have become normal, and I can move them perfectly."

"On October 23, 1968, Giuseppe Scatigna from Palermo underwent surgery to remove a lymphoglandular tumor in his abdomen. The pathology report was not very hopeful. The patient prayed to Padre Pio. On November 8 he was admitted to the House for the Relief of the Suffering for a checkup, and there was no sign of the disease. He was discharged."

Although these healings may have been medically documented, the healings described in letters of personal testimony sent in to San Giovanni Rotondo may or may not be medically verifiable. The postulators choose some to follow up for verification. They do not have staff or resources to follow up on the overwhelming volume of testimony to the generous overflowing of the healing power of God.

Padre Pio in Texas: Tony John Colette

Diagnosed in 1969 in Houston, Texas with an incurable disease so rare that his case was written up in a medical journal, Tony John

Colette's muscular nervous system was being eaten away and as a result he had pain throughout his whole body.

Twenty years old at the time of diagnosis, Tony spent his young adulthood having surgeries and being subjected to medical tests as part of research projects. He was able to walk on crutches with great difficulty, helped by metal supports for his back and braces on his lower limbs.

Treated at St. Joseph Hospital for a long period of time, Tony was discharged in 1973 with the devastating news that doctors had done all they could do for him. There was no hope of a cure.

Early one morning, in terrible pain, Tony was startled when a man walked into the room. Devoted to Padre Pio, Tony recognized the person smiling at him as the deceased saint.

The apparition said, "I want to help you. Don't be afraid." While Padre Pio watched, Tony's whole body shuddered. Indescribable peace replaced the pain. After a few minutes, Padre Pio left. Completely relaxed and peaceful, Tony dozed off.

The next morning, Tony surprised the doctors at St. Joseph Hospital by walking in quickly, painlessly, and easily without the metal paraphernalia of braces and crutches.

*   *   *

Bedridden for thirty-three years, Antonio Paladino had been completely paralyzed as a result of an accident at work. After the death of Padre Pio, on the night of December 12, 1968, Antonio felt someone touch him on his left shoulder. He saw an apparition of Padre Pio. The saint said, "Get up and walk." Antonio Paladino was healed: he got out of bed for the first time in thirty-three years and walked.

Father Gerardo Di Flumeri, who was the vice-postulator for the cause of Padre Pio's beatification, said, "I can continue reading for hours . . . All the letters are like this, full of mysterious events and healing that cannot be explained."

&

Renzo Allegri, *Padre Pio: Man of Hope* (Ann Arbor, MI: Servant Publications, 2000), 13-14, 36, 42, 44, 71-72, 104, 163-164, 166, 171-176, 180-181, 183, 187, 243, 257-265, 267-268.

Sister Francis Clare: Is It Okay to Heal VD?

The Federal Correctional Institution in Milan, Michigan was an unlikely setting for an eruption of Pentecostal power, but in July 1972, the chaplain, Father Granger, asked Sister Francis Clare, S.S.N.D. (School Sisters of Notre Dame) to ignite that power every week at the prisoners' Saturday afternoon prayer meeting. Such a task is challenging anywhere, but especially at the Milan Prison that housed 650 men, ages 18 to 28, incarcerated for crimes ranging from smuggling heroin to murder.

Every Friday night, Sister Francis Clare and her colleague, Sister Lucienne, prepared by spending several hours praising God for what He would do the next day, binding the powers of darkness, and waiting for God's direction.

Sister Clare says, "I can't recall one prisoner we prayed for whom God did not physically heal or set free emotionally or spiritually."

God had told her, "Your only problem will be to believe what I am ready to do or to get in My way by claiming any of the glory."

The Sisters sought to be the hands and feet of Jesus.

The only time immediate healing (a miracle) did not take place was when unforgiveness on the part of the one seeking healing delayed God's work. Once the prisoner worked through the process of forgiving, Sister says she cannot recall anyone who was not completely healed. There were even proxy healings: A prisoner whose twin brother had a brain tumor stood in as proxy as they prayed for the brother's healing. The twin was healed the same day.

As healings occurred, the good news spread. More and more men came to the Saturday meetings. Sister regrets not having a camera to take before-and-after pictures of the men aglow with the Spirit.

The Sisters were quite uneasy approaching the prison the first time. On the way to the parking lot, they heard a voice boom from the watchtower, "What's your business?"

"' . . . We bring the good news.'

"'Any alcoholic beverages? Ammunition? Cameras? . . . Weapons? Explosives?'

"Later when the Sisters felt more at ease, they would reply, 'Nothing explosive, but the Love of God.'"

A prisoner scheduled for surgery for torn ligaments in his knees asked for prayer. As the Sisters prayed, vibrating heat poured from their hands into his knees. Doctors confirmed he no longer needed surgery. He had been healed.

A man with VD (venereal disease) too advanced for medical help asked for prayer. Sister hesitated at first, thinking it might not be right to pray for VD, then chided herself for being uncharitable. They prayed. Doctors confirmed the impossible: the prisoner had been healed.

* * *

"Give to the Lord glory and praise. Give to the Lord the glory due his name . . . The voice of the Lord is over the waters, the God of glory thunders . . . The voice of the Lord is mighty . . . in his temple all say, 'Glory!'" (Psalm 29)

Sister Francis Clare: Double Play

In 1972, Srs. Francis Clare, Lucienne, and Marge went to the Milan Federal Correctional Institution every Saturday afternoon. The sisters would begin the service in the chapel asking if any of the prisoners wanted prayers.

Dave, a twenty-three-year-old who had been in and out of prison since he was thirteen, asked for prayer to stop the hatred that drove him back into prison every time he was released. The prisoner also needed prayer for an ulcer for which he needed an entire bottle of Maalox daily despite following a bland diet. Medical records showed recent transfusions of seventeen pints of blood. The doctor had told Dave that morning that his stomach was one ulcerated mess and nothing more could be done by doctors. He'd have to learn to live with it.

Quoting one healing Scripture after another, without hesitation the three Sisters took on the double challenge of hate and ulcer.

"God is bigger than any hate and God is bigger than any ulcer! God is in the miracle business and so let's ask Him for a double right now!"

Three Sisters and twenty prisoners joined hands and prayed. First, they told Jesus they knew he was present as Healer. They praised and thanked Him for His great love for all and especially for Dave. In the power of Jesus' Name, they came against hate in Dave. They claimed an anointing of Jesus' Love to fill in places where hatred existed. Then they thanked Jesus for doing what they asked.

For a few minutes, they prayed spontaneously in English and in tongues, sensing God's Presence. Then they claimed healing for Dave's ulcer.

"Jesus, You are not only the Savior of our souls but the Healer of our bodies. We claim Your healing love and your healing light to enter Dave's body right now to destroy that ulcer. Touch him, Lord, with the fullness of Your resurrection power in every cell of his body, destroy all that needs to be destroyed, and recreate all that needs to be recreated.

We believe Your word that says: 'Where two or three are gathered and you ask for anything in My Name, it will be done.' We have asked in Your Name and we thank you that it is done. We accept this healing in whatever way you are giving it for the glory of the Father. Amen."

Their prayers were usually like this, just believing the power of God's word. Later that day, Sister prayed with Dave to accept Jesus as his Savior, and for inner healing of what led to his hate and the ulcer.

The following Saturday, Dave was radiant. The hate and the ulcer were both gone. And he couldn't stop praising God.

"The doctor had told me I would never again eat any pizza or any spicy food. I eat it every day with no effect on my stomach. I was taking a bottle of medicine a day, and since I was prayed over, I don't have to take any medicine . . . He has taken away my crime thoughts and restored my mind with love and kindness . . . I talk to God every day and he also talks to me. God helps me with my work and many other things. I thank God every day for what He has done for me. As it has happened to me, it will also happen to you if you will turn your life over to God. My friends, it is so great!"

Sister Francis Clare: Cathecostal

When asked if she were a Catholic or a Pentecostal, Sister Francis Clare responded, "I'm a Cathecostal!"

Filled with the Cathecostal's awe at the might and mercy of God, Sister witnessed healing after healing at the prison.

On Saturdays at the prayer meeting where Sister says all were healed, "God proved himself the Divine Chiropractor."

"Adjustments were made in seconds."

One of the prisoners' legs was 1 to 1½ inches longer than the other. The fellows seeking an adjustment would sit down and extend their legs into another's palms, then "Praise a bit and claim a bit."

Another prisoner had his eyes closed. As the group prayed, they watched his shorter leg lengthen. The prisoner opened his eyes and called out, "Hey, you're pulling my leg." But there was no one touching him, only Jesus.

After one prisoner was healed, Sister Francis and Sister Lucienne would have the one healed pray for the healing of the next one seeking healing. One man said, "But I ain't never said a prayer out loud in my life." Sister told him to say whatever came into his heart.

"Lord, what you did for me, you can do for my brother," the prisoner said. They all stared in awe as the other man's shorter leg shot out an inch to equal the length of the other.

The head of the prison's AA unit had been arrested for drunkenness seventy times in seven years. A charming man, Bob heard that God had healed his friend Dave's ulcer and asked prayer for the healing of his own ulcer.

As they prayed in the prison chapel, Bob felt gentle warmth, then burning heat penetrating the area of the ulcer. The doctor confirmed that Bob's ulcer had been completely healed. Then Bob asked to know Jesus as his Baptizer in the Holy Spirit. Sister suggested he spend time increasing his hunger for the gift. Then the group prayed for the healing of all memories and circumstances that had made him an alcoholic.

Finally, they prayed for his Baptism in the Holy Spirit. God poured in the fullness of His love. Reeling under a heavy anointing, Bob enjoyed a new form of drunkenness. At the next AA meeting, he was "literally catapulted" off his chair with a new boldness to give witness to what God had done.

*　*　*

Sister elaborates on King David's prayer, "I give thee thanks for I am fearfully, wonderfully made" (Psalm 139) by adding today's scientific facts: 60,000 billion living cells each contain the DNA blueprint for our entire body. Our 10 million brain cells are as complicated as any computer. Two thousand gallons of blood are "pumped through 60,000 miles of blood vessels daily by a heart the size of a fist."

"He who created us can recreate any part of our mind, body, or spirit freely out of love . . . He speaks to us as a most loving Father. He awaits our prayer of surrender. It's Your move, God!"

Sister Francis Clare: Wow, God (American Idiom for "Hallelujah")

There has to be something more. Sister Briege McKenna said it and Sister Francis Clare of the School Sisters of Notre Dame felt it. Like Sister Briege, Sister Francis Clare knew it would never be with "them," Catholic Pentecostals, a weird bunch.

Years before the Charismatic renewal in the Catholic Church, on the night before taking her final vows, Sister Francis Clare had a transforming spiritual experience that filled her with constant joy for the next twenty-five years. Then it vanished.

Feeling empty, Sister decided to leave religious life. Bored while waiting out her promise to stick it out until Christmas, Sister went to a talk on Catholic Pentecostals led by nuns. After the talk, Sister railed on and on against the movement, "I can't believe . . . the . . . things you were talking about can really happen."

The other nuns gave Sister a copy of the *The Cross and the Switchblade* by David Wilkerson and *They Speak with Other Tongues* by John Sherrill. Sister Francis tossed the books on the shelf unread.

One night, bored with God, Sister began *The Cross and the Switchblade*. It made her furious. "Here was . . . Nicky Cruz . . . who had broken all fifteen of the Ten Commandments, in a relationship closer to God than I was."

Sister prayed, "This isn't fair. Here I have been a nun for twenty-five years, and whatever You've done for Nicky Cruz, You've never done for me! . . . Father, I want it. I want what that gangster's got."

One of the other nuns warned her not to make her doldrums worse with "this Pentecostal thing." Sister ignored her, took the plunge, and attended an inter-faith Charismatic prayer meeting.

Some things Sister liked, some things she didn't like. Then she went to an inter-faith Charismatic weekend. When Sister first heard tongues, she thought, "Weirdo! I can't buy that!"

Then Francis Clare started thinking about having sung in Latin for years without really understanding. All Sister had known was she was praising God, like speaking in tongues. Conflicted, Francis Clare told God she would not go back to Charismatic meetings until He spoke to her about it and spoke clearly. To get a message from God, Sister "cut the book," not knowing people did that, opening the Bible at random to Luke, "Stay in Jerusalem until you are endued with power from on High." (Luke 24:29)

All Sister could say was, "Lord, You do speak clearly!" Intense fear of Baptism in the Holy Spirit lifted as she heard others at the meeting sharing the same feelings. Everyone had moved first toward and then away from the experience.

The group described how their lives had been changed since: Scriptures came alive, the incredible love and Presence of God filled them. The desire to praise God was constant, chains of the past dropped off.

As Sister listened, she heard them describing what had happened to her the night before she took her final vows. ". . . that experience of a mighty outpouring of light, Grace and glory . . . that feeling that had left her so 'happy.' That incredible walk in light, love, Presence and power prior to the dark night . . . This was that." Sister Francis Clare realized she had been baptized in the Holy Spirit twenty-five years before. Now Sister had a name for the glory she missed so desperately.

Sister Francis Clare: Nun-Catholic Rediscovers Fire

Sister Francis Clare had it again. The joy of twenty-five years returned multiplied many times over. Sister was once more, this time knowingly, baptized in the Holy Spirit.

Fall of 1969, Sister's three months' hunger was satisfied: Filled again with glory, Sister knew she stood under a cloud constantly baptizing her in the Holy Spirit.

"I knew only light-joy-Presence. The Lord spoke through Isaiah 60, 'Arise, shine; for your light has come, and the glory of the Lord has risen upon you . . . you will have the Lord for an everlasting light.'"

"In Jesus, in the Word, in the new Pentecost, I had rediscovered 'Fire.'"

The change in Sister was evident to everyone around her. She was a nun on fire. One of the things God said to her was, "I have given you my gift of evangelism to go forth to spread My word and to think not of what you will say for I will give you the words . . ."

God told her to write a job description using the Bible and the 1970 Acts of the School Sisters of Notre Dame. Not really sure it was what God wanted, Sister wrote words that made her cringe and made her Superior gasp: "Traveling with an inter-faith team across the United States in a 'revival USA' program."

Sister's Superior suggested Sister leave the convent. Crushed, Francis Clare turned to prayer with another Spirit-filled nun. Sister Ethel gave a word of prophecy, "Do not be shook. In a few days, I will give you more light . . . do not weep . . ."

Sure enough, in a few days Bishop Waters responded positively. Sister Francis Clare left high school English teaching for full-time work in the Charismatic renewal.

At a house of prayer experience center in Goshen, New York, Shelley Cohen, Jewish pianist for the *Tonight Show*, shared his testimony. A newly-converted Catholic Charismatic, he and his wife were having lunch with Sister Francis Clare. The couple were leaving Goshen to evangelize friends, but both had severe headaches that nothing seemed to help.

"'Do you know that Jesus could lift that?' I asked.

"'You've got to be kidding.'

"'No, really it is very simple for Jesus to take away the pain' . . . (we) lifted our minds to the Lord. I rested my hand on Shelley's head, asked Jesus to take the pain, and the pain was lifted!

"'Incredible! Wow! What a God we serve!' Shelley rejoiced.

"'To show you that I had nothing to do with it, Shelley, you rest your hand on your wife's head and ask The Lord to take her pain.' He did. And God did."

* * *

One day God gave Sister a blank page as a message. "That is the way I want you to come before me every day—like a blank page. And when you stop writing on it what you want Me to do with your life then I will indeed be Lord of your life."

Sister Francis Clare: ". . . Think not what you will say for I will give you the words"

Scary under any circumstances, these words from God terrified Sister Francis Clare before she gave a nun's witness to non-Catholics at the International Assembly of God conference in Chicago, Illinois.

The Sister in charge insisted on an outline, so Francis Clare prepared one. But on the day of the talk, Sister threw it away. All Francis Clare could remember was another prophetic word, "You have given Me your heart; now give Me your mind."

Sister stood before the International Assembly of ministers without an organized thought in her head. Through the hour and a half talk, two leaders of the conference wept, Drs. Quanabusch and Rasmussen, realizing God was pouring out His Spirit on a Church they had studied only as "the whore of Babylon," the Roman Catholic Church.

From Sister's talk came invitations for evangelism around the world, her heart's desire. But discernment of the team said Sister should live for a time in the Word of God community in Ann Arbor, Michigan.

Not in the least interested, nonetheless Sister Francis Clare obeyed the Will of God and spent nineteen months there in what she calls the most Abrahamic thing she had been asked to do and not do.

Father Bob sensed God wanted him to pray with Sister Francis Clare for a special anointing for a ministry of healing. "No sooner did Bob rest his hand on my head with a prayer of anointing when God's power shot through me as if I were a lightning rod. I couldn't deny that there was something there that had not been present before!"

But Sister was worried. What if it didn't work?

"'Don't be silly. You don't heal, the Lord does,' Bob said.

"'How will I know when to pray with people?'

"'Whenever you see anyone suffering, if the Lord moves you or they ask, just reach out in love as Jesus did.'

"And all I needed do was . . . pray a bit, believe a bit, and praise a lot."

Sister Francis Clare's first workout came that day. On their way into St. Mary's Convent, Sister Francis and another nun ran into a little old crippled nun. When Francis Clare saw the old nun's hands, she panicked.

"'Oh Lord! You wouldn't be expecting me to pray for her!' It was just a thought. I tried to drown it out."

We chatted. Finally Sister Francis Clare got up the courage to say, "Sister, you really have arthritis haven't you?" The little old nun said the doctors couldn't do a thing but give her more pills.

"'Would you believe Jesus could heal you?' I volunteered almost apologetically.

"'. . . If He wanted to.'

"'Would you believe He would do it right now if we prayed for you?'

"'Why yes. He could. Do pray for me.'

"'God, You poured it in. Now pour it out.' That was all I said. I felt the surge of God's power pour forth from my hands to the gnarled, twisted, arthritic hands of the old Sister I was praying with, and those buckled joints unbuckled, the fingers straightened, and the hands became as soft as a baby's."

Sister calls this the ". . . first of the signs given by Jesus in the convent of St. Mary's at Notre Dame in Indiana, to let His glory be seen, and His Sisters believed in Him."

Sister Francis Clare: Holy Rollers—More Healings

A week later, rolling along on the Greyhound bus to Chicago, Sister Francis Clare sat next to an elderly lady who was unable to make conversation. An operation had left her deaf in one ear. Through lip reading and head turning, the old lady finally understood Sister when asked, "Do you believe that Jesus could heal you?"

"'Yes, He could.'

"'Right now?'

"'Yes. Right now.'"

They prayed and as the bus rolled down the mountain slopes of West Virginia, "I reached over to put my hand on her ear. It was as if a gentle bolt of 'healing vibes' shot through the deafened ear. Between the two of us, the rest of that trip was one jolly Greyhound prayer meeting."

Despite the healing of arthritis in the convent at Notre Dame and this healing on the Greyhound, in the next year there were many times Sister was chicken about attempting healing, even though at other times she saw healing after healing.

There were also times when Sister prayed for healing and nothing happened. At first she was upset when this happened, but then Francis Clare learned to simply respond with compassion, pray the prayer of faith, and let go.

At the House of Prayer in Goshen, while cooking for eighty Sisters, Sister Francis Clare was face to face with a gas broiler that was not lighting. The gas exploded, spitting a ball of fire on her face, head, and hair.

Through excruciating burning pain on her face and right hand, Sister began praising the Lord. She apologized to the ambulance driver for praising out loud in tongues all the way to emergency. Then the nun apologized as she prayed in tongues in front of the doctor. As Francis Clare lay agonizing on the table praising in tongues, the doctor thought her a foreigner praying in her own language.

Released from the hospital with pain prescriptions, Francis Clare went back to the prayer community to suffer. One look in the mirror told Sister she'd be out of commission for a long time. A group gathered in her room to help her in her agony.

Quoting, "They will lay their hands upon the sick and they will recover," Sister Francis Clare asked those gathered to pray that she believe God would heal her. They began praying, "More out of pity than belief."

Suddenly Sister realized the pain was gone. She was healed. Francis Clare threw away the pain prescriptions! Her face was still a mess, but in the next few days, two or three layers of skin peeled "very gently." Several days later, to the doctor's amazement (and everyone else's), Sister Francis Clare had new skin and no scars at all.

* * *

"Sometimes your love for Me fades; sometimes your love for Me is doubtful. My love for you is not that way. My love for you is constant. Even when you are asleep I am loving you . . . I am always mightily in love with you."

Sister Francis Clare: Five Days to Healing—Divine Tutoring

The amazing healing of Sister Francis Clare's burns made Sister Francis and two other nuns (one a nurse from Hong Kong) hungry for more learning about healing. They asked Father Ferry for instruction. The priest refused. Instead, Father Ferry suggested the four of them go to the Source by praying together, hands resting on the Bible for half an hour a day. (What God said to them as prophetic words begins each chapter of *Wow, God*.)

A few days into their healing lessons, God sent "lab work," a paralytic Sister of Charity whose left arm and the left side of her face were paralyzed. The group prayed with her five times.

"The first day we saw no signs but we believed for God's timing, for God's way. The second day we saw no signs but we were thankful for what God was doing. The third day Sister encouraged, 'People say I'm looking different.'

"The fourth day we said, 'Margaret, you are looking different.'

"The fifth, the paralysis was completely gone."

What Sister learned helped her as she prayed Saturdays for healing of inmates at the prison in Milan, Michigan. In prison, Mike was the head of a gang of seventy-five. Even in prison he was outstanding in toughness. He wanted Jesus in his life. His eyes shone; his skin glowed. It was his twin whose brain tumor was healed by proxy.

Inner healings matched and sometimes exceeded physical healings. Willie Norman was due to be released in a month. He wanted to go to church to attend Mass. Men about to be released could go on a field trip of this sort. The sisters sponsored him. During his seven-hour leave, he went to the 1 p.m. Mass.

A professional ball player, the inmate had been adopted because his natural parents were blind. He wanted to get rid of all that hurt. Willie told the sisters all his life he'd wondered about people knowing Jesus. Sister told him today he would know he knew Jesus. The nuns told him how to ask for Baptism in the Holy Spirit.

"'I'm clean,' he shouted."

"The sisters prayed for his inner healing. 'It's like a volcano erupting in my insides.'"

"They returned a new Willie to the prison. Sister told him, 'He who began a good work in you will protect it.'"

"Willie was a win."

* * *

"I know that you have been busy about My work. Now you must rest for a while. I would speak to you in silence: you must learn to listen to Me in silence. I can be a God of thunder but my preference is gentleness. I want to speak to you in quiet. I want to train your ear to listen to Me in silence."

Sister Francis Clare: Converting the Nuns

Sister Francis Clare sees a great divide between Charismatic and non-Charismatic religious in the Roman Catholic Church. For some time, Francis Clare was the only Sister in her convent of forty who had been baptized in the Holy Spirit. Some of the healings Sister has witnessed in convents she feels were intended to testify to the non-Charismatic Sisters the healing power of God at work today.

Francis Clare quotes the testimony of an American nun who fell from a horse at the age of six, injuring her back.

"When I came to this retreat my back was like an S. Now it is straight as an arrow! And that isn't all . . . I knew when you prayed . . . something happened for I felt a penetrating heat. But when Sister Marie and I were kneeling in the back of the chapel after the prayer we both actually heard a clicking of the bones. There was no denying the sound. Click! Click! Click! All through that first night every time either of us awakened there was this audible clicking of vertebrae telling us God was doing a miracle.

"The next morning was the first time in forty years I was able to bend from the waist down . . . Every chiropractor I have gone to had the same story. 'Sister your back is like an S.' Now they all have the same comparison—straight as an arrow! Praise God!"

In one percent Catholic Sweden, at a convent in Göteborg housing School Sisters of Notre Dame (nuns from Sister Francis Clare's own order), after a day of Charismatic sharing, Sister asked if the nuns would like to pray for physical healing.

"'Physical healing, nothing, I would like this baptism of the Holy Spirit.'

"'No need to make a choice, you can have both.'"

All nine Sisters experienced the baptism of the Holy Spirit and all nine Sisters were healed of some physical complaint.

Father Woodford, a local American priest, said that when Francis Clare's prayer group insisted on praying for his phlebitis, he almost rebelled, thinking with all the suffering in the world he should be able to suffer this lesser affliction. As the priest was driving home, the Lord asked did Father Woodford think healing phlebitis would lessen God's power so He wouldn't have enough power left over to heal the rest of the world?

Sister Francis Clare says we were saved 2,000 years ago and we were also healed 2,000 years ago. "The day we claim salvation, it is ours. And the day we claim healing it is ours." She feels God hasn't worked frequent miracles all these hundreds of years because of our unbelief.

* * *

"Give glory to My Name and extol My Wonders. Every day of your life give glory to My Name and thanks to your God for the mighty deeds He has wrought. Look about you and see Me in every good thing. Look about you and see where I am not and put Me there."

Sister Francis Clare: Boy Sees Through Glass Eye

In a fire-cracker accident in 1969, Dave Pelletier lost the sight in one of his eyes. Healed through a miracle, "Today he not only sees with

20/20 tunnel vision through his glass eye, but he also reads through the empty socket."

Sister and thousands of others, including twelve ophthalmologists, ten American and two Swedish, have witnessed the validity of this miracle. In front of a large international gathering in Sweden, with the good eye covered, David opened Sister's Bible at random and read through his glass eye.

Then the miracle boy opened the Scriptures at random a second time, removed his glass eye, and read from Sister's Bible through the empty socket. What David read at random from the Bible the second time was Acts 2:11-12 (Remember, this was an international, multi-language conference):

"And we all hear these men speaking in our own languages about the mighty miracles of God. They stood there amazed and perplexed. 'What can this mean?' they asked each other."

The following day, the Swedish newspaper, *Dagen*, reported the incident. Their headline was "Boy Sees Through Glass Eye."

Another miracle that touched Sister deeply was the healing of Rogelio Parillo, who had been a leper for fourteen years. Francis Clare heard him speak at the Americana Hotel in New York City in the summer of 1973.

Afflicted with leprosy at the age of ten, Rogelio became the most repulsive-looking of all the lepers in the colony. The other lepers protested his eating with them in the common dining room.

Rogelio Parillo's voice mechanism was almost entirely eaten away by the disease so that he could no longer sing. He hoped for an early death.

Then a group of Christian people conducted a service at the leper colony and preached about Jesus saving, filling, and healing. With newfound hope in Jesus, Rogelio waited at the "very end of a very long line."

"Finally two hands were placed on his head as Pastor Torres said this prayer: 'Spirit of leprosy, I cast you out of this man in the Name of Christ Jesus!'"

When Rogelio returned to his quarters that night, he told the doctor he had been healed. Many tests, examinations, and conferences took place before doctors agreed that Rogelio Parillo really had been healed. Even his voice was completely restored. Not only was Rogelio cleansed of his leprosy, but he returned to sing thanks to Jesus with his restored voice.

*   *   *

"I have taken possession of your heart. Now you must give me your mind. Do not contrive thoughts to figure out My plans. Do not question what I do. Do not debate within yourselves. Be simple. I will be with you moment by moment. Do not look for My message tomorrow in the today. Every day I have something new to tell you but it will be for today, for this moment. In this way I will lead you."

Sister Francis Clare: A Nun-Catholic with Non-Catholics

"Once we all put more stress on the *Who* we believe in rather than the *whats*, a lot of the *whats* that have separated us become so-whats. So what if you believe in (what do you believe in?) what I don't. So what if you believe in immersion and I believe in pouring. It is not so much how we get it as long as we are born again into the family of God, and who we walk with after we are in . . . and in what measure of God's power."

Sister went to Scandinavia with 170 Spirit-filled Christians of all denominations. They didn't ask about the whats, they asked, "Do you know Jesus?

"'Are you a born-again Christian?'

"'Have you experienced the Baptism in the Holy Spirit?'"

At dinner, a young man who had attempted suicide a couple of weeks earlier, asked Sister to pray with him that he might know Jesus. As they prayed, the youth was baptized in the Holy Spirit and without any special prayer for healing the boy's vision was healed. When the young man reached for his glasses after prayer, he realized he no longer needed them. God healed his vision without being asked.

In a Pentecostal church in St. Peter, Minnesota, Sister prayed for the healing of the pastor's little boy, Stevie, who had never been able to walk on his heels because the tendons in the back of his legs were too short. The child was healed.

An old lady wept tears of joy when she saw Sister praying with the minister's son for healing. She felt a Catholic nun praying with a Protestant minister for the healing of his child was much more of a miracle than the physical healing of the little boy.

In the summer of 1970, at Sister's first Full Gospel Businessmen's Convention in the Chicago Hilton, a Protestant clergyman asked, "Are you saved, Sister?"

As a baptized Catholic of forty-four years and a Catholic nun of twenty-five years, Sister was taken aback. Peter Marshall, Jr. rescued her from the gentleman, patted her on the back, and said, "That's all right, Sister. Stay just the way you are."

Sister found out later that the minister with the "question" had been preaching for fifty years without knowing Jesus himself.

"It is possible for a Sister or any other baptized person to be preaching Jesus and to know a lot about Jesus without knowing Jesus Christ Himself."

"It is possible to miss heaven by seventeen inches—the distance between the mind and the heart, the difference between the 'what' and the 'Who.'"

*   *   *

"God is doing a sovereign work. We cannot program it. We cannot halt it. We can say, 'Do it, God! Do it!' We can move when He says, 'Move!' We can praise God for what we see happening!"

∾∾

Sister Francis Clare, S.S.N.D., *Glory to Glory: Personal Meditations for the New Millennium* (Williston Park, NY: Resurrection Press, 1998), 91.

Wow, God (a 6-audio C.D. series), Forge Recording, Valley Forge, PA [adapted from her book, *Wow, God*], from Ch. 17.

Sister Francis Clare, S.S.N.D., *Wow, God* (Green Forest, AZ: New Leaf Press, 1975), 14, 46-47, 51-52, 56-57, 76, 80, 82-84, 87-88, 109-113, 115, 148-149, 152, 160, 164, 166, 168-169, 174, 177-179, 181.

Sister Francis Clare, S.S.N.D., *Your Move, God* (Green Forest, AZ: New Leaf Press, 1982), 108.

Betty Seton Danced with George Washington

The first saint born and bred in America, St. Elizabeth Seton was a politically connected WASP (white Anglo-Saxon Protestant) from an Anglican family. Born August 28, 1774, two years before the American Revolution, Elizabeth, a Bayley of the wealthy New York Bayleys, grew into a lovely society belle. The daughter of a professor of medicine, Betty enjoyed wealth and popularity, but was aware of the needs of the less fortunate. Always deeply religious, she and a group of her young socialite friends, calling themselves Sisters of Charity, worked to help the poor.

At twenty, she married William Seton and after their wedding the happy young couple hosted a birthday party for George Washington.

Several years later, Mrs. William Seton's life turned tragic. The mother of five children under the age of ten, her husband bankrupt, Betty took William to Italy to recover from tuberculosis. Ten years after their marriage, he died in her arms in Pisa.

Introduced to Catholicism in Italy, the widow Seton returned to the United States and became a Catholic despite ostracism from outraged friends and family. Because anti-Catholic feeling was so strong in New York City, Betty moved with her children to Baltimore, Maryland where their religious practice was accepted.

There the young widow opened a school. Three of the seven girls in Elizabeth's first class were her own daughters. In 1809, a few women, including two of her sisters-in-law, joined her, took vows, and formed the Sisters of Charity of Saint Joseph. As a religious, Elizabeth Ann

Seton was granted the unusual privilege of raising her own children and was elected first superior of the community.

A concerned single parent, Mother Seton protested that her need to care for her family made it impossible for her to head a religious order. Her protests ignored, Elizabeth remained leader for life of the first order of religious women established in the United States.

In the summer of 1809, the new order moved to Emmitsburg, Maryland where they opened a free school and a private academy. Like George Washington, first in war, first in peace, and first in the hearts of his countrymen, Mother Seton was "first." She established in the U.S. our first order of religious women, our first parochial schools, and our first Catholic orphanages. Six branches of the Sisters of Charity in different parts of the country came from her seminal group.

Tens of thousands of women have served as dedicated teachers, nurses, social workers, and administrators under her inspiration. In 1963 there were 11,000 Sisters of Charity in the United States running school systems, colleges, hospitals, orphanages, and facilities for the handicapped and the aged. Her accomplishments are even more amazing considering the shortness of her life: St. Elizabeth Ann Seton died at the age of forty-six on January 4, 1821.

What Betty Seton accomplished in her sixteen years as a destitute widow and single parent of five little children is a marvel of trust in God's Love. Refusing to be embittered by the death of her husband, the young widow turned to God for comfort, seeking always "His Will." When her family and friends rejected her after her conversion, Elizabeth forgave them and went where she could serve God as her conscience dictated. In Maryland, prior to telephone, radio and television, the saint inspired valiant women to join her and serve as instruments of God's Love all over the country. Two hundred years later, Mother Seton leads them still. Her life is a miracle.

Mother Seton Flexes Her Muscles

One of six branches of the Sisters of Charity in Emmitsburg sprang from a group of Sisters sent to New Orleans, Louisiana in 1830, nine years after the death of Mother Seton. Called the Daughters of Charity of St. Vincent de Paul, the Sisters assumed the big winged bonnet of the flying nun, took charge of the mental hospital, and were assigned to Charity Hospital.

One hundred years later in 1934, the administrator of the 250-bed mental hospital, Sister Gertrude Korzendorfer, was desperately sick. Her health had been deteriorating for months. Jaundiced dark yellow, nauseous, and in intense pain, Sister suffered chills and high fever.

On December 27, 1934, her doctor, James T. Nix, M.D., ordered her to Hôtel-Dieu, the Sisters' hospital in New Orleans. Nothing helped. She could not retain food. The sixty-year-old woman was melting from 165 pounds to 118. Four renowned physicians, including Dr. Nix, suspected cancer of the pancreas and recommended exploratory surgery.

The three doctors who attended at the surgery on January 5, 1935 saw the accuracy of the initial diagnosis. Sister Gertrude's case was hopeless. She had an inoperable cancer the size of an orange at the head of the pancreas. A tissue sample of the tumor was taken for laboratory analysis. The incision was closed. At three different laboratories, three pathologists examined the slides and reached the same conclusion: Sister Gertrude had terminal cancer. She would be dead in three months.

The Daughters of Charity at De Paul Sanitarium and Hôtel-Dieu began a novena [nine days of prayer] asking Mother Seton to intercede with God to cure Sister Gertrude. As soon as the novena began, Sister Gertrude rallied.

"The hospital records document a sudden change in the patient's condition. Her fever dropped; her color became normal. 'From the second day following the operation,' Sister Gertrude . . . said . . . 'I felt neither pain nor nausea. My strength returned.'"

To the amazement of the doctors, she soon appeared in good health. Sister Gertrude returned to work two months later.

"Doctor Nix wrote to Sister Gertrude on June 11, 1937, 'Your cure, as I see it, was the result of Divine intervention.'

"Two other doctors . . . Doctor Marion Souchon, a surgeon of great experience and ability and Doctor A. L. Levin, a noted gastroenterologist . . . both of whom witnessed the operation by Doctor Nix, have declared that in their opinion the recovery of Sister Gertrude Korzendorfer could not be attributed to medical or surgical intervention."

"'I have never believed in miracles,' said one of the surgeons, a Jew, 'but if ever there was a miracle this was one.'"

From 1927 to 1942, Sister Gertrude ran the mental hospital. She enjoyed good health for the last seven and a half years of her life. Her illness never recurred. Sister died in an instant of a pulmonary embolism at the Villa Saint Louise, Normandy, Missouri. With the original biopsy section showing an adeno-carcinoma of the small ducts of the pancreas, an autopsy found no evidence of cancer and no evidence of a scar in the pancreas where the tumor had been. The doctors called it a complete spontaneous cure of cancer of the head of the pancreas, a miracle.

Doctors are Unanimous: It's a Miracle

Nothing could be done to help the child. In January 1952, the four-year-old from Baltimore, Ann O'Neill, was taken to St. Agnes Hospital, a Sisters of Charity facility, and given blood tests that proved the doctor's reading of her symptoms to be correct. The low grade fever and skin hemorrhages over her whole body indicated acute leukemia.

Dr. Milton Sacks of University of Maryland Hospital, an expert on leukemia, suggested Ann be transferred to his hospital, an excellent facility for blood diseases. The O'Neills bundled her in blankets and drove the delirious child there themselves. Mrs. O'Neill was pregnant with their third child.

"'She'd call my name,' says Mrs. O'Neill. 'One night when I was with her the baby began to come and I had to leave. It was terrible, terrible to tear myself away when she needed me.' After the birth the doctors told Mrs. O'Neill what she had suspected: Ann was dying . . .'"

When Dr. Sacks tried a new drug, the symptoms began to recede. The O'Neills begged him to let them take the child home. He agreed reluctantly. Ann went home on March 27 and returned a few days later, worse than ever: gasping for breath and covered with strange new sores diagnosed as a virulent form of chicken pox.

On April 9, the child was re-admitted to St. Agnes Hospital. The next day, Sister Mary Alice Fowler, supervisor of the pediatric wing, asked Mrs. O'Neill if she would like to join in prayers asking Mother Seton to intercede with God for Ann.

"'I had seen the child when she was readmitted,' says Sister Mary Alice, 'a really pitiful thing, her little face all pale and puffy, and sores from the top of her head to the soles of her feet . . . the feeling came over me that this would be a good case for Mother Seton to show her power with God.'"

Sister pinned a little piece of ribbon on Ann's hospital gown. It was cloth touched to a bone from Mother Seton's body. Then Sister Mary Alice asked all the sisters and all the children of the order's many schools and orphanages to pray for Ann's cure.

The blood count that day showed a dramatic change for the better. By Easter, April 13, the child was obviously improved. Ann left the hospital on April 27. Doctors told the parents the child's remission would not last. When the disease recurred, the child would die. Everyone kept praying.

On June 2, Dr. Sacks was amazed to find her blood count normal. Twenty-three years later, it was still normal and Ann O'Neill Hooe was the mother of four children.

In 1960, the Church called a local tribunal to investigate the miracle. Before six investigating judges and two devil's advocates (all priests), Dr. Milton Sacks, who is Jewish, testified there was (in 1960) no known cure for leukemia.

"'It is inevitably fatal . . . The case has defied the normal course of events. (Ann's extremely long remission) is the only one of its kind in my experience.'"

"The general practitioner, an Episcopalian, testified, ' . . . It's a miracle, I've seen many other cases. None got well.'"

After all witnesses had been heard, the tribunal's next step required fresh medical examinations by two giants in the field of leukemia: Drs. Farber of Harvard Medical School and Dameshek of Tufts (both Jewish).

Ann took further tests, including a painful bone marrow test. All signs of cancer were gone. Both Drs. Farber and Dameshek agreed there was no medical explanation for her cure. Only then did the local tribunal decide, "God did it!" The case was sent on to Rome.

The Difference Between an HMO and a Wrap-Around Plan

On March 17, 1963, healthy fifteen-year-old Ann O'Neill, healed of leukemia, flew to Rome with her mother for the beatification of now Blessed Mother Seton.

On October 9, 1963, a Protestant sixty-year-old Con Edison employee, Carl Kalin, was admitted to St. Joseph's Hospital in Yonkers, New York, run by the Sisters of Charity of Mount St. Vincent-on-Hudson. Carl Kalin had a brain disease so rare the medical literature cites only five other cases. "All five died."

His wife, a Catholic, pinned a relic of Blessed Mother Seton on her husband's hospital gown. At 6:45 p.m., he took a turn for the worse and Sister Dominic Rosaire called for the administrator to comfort Mrs. Kalin. While doctors worked feverishly over Carl, whose face was purplish-black, the Sister Administrator and Mrs. Kalin prayed for his recovery in an adjoining room.

Their prayers were interrupted by the attending physician, Dr. Frank Flood, who said Carl might die before midnight. Sister Dominic Rosaire immediately called the motherhouse at Mount St. Vincent to ask prayers of the Sisters that Mother Seton intercede with God for the full recovery of Carl Kalin. Sister Dominic placed a first-class relic [part of the physical remains of a saint] of Elizabeth Seton on Carl's head, then fastened it on the wall above his bed.

The coma was broken only by almost continuous convulsions. A neurologist and an anesthesiologist consulted, examined the patient, and agreed that the massive infection in Carl Kalin's brain would kill him shortly. Carl lived two more days in extremely critical condition as the novena begun on October 9 continued.

Finally the evening of the 11th, the night nurse placed the first-class relic of Mother Seton on Carl's head and chest again. His convulsions stopped immediately and his temperature took a dramatic drop. Before morning, it was normal.

The morning of the October 12, Carl awakened from the coma but couldn't recognize anyone, did not know where he was, and had lost all concept of time. For the next three days, he could not sleep.

Finally on the 15th, Carl fell asleep until noon the next day. He awakened alert and coherent. The last day of the novena, October 17, Carl Kalin was out of bed and walking around the hospital, fully alert.

On November 2, 1963, he was discharged. Alive for the canonization of Mother Seton on September 14, 1975, Carl Kalin was retired in Florida and showed no ill effects from the ordeal he had endured.

Miraculous cures must be complete, permanent, and beyond the powers of medicine. Seven doctors in the United States testified in the case of Carl Kalin. Ten years must pass to prove the cure permanent. Then Carl Kalin's case went, as Ann O'Neill's had, to a medical board of nine doctors in the Vatican who judge the validity of the evidence. Only then does the Sacred Congregation for the Causes of Saints recommend to the Pope that the event be declared a miracle. Pope John XXIII accepted their recommendation and Blessed Elizabeth Seton became St. Elizabeth Seton. It was official: the Church had the proof it needed that Betty Seton is with God and can intercede for those who pray.

Mother Seton trusted "His Will" and kept her eyes on Him through bankruptcy, widowhood, single parenthood, bigotry, and the death of two daughters.

The miracles associated with her prove God is with us for the journey, no matter how tough it is. He is listening!

❧❧

Thomas Congdon, *Saturday Evening Post*, March 23, 1963, 76-77.

Mother Seton Guild Bulletin, March 1943, 3.

Archconfraternity of the Holy Agony, January 1965, 23.

Healing is the love of the Blessed Trinity released as seen fit by God. Nobody truly knows when, where, or how such healing may occur. Most times, healing is spiritual, mental, or emotional. Sometimes it is observable and physical.

When touched by God, all souls know that something unusual is occurring. They experience Divine touches internally, intimately, and peacefully.

Rose Ann, while dying of brain cancer, many times would say, "John, I can feel His Presence in me." She would point to her heart.

She received the ultimate healing in 2009. She went Home. Her book is a testimony to her belief that God answers all prayers His Way and in His Timeless Love. Thus, even though Rose Ann was not healed in her life in time, she is totally healed by God and is with Him in His New Jerusalem forever!

Appendix

The Catholic Church is Strict about Miracles Required for Canonization

Just any old healing doesn't get the title of miracle. The requirements include the fact that the patient was sick, there was no known cure for the ailment, prayers were directed to the Venerable, the patient was cured, the cure was instantaneous, complete, and permanent, and the cure was without natural explanation.

Who Decides if a Cure is a Miracle?

Decisions about what cures meet the criteria are made by a board of eminent physicians with expertise on the disease in focus. Their religious belief or lack of religious belief is not important. A court hearing is held and doctors who treated the cured person testify before the tribunal. However, testifying doctors do not make the decision. The decision is made by the board of impartial physicians with no emotional ties to the patient and is based on examination of the patient, medical testimony, and medical records.

The Sainthood Process

The sainthood process is a rigorous one that involves four steps. The cause of the candidate for sainthood begins in the diocese where the person lived and died. The person must have possessed sanctity demonstrated by sufficient compelling documented evidence. The person is referred to as *Servant of God* when the cause is officially introduced in the diocese.

If at the end of evaluation and research into the person's heroic virtue as well as the primary documentation it is determined all is satisfactory, documentation is submitted to the Congregation for the Causes of Saints at the Vatican, where it is studied and evaluated. The determination of the person becoming *Venerable* is made by the Holy Father.

Once proclaimed Venerable, the person is eligible for beatification, which necessitates a miracle verified by a medical commission and theologians and affirmation by Congregation officials. The final decision is made by the Holy Father for the person to be declared *Blessed*.

One more verifiable miracle is needed to be extensively examined at the Vatican in order for the person to be canonized. The Holy Father makes the final decision for the person to be declared *Saint*.

* * *

Praise God Who sees our need, hears our prayers, and heals our infirmities!

I had no idea at the outset of working on this book what a job it would be to secure permissions for quoted materials. I am indebted to the copyright holders for their kind permission to reprint material quoted in this book.

Every effort has been made to identify and contact copyright holders and publishers (even when the material was in the public domain or the subject of fair use). I apologize for any possible errors or omissions and will correct these should there be any further editions of this book.

༺༻

Excerpts from *Testimony of Father Robert DeGrandis* and *The Gift of Miracles: Experiencing God's Extraordinary Power in Your Life* by Robert DeGrandis, S.S.J., reprinted by kind permission of the author.

Excerpts from Emiliano Tardif's *Jesus Lives Today!* (Greenlawn Press, 1989) and *Jesus is the Messiah!* (Greenlawn Press, 1992), reprinted by kind permission of Greenlawn Press.

Excerpts from *Miracles Do Happen* by Briege McKenna, O.S.C. with Henry Libersat, reprinted by permission of Franciscan Media.

Excerpts from *Healing* by Francis MacNutt, copyright 1974 by Ave Maria Press, P.O. Box 428, Notre Dame, IN 46556. Used with permission of the publisher.

Excerpts from *The Power to Heal* by Francis MacNutt, copyright 1977 by Ave Maria Press, P.O. Box 428, Notre Dame, IN 46556. Used with permission of the publisher.

Excerpts from Agnes Sanford's *Sealed Orders* (Logos International, 1972), reprinted with kind permission of Bridge Logos.

Excerpts from Agnes Sanford's *The Healing Light*, reprinted with kind permission of Macalester Park Publishing Company.

Excerpts from *A Man of Miracles* by Heather Parsons, reprinted by permission of Father Peter Mary Rookey, O.S.M.

Excerpts from *Solanus Casey: The Official Account of a Virtuous American Life* by Michael Crosby, O.F.M. Published by The Crossroad Publishing Company, 2000. Reprinted with permission by The Crossroad Publishing Company. www.crossroadpublishing.com

Excerpts from *Wow, God* by Sister Francis Clare Schares, S.S.N.D., reprinted by kind permission of the author.

Rose Ann Palmer, Ph.D., researched the materials on healing and healing testimonies across religions and across time. The book *God Did It* reflects three years of research work. Rose Ann finished the original copy of the text on Memorial Day weekend in 2007. The following Monday she was diagnosed with brain cancer and died on May 14, 2009.

Rose Ann married Eddie Hubbard and had one son, John, to whom this book is dedicated. Some years later, she met and married John Palmer, who had three children during his first marriage. John T. Palmer, Ph.D., Psychologist, fulfills his promise to her to finalize the book and have it published. This book completes the work of Rose Ann.

Rose Ann Palmer received her doctoral degree in Deafness Rehabilitation from New York University. She was an English teacher, an on-air instructor of the homebound on WYNE (NYC educational radio station), and an itinerant speech and hearing impaired teacher for the NY Board of Education. She was an active Catholic, an avid tennis and bridge player, and a proud member of MENSA.

Upon retiring, Rose Ann was a television producer for a diocesan television station for the show, *Father Tom, Faith*, where many of the guests were people who had the "gift of healing." That is where the idea for this book generated. She wrote the book in the style of *Chicken Soup for the Soul*. It is quite an uplifting publication that offers hope to those in need of healing.

John Palmer works for the Renewal Apostolate of the Diocese of Rockville Center. As such, he coordinates the activities of over 200 prayer groups across the diocese. He finalized the book in its current form and is publishing it for he believes it will inspire all who read it.

We are from Long Island, New York. It is my hope and I know the hope of my late wife that this book be an instrument of peace in the hearts, minds, and souls of all who read it.

—John Palmer

❧❧

John Palmer

jpalmer@holyspiritwithin.net

107 Rockywood Road, Manhasset, NY 11030

www.GODDIDIT.com

❧❧

You may purchase copies of
God Did It
at your local bookstore
and order online at websites, including
www.iUniverse.com
www.BN.com
www.Amazon.com
www.AdventShop.com

❧❧